"WE'RE TAKING FIRE."

WE'RE
TAKING FIRE

A Reporter's View of the Vietnam War, Tet and the Fall of LBJ

PETER ARNETT

ASSOCIATED PRESS

To my journalist colleagues whose efforts make democracy stronger.

CONTENTS

1

TET '68: THE FIRST 36 HOURS

THE BLAST OF STRINGS OF EXPLODING FIRECRACKERS jerked me awake as Vietnamese neighbors continued their celebrations into the early hours of the morning. It was Saigon, January 31, 1968, the first day of the year of the traditional lunar calendar, Tet Nguyen Dan, and the most important Vietnamese festival. Amid the cacophony I noticed a loud, methodical rat-tat-tat that shook our apartment shutters as though someone was banging on them with a hammer. I'd heard that sound before in the battlefield, the roar of a heavy-caliber machine gun, and it seemed to be shooting up Pasteur Street just three room-lengths away. A weapon that lethal had not been discharged in Saigon since the overthrow of President Ngo Dinh Diem four years earlier. I opened my bedroom window and watched as war came to Saigon from the jungles and paddy fields and peasant villages where it had lingered for years. Red tracer bullets zipped through the sky and firefights were erupting near the centers of power in South Vietnam's capital, the presidential palace and the American embassy. As the sounds of exploding grenades and rockets vibrated through the darkness, I bundled my wife Nina and my young children, Elsa and Andrew, and our maid into the bathroom, which I hoped was safer than the rest of our small apartment, and I covered them with mattresses from the beds. I phoned the Associated Press office, and bureau chief Robert Tuckman answered, his voice high-pitched and excited: "They're shelling the city, for God's sake." I told him I was on my way.

1

I wasn't the only one so rudely awakened in total surprise at around 2:30 that morning. Only those in the know—the attacking Vietcong guerrillas and North Vietnamese military forces and their allied clandestine networks in the city—had any idea of what was happening. By quietly moving combat troops through the supposedly secure countryside into the heart of Saigon, they were able to strike without warning. General William Westmoreland, the increasingly confident commander of all American combat forces fighting in Vietnam, was asleep in his comfortable villa at Tran Quy Cap street when attacks began all around his neighborhood. Just nine weeks earlier, the general visited the United States on the orders of President Lyndon Johnson to participate in a "success offensive," a concerted effort to bolster public support for the war. In an address at the National Press Club, he asserted that the Vietcong were "unable to mount a major offensive" and that the point was reached "when the end begins to come into view." But on this early morning, Westmoreland was stuck, unable to reach his Saigon headquarters as gunfire roared in the street outside. By telephone, he learned of the spiraling crisis, particularly a fierce attack on the six-story American embassy at Thong Nhut street several blocks away. He later said, "My Marine aide was talking to the Marine guard inside the embassy, and by my numerous telephone conversations with U.S. Army MP command I was able to follow the course of the battle and direct action."

Ambassador Ellsworth Bunker was similarly blindsided by the ferocity of the enemy attacks, particularly the assault on his embassy. He was asleep in his villa four blocks away when his security team rushed into his bedroom and ushered him down to the basement in his pajamas. Wearing his bathrobe, he was soon loaded into an armored car and driven to a safe house. Bunker had been in South Vietnam less than a year, and in that time he had worked closely with Westmoreland and endorsed his views.

In Washington, D.C., half a day behind Vietnam in time, it was the early afternoon of January 30. President Johnson was presiding over a meeting of his closest security advisors, their biggest Vietnam concern the struggle to avoid the loss of the U.S. Marine combat base of Khe Sanh that over the weeks had been threatened by a growing number of

North Vietnamese troops. Nearly half of all American combat troops in Vietnam were being moved to the northern provinces to support Khe Sanh and other border bases. It was during the meeting that President Johnson first heard the alarming news from Saigon. His special assistant for national security affairs, Walt Rostow, returned after taking a call from the National Military Command Center. It was 2:35 p.m. Rostow, a hawk on Vietnam who late in 1967 had used the phrase "light at the end of the tunnel" to describe the war policy's successes, announced, "We have just been informed that we are being heavily mortared in Saigon. The presidential palace, our bachelor officers' quarters, the embassy and the city itself have been hit. This flash was just received from the NMCC."

The minutes of the meeting record President Johnson as responding, "This could be very bad. What can we do to shake them from this? This looks like where we came in. Remember it was at Pleiku that they hit our barracks and that we began to strike them in the North. What comes to mind in the way of retaliation?" He was recalling that it was at Pleiku in the Central Highlands in the early morning hours of February 7, 1965, that 300 Vietcong troops attacked the helicopter facility at Camp Holloway, killing eight Americans, wounding 126 and destroying 16 aircraft. President Johnson ordered retaliatory airstrikes against North Vietnam by carrier-based Navy fighter-bombers in a response that foretold America's full-scale entry into the Vietnam war.

At the White House meeting, the chairman of the Joint Chiefs of Staff, Earle Wheeler, downplayed the news. "It was the same type of thing before. You remember that during the inauguration, the MACV (Military Advisory Command Vietnam) headquarters was hit. In a city like Saigon people can infiltrate easily. They carry in rounds of ammunition and mortars. They fire and run. It is about as tough to stop it in its entirety as to protect against a mugging in Washington, D.C. We've got to pacify all of this area as get rid of the Vietcong infrastructure. They are making a major effort to mount a series of these actions to make a big splurge at Tet." Defense Secretary Robert McNamara, the primary architect of early war policy whose growing doubts about the morality of the American effort had led to his announced replacement, gave little weight to the initial information, suggesting it should be handled as "a 'public relations' issue."

Around the same time, William Colby, the CIA's chief of the Far East Division, at work at the agency's Langley, Virginia, headquarters, received a flash message from Saigon station reporting that "a violent attack against the American embassy is in progress with the attackers possibly within the embassy itself." Colby advised them in a flash return message that the Communications Center should button up its steel doors. Colby was a former CIA station chief in Saigon, a confidant of the slain President Ngo Dinh Diem, and a proponent of a counter insurgency strategy that relied less on American combat troops. Within days, he would be on his way to South Vietnam to help pick up the pieces of a crumbling policy.

As the 3 million people of Saigon became abruptly aware of the brutal enemy intrusion in their Tet holiday celebrations, there was confusion within the South Vietnamese security ranks. Many of the military police primarily responsible for city protection were at home celebrating with their families. President Nguyen Van Thieu, who was also the commander of Vietnam's armed forces, was on a Tet holiday with his family and could not be immediately located. A month earlier, the American military command had handed over the security of the nation's capital entirely to the Vietnamese paramilitary police forces, and Thieu's authority was necessary to facilitate supporting troop movements from outside. Vice President Nguyen Cao Ky complained later, "Catastrophe loomed. In expectation of the usual Tet truce, half of our armed forces had gone on leave. To make things worse, most of our army's combat forces were not deployed in or near big cities." General Westmoreland was particularly unhappy about President Thieu, who had been informed of security concerns in the northern region and had agreed to cancel the Tet ceasefire there a day earlier. The day passed with no notice of the cancellation, and according to Westmoreland, "I telephoned the American embassy to find that the South Vietnamese government had provided its press officer with a release but that the press office was shut tight, closed for Tet. President Thieu had departed to pass the holidays in My Tho, his wife's hometown in the Mekong Delta. Such a lackadaisical attitude on

4

the part of the government was shocking and frustrating yet indicative of the state of mind, to near euphoria, that envelops the Vietnamese at Tet."

Not all the Vietnamese, however, were euphoric celebrants, certainly not the Vietcong who were violating their own announced seven-day Tet truce with surprise attacks across the country. We would soon learn that the Saigon attacks were just the point of the spear. The Vietcong and the North Vietnamese, who had until now avoided attacking major population centers, were using an estimated 80,000 fighters in a coordinated assault against 39 of South Vietnam's 44 province capitals, 64 district headquarters, almost every allied airfield, and Saigon. A puzzle was that the only American installation attacked was the embassy.

I said goodbye to my family to begin my reporting day, and opened my apartment door as a burst of heavy machine-gun fire flashed through the darkness in the direction of the presidential palace two blocks away. I waited for a break in the shooting and stepped out into the lamplight, raising my arms in a friendly gesture to the invisible gunners behind the sandbags just down the street. I was in shirt sleeves and slacks and I smiled and shouted "journalist" in Vietnamese. There was no reaction so I just walked past them on my way to the AP office. Our staff were on the telephones, reporting what best they could to our news headquarters in New York City. The American embassy was under attack; so was Tan Son Nhut airport and the main Saigon radio station, the presidential palace, and Vietnamese security installations. We needed eyewitness stories, bureau chief Tuckman told me.

I was joined by reporter colleague John Nance and photographer Joe Holloway, grabbing the keys to the office mini-jeep and setting off across the embattled city, the night sky bright with tracer bullets and the swinging arcs of parachute flares. We drove up a side street behind the presidential palace to get closer to the action. A South Vietnamese soldier stepped out in front of the jeep and signaled us to turn back, indicating that the Vietcong had moved into a nearby unfinished building, after their attack by rockets and hand grenades against the palace gate had been repulsed. As we turned, a hail of bullets splattered the street around us, sending us quickly on our way. One of the Vietcong combatants who fired at us was a woman, Vu Minh Nghia, 21 years old, who was among the eight

Vietcong attackers who survived. She told her captors her assault team had sneaked into Saigon the previous evening, worried by the last-minute order to attack the well-defended palace. They were briefly fighting around the gate, she said, before retreating to the nearby house after seven of their number were killed. They were shooting at anyone who approached until later in the day when they gave up.

When I returned to the AP office at 4:30 a.m. I received a call from Barry Zorthian, the chief of the joint U.S. information office, offering me a scoop, a phone interview with a top American official trapped in his two-story cottage in a corner of the courtyard of the embattled embassy. "We just want you to get the story straight, Peter," Zorthian said. There were gunshot sounds and explosions in the background when I interviewed George "Jake" Jacobson, the veteran embassy coordinator, who told me that several enemy commandos had blown a hole in the embassy wall an hour or so earlier and were roaming the grounds outside his cottage, firing bazooka shells at the façade of the shiny, new eight-story embassy chancery building. And the attackers were exchanging fire with snipers in buildings across the street.

"They know I am here," Jacobson, a courtly older man, told me in a whisper on the phone. He said his upstairs bedroom windows were already shot out by a rocket. He had armed himself with a hand grenade for a last-ditch stand. He was a cool one, a veteran of nine years' service in Vietnam. His last comments to me were that, "The Vietcong are calculating a big splash all over the world with their activities." I was intrigued by these comments from a senior official crouching in his bedroom and fearing for his life but also figuring out a credible explanation for what was going on—that it was a communist publicity stunt. As I wrote the story for the AP, I could hardly believe the audacity of the Vietcong, who were not only assaulting the American embassy, but also launching vigorous attacks against a dozen other targets across Saigon, all at a time when conventional wisdom had them pushed to the ropes.

The fate of George Jacobson and that of the embassy itself in the developing battle became an immediate priority for our coverage because it was the highest profile target in the first hours of the offensive, and it was just five blocks away from the AP office. We set off for the embassy on foot, heading up Tu Do street past the towering red-brick Roman Catholic basilica, noticing security men in the adjoining park hiding behind trees; but they made no effort to stop us. Bursts of rockets and the crack of small arms drew us down Thong Nhut Boulevard, past the headquarters of the Texas construction giant RMK-BRJ to Hai Ba Trung street, and the corner of the block where the embassy, behind an eight-foot concrete wall, loomed above us in the darkness. We edged along the street and crouched down as small as we could make ourselves. The boulevard was a shooting gallery; gunfire crackled over our heads and thudded into tree trucks and walls. American military police from the 716 battalion had occupied an upper floor of an apartment building across the street and were directing fire into the embassy grounds. The Vietcong inside were returning fire.

The senior Marine guard at the embassy, Staff Sergeant Ronald Harper, was taking cover in the floodlit lobby when a rocket smashed into a window next to the wooden door, wounding a fellow Marine in the arms, face and legs. A few seconds later the attackers dropped a hand grenade through the broken window as another rocket exploded against the door. Harper said later, "I figured the Vietcong were coming in. I moved back to the armory to get my 9mm Beretta submachine gun, then I helped move my buddy upstairs. I figured we were in for it." He returned and fired a test burst from his machine gun and backed into the corner of the lobby, able to see through the steel grills in the open window. As more rockets thumped into the fragile concrete latticework on the embassy façade, Harper said, bits of searing, hot metal took their toll on these trapped in the embassy. "One Marine guard fell dead; six others were wounded," including himself.

The first glow of a gray dawn lit the scene. We saw a bullet-riddled black Citroen sedan in the middle of the street, its driver slumped over the steering wheel. Outside the embassy gate were two other immobilized vehicles. There was concrete rubble scattered near them and a haze of dust in the air from the blasting the Vietcong had done to make their way into the embassy grounds. I wondered what had happened to George Jacobson, and I was told by a Marine captain, Robert O'Brien, who had arrived with Marine guard reinforcements, that he had been in radio communication with Jacobson and the handful of embassy staffers in the chancery on overnight duty. He said, "I've relayed to them the word from command headquarters they would have to hold out because a counterattack would be too dangerous in the darkness."

Inside the embassy, the duty officer, 32-year-old Allan Wendt, was asleep in a cot in room 433 on the fourth floor of the embassy when the attack began. He later recalled, "Suddenly the building was hit by a loud explosion. Automatic weapons fire broke out and rockets began to thud into the building. I quickly retreated to the more secure and better equipped communications room where a specialist, James A Griffin, was on duty. A call to the ground-floor Marine security guard post revealed that at least one Marine guard, Staff Sergeant Ronald W. Harper, was alive and functioning. The Vietcong attackers, at that point, were not in the building. I placed and received phone calls from the White House Situation Room, the State Department operations center, and the American military command in Saigon. I spoke regularly to embassy officers at the off-site command post setup by Ambassador Bunker. As the siege wore on, we pleaded with the U.S. military command for relief. We were told an armored column was on its way. It never arrived. One helicopter finally did land on the roof and evacuated a wounded Marine. But to my consternation, I also discovered that two armed American military personnel including a Marine whose presence I had not detected, also took off on the chopper, leaving the lone Marine on the ground floor and a few civilians and me to fend for ourselves." (There is no available record on whether this incident was followed up)

As the morning brightened, John Nance and I, still concealed near the outside wall, saw military policemen crawling along the exposed gutters and the sidewalk next to the embassy wall up ahead of us, moving into position for a counterattack while others were gathering in formation to assist them. A dozen Huey helicopters came in low over the gardens at the Saigon zoo end of the street, heading towards us. I realized they were going to attempt an infantry assault against the embassy. Nance, who had taken shelter behind one of the immobilized vehicles, watched as an MP rose to his feet and slammed his shoulder against the wrought iron embassy gate. It swung open and the military policemen rushed inside as the roar of exploding hand grenades and automatic weapons fire erupted. I could see the first of the helicopters hovering over us, trying to land on the embassy roof. In a barrage of gunfire from the courtyard it pulled away and was gone, and soon many of the soldiers who had stormed through the gate were back outside, pointing to the middle floors of the chancery building. Not only were the Vietcong inside embassy grounds, but they had apparently penetrated the embassy itself and were upstairs. I asked a disheveled officer if he was sure and he said, "My god, yes, we're taking fire from up there. Keep your head down."

I ran to the construction building down the street where the Indian night porter let me use the phone to send my story. Ed White calmly took my dictation, and I returned to the corner of Hai Ba Trung where newspaper and television colleagues were assembling to cover one of the most sensational actions of the whole war. An hour later, a second helicopter assault was launched, and we saw soldiers from the U.S. Army's 101st Airborne Division jumping to the chancery roof and beginning their descent through the building. I saw correspondent Howard Tuckner of NBC and his cameraman Vo Huynh follow a military police squad through the front gate into the embassy grounds, and we were all soon joining them, gasping at the evidence of the fierce struggle inside.

A large hole had been blasted through the protective wall, the Great Seal of the United States was bullet-riddled and knocked down from above the door, and the lobby was a tangled wreck. There was a score of dead Vietcong in green and brown clothing and red armbands and several dead Americans, their blood splashed on the pathways and walls. We heard gunshots from the rear of the courtyard. We saw a pale George Jacobson emerge from his villa, the victor over a lone, wounded Vietcong gunman who had entered his house and hidden in a bathroom, and then attempted to kill him with an automatic weapon. Using a hand gun thrown up to him as he leaned from his upstairs bedroom, Jacobson killed his attacker who was coming up the stairs. Nineteen of the Vietcong attackers were killed and one was captured. Five American soldiers died.

When Westmoreland arrived at the scene soon afterwards, anxious to return to a scene of normality, he instructed Allan Wendt to have the embassy cleaned up and the employees back at work by noon. Wendt said later, "This was quite unrealistic. Fighting was raging all over the city." At mid-morning, the 32-year-old diplomat drove home in his bullet-scarred car parked at the back of the chancery. Its windshield was shot away but at least he could drive it. In a report to the Department of State a few weeks later, Wendt said, "The attack on the embassy revealed our lack of military and civilian preparedness. As civilian duty officer, I was ill-prepared. I was given no useful intelligence. I had no training in the use of weapons or first aid. I was lucky to survive; the odds were against it. But a few good decisions saved us. At the first shot, a quick-thinking Marine at an adjoining building in the compound had rushed across the compound and closed the embassy's thick wooden doors. The architecture of the building with its lattice work concrete absorbed the rocket rounds fired into it. The Vietcong attackers were not of World War II caliber and fortunately for us were hit by Vietnamese and American personnel firing down on them from adjoining rooftops."

A concerned President Johnson — glued to the three wire service news printers running in his office, checking the evening newspapers and watching television news — was impressed by Westmoreland's strident assertions of victory while standing amid the bloody carnage of the American embassy courtyard and saying that no Vietcong had penetrated the inside of the chancery. The general described the enemy attacks across the city as "a diversion" to draw attention away from what he described as the "real intentions" of the enemy, which he said were to secure a victory against the Marine combat base at Khe Sanh. Westmoreland had warned for weeks that the communists were looking to achieve a success at Khe Sanh similar to that of the 1954 battle of Dien Bien Phu, also an isolated stronghold located in a border area. The major defeat there had forced the French to withdraw from Vietnam after a 10-year struggle to re-establish its colonial territories following World War II.

In Washington, President Johnson saw Westmoreland's confident assertions of victory as an antidote to the rising clamor of criticism in Congress and in the media over war policy. He messaged Saigon that the general should give two news briefings each day rather than the planned single appearance. Accordingly, Westmoreland appeared at the press center auditorium where the official daily late afternoon briefing, nicknamed "the five o'clock follies," was being held. He doubled up on his optimism, describing the massive attacks as "a major go-for-broke offensive, but I anticipate that the enemy will shortly run out of steam." He also announced that the important central Vietnamese city of Hue had been cleared of enemy forces. But officials later had to retract that statement because the old imperial capital had already fallen to Vietcong and North Vietnamese troops after a few hours' battle. Control would be relinquished there only after a brutal 24-day struggle primarily fought by U.S. Marines. And fighting was continuing in several other provincial capitals including Kontum, Ben Tre, Phan Thiet, Ban Me Thuot and Can Tho, all indications that this was more than a communist diversion but a major offensive planned and implemented over several months while America's attention was on the northern provinces

Westmoreland would soon personally experience the persistent dangers existing in Saigon at this time. He was required to move to the headquarters of the American military assistance command because his own residence remained insecure. Lewis Sorley, who wrote a biography of the general, quoted Brigadier General Zeb Bradford, then a field grade officer and aide-de-camp: "It was humiliating for Westmoreland. He couldn't get out of his own headquarters. That first day, the senior generals assembled in a makeshift dining room for the evening meal. The mood was grim, even despondent. It appeared that all that had been achieved over the years had been for nothing. The gloom was made complete when a stray bullet smashed through the window in the room where the generals were eating. With as much dignity as possible these senior officers had to evacuate themselves to a safer part of the building." On February 1, according to Sorley, Brigadier General John Chaisson wrote to his wife, "Our HQ has been under continuous attack all day. We are all holed up here, including Westy." The next day the general wrote, "General Westmoreland had to shift his office. He was getting sniper fire."

In the morning of day two of the offensive, Associated Press photographer Eddie Adams and an NBC television crew encountered General Nguyen Ngoc Loan, the cold-eyed national police chief, on a street near the An Quang pagoda. He was directing a clean-up operation by some of his uniformed and heavily armed police units, and stopped to chat with the newsmen. General Loan had friends in Washington. President Johnson, at the White House meeting where he first learned of the Tet Offensive, was urged to make sure General Loan kept his job as national police chief, despite criticism from American officials in Saigon who had previously sparred with him over security issues and his heavy-handed behavior. Secretary of Defense Robert McNamara said, "I recommend that we need to keep General Loan in charge of the Saigon police. He should not be removed, as some of our people in the State Department are recommending. At least until we find someone better." CIA Director Richard Helms said, "I agree." McNamara said, "He is the best security chief since Diem's time. He has cleaned up Saigon well." Secretary of State Dean Rusk said, "He is a good police chief, but he has been rather uncooperative with some of our people."

Standing alongside General Loan in the late morning heat on a street empty of traffic and civilians, as gunfire echoed around the silent buildings, Adams saw a group of helmeted police talking loudly as they approached with a handcuffed Vietnamese man in civilian clothes in their midst. They placed him in front of the general who questioned him briefly. Adams saw that the police chief was holding a .38-caliber revolver in his right hand, and watched as the officer's right arm swing up. So, too, did Adams' hands swing up, clutching his camera. He snapped a picture as General Loan murdered the prisoner standing in front of him with a single shot to the head. The general turned to Adams and said, "These guys kill a lot of our people, and I think Buddha will forgive me," and walked away. The NBC crew, camera rolling, caught the whole sequence of events on film.

I was at the Saigon AP bureau when Adams returned with his film. He was pale-faced, wide-eyed. "I just saw something unbelievable. But I don't know if I got the picture," he said. Fifteen minutes later his film emerged from the darkroom, revealing the horrifying image Adams had captured, the photo of South Vietnam's top police official with his outstretched arm holding a firearm inches from the face of a man whose head had been snapped back the split second a bullet entered his brain. The photograph was quickly fed into the Associated Press's international news distribution service and used widely in newspapers and on television. The victim was later identified as Nguyen Van Lem, said to be the leader of a clandestine Vietcong execution squad that was targeting Saigon government officials. The photograph of his public execution by one of those officials brought home to the world the horrors of a continuing brutal war that had emerged into the daylight of South Vietnam's biggest cities from the shadows of the countryside.

Many thousands of communist soldiers were killed in the first month of the offensive, with the Saigon government and the American command claiming a decisive victory based on the body-count formula that was in use to chart the progress of the war. But allied casualties were also high. In the first month's combat, more than 2,100 American soldiers died, along with 4,000 South Vietnamese troops killed and tens of thousands of Vietnamese civilians killed and wounded. But the psychological victory went to the communists who had achieved almost complete strategic surprise in the Tet Offensive, with some military commentators soon labeling it "the worst intelligence failure for the United States since the attack on Pearl Harbor."

Harry McPherson was a special counsel for President Johnson who served in his administration from 1965 to 1969 and was with him in the White House as the Tet Offensive ran its course. He reflected on the rapidly-growing controversies in the early days of the Tet Offensive battle, in an interview for the Lyndon Johnson Presidential Library in Austin, Texas. "There were competing views and opposing phenomena all over the place," he said. "The embassy in Saigon and the military operation in Saigon were telling us that we had really beat the hell out of the enemy and they have taken tremendous casualties. They lost an enormous number of people including some of their best people. They surfaced a lot of assets, to use a military phrase. A lot of people who were in the infrastructure in South Vietnam and living apparently normal lives while being VC agents came out into the open and were either killed, captured or at least identified and chased out of their villages. They (the enemy) lost a lot; they did not achieve what they expected to achieve or hoped to achieve at the outset. The South Vietnamese did get a momentary shot in the arm; they did work harder. When it was over they got together more effectively. A number of citizens efforts were begun for the first time. All of this was a plus.

"The negative was tremendous and was underplayed by Saigon. The negative was essentially here in this country. It was the feeling on the part of vast numbers of Americans, particularly after Westmoreland and Bunker had come back in the fall of the previous year and said things were just looking really good. I believe they used the expression 'light at the end of the tunnel.' After all of that, and after a tremendous commitment for three years — air power, 550,000 men, and all the rest of it — that this crowd (the Vietcong) was still able to mount a major offensive that smashed into cities and secure hamlets and such things. That they were able to hold Hue for a long time while the U.S. Marines encircled them. They were able to get into Saigon and terrorize the population, all that, and the awful picture you may remember of General Loan, the national police chief, executing a VC on the street.

"The terrible quality of the war in Vietnam came home to people. It appeared that these guys didn't want to quit at all and were never going to quit, and that our crowd was as caught off guard as ever."

2

AT THE BEGINNING

TWO YEARS AFTER HIS ELECTION VICTORY IN 1952, won partly on his promise the end the unpopular Korean War, President Dwight D. Eisenhower denied desperate French entreaties to send American warplanes to save the besieged outpost of Dien Bien Phu in northwest Vietnam from being overrun by a communist peasant army. Another overt war for the United States was not on Eisenhower's agenda.

The leading security concern of the major players on the world scene at that time, the Soviet Union's Nikita Khrushchev, Mao Zedong of mainland China and Eisenhower of the United States, was the drama of the Cold War, where a serious miscalculation could face mankind with nuclear annihilation. In the scheme of things, Southeast Asia was a sideshow compared to the continuing military confrontations in Europe. The small nations in the region were emerging from colonialism under various forms of government: autocratic in Indonesia, democratic in the Philippines, Malaysia and Singapore, authoritarian in Burma, and paternalistic under monarchies in Thailand, Cambodia and Laos.

The remaining country, Vietnam, an ancient land colonized by the French for nearly a century that had won independence in 1954 after a decade-long struggle, was left with an uncertain future. Great Power agreements in Geneva gave the northern part to the communists. The future of the south was to be determined in elections aimed at unifying the new nation. But faced with a potent anticommunist political environment in the U.S. fueled by the strident congressional hearings of Senator Joseph McCarthy, the Eisenhower administration chose to intervene assertively in the political affairs of Vietnam. The intention was to establish a new, independent, pro-Western nation named South Vietnam, and to see to its survival. A succession of U.S. governments in the 1950s the 1960s and the 1970s invested billions of dollars and eventually more than half a million of its combat troops in the attempts to achieve that goal.

As a young reporter for the Associated Press, I covered news stories in Southeast Asia as the emerging American military involvement became apparent. One was the establishment of the Southeast Asian Treaty Organization (SEATO) based in Thailand, the creation of U.S. Secretary of State John Foster Dulles, that brought several regional anti-communist states together in a military and economic alliance. I watched the arrival of several hundred American soldiers in Vientiane, Laos, in 1960, dressed in civilian clothes in a transparent attempt to avoid violating the Geneva Agreements. Their mission was to prop up the U.S.-backed military government that was worrying about Chinese military road-building along the northern border and the appearance of North Vietnamese troops inside the Laos border from a region near where the famous battle of Dien Bien Phu had been fought in 1954. There were continuing concerns about Laos and its importance to the emerging anti-guerrilla struggle in neighboring South Vietnam, and a battalion of U.S. Marines was sent to Thailand's Mekong River border with Laos in 1962. That is where I had my first opportunity to write about American soldiers in foreign deployment. And later that year, I was assigned to Saigon to cover the efforts of the new administration of President John F. Kennedy, which had inherited America's commitment to stay the course in South Vietnam.

As a foreign correspondent, you cover the facts as you see them, or from reliable sources who know more about what's going on than you do. With that intent, after the war I interviewed many of those involved in making decisions during the critical years of the war. One of them was John Kenneth Galbraith, an outspoken liberal intellectual who was a confidant of President Kennedy and served as his ambassador to India.

Galbraith told me, "The view of Southeast Asia at that time in Washington was in my view simplistic. There was a notion that this was part of the great revolution of the times, that the revolution stemmed from the monolithic expression of the power of China and Russia. No distinction was made between them at that time. They were all thought to be the same. It attributed much more military and political and social power to these new countries than they actually had. If you were living there, in the countryside, one had doubts about the importance about whether Vietnam called itself communist or socialist or otherwise."

Kennedy came to power in 1961 with a very slender vote margin, Galbraith noted, adding that during the first year he had the Bay of Pigs disaster in Cuba and had sent diplomat Averill Harriman to Laos to work out a neutral political solution there. "And these were being criticized as being in some sense a surrender. Kennedy was reluctant to be seen to do the same thing in South Vietnam, but he referred to the relative unimportance of South Vietnam," Galbraith said. "I made the argument they if the country had been unified at the time of the French departure, the phrase that I used was, 'It would never have been retrieved from the obscurity that it so much deserved.' Kennedy said, 'I agree with you,' or words to that effect. But the president also mentioned that there was the political problem, and that 'I can only have so many political defeats in one year.'"

Kennedy asked Galbraith to travel to South Vietnam on his way to his ambassador's post in India and make his own assessment of the situation. Galbraith's visit was in late 1961, and he told me, "One did have a strong impression of the pathological incompetence of the government. Just a few thousands of Vietcong guerrillas, scattered over that still large country, and a vast array of armed men already incapable of doing anything about them." In his report to the president, Galbraith did not urge a complete pullout of the several thousand military advisors America had already sent. "But I urged that we detach ourselves and limit our liabilities there just as much as possible. We must very much limit our commitment there and be on the side of good things such as land reform."

Galbraith remembered coming down strongly on the military question when he later personally briefed Kennedy at the White House, insisting that "we do not commit any of our own forces there, on the grounds that this was the kind of social condition with which one could not contend in any military way. I was also against the regime of President Ngo Dinh Diem."

President Kennedy's frequent use of his personal friends to assess the situation in Vietnam angered the American ambassador, Frederick Nolting, who later wrote that Galbraith arrived in Saigon unexpectedly in the midst of delicate negotiations with the Diem government. Those talks dealt with accountability for American funds, the broadening of the government, the role of the National Assembly and the accumulation of power in the hands of the president; in addition, the role of Diem's brothers, particularly Ngo Dinh Nhu and his wife Madame Nhu, in the power structure.

Nolting told me in an interview, "Galbraith was on his way to his ambassadorship in India and stayed in our home and was a stimulating house guest, later sending a number of books, including several of his own. He came at the president's request and I suppose to check up on us and see how we were doing. From this small incident, I began to suspect that the president relied more on news stories and reports from his cronies than he did on our cables which were normally sent through the State Department."

A few months earlier, Nolting had hosted a more acceptable visitor officially sent by Kennedy to assess the situation in South Vietnam. He was General Maxwell Taylor, a distinguished military officer who had written a book on military policy called "The Uncertain Trumpet," advocating a more flexible military policy as a change from the Eisenhower years. The president and his brother Robert Kennedy found the general to their liking. Taylor's report to the president, co-authored by Walt Rostow, a hawkish National Security Council member, significantly raised the stakes.

General Taylor recalled that trip in an interview with me after the war in his Washington, D.C., apartment, where mementoes from a long life of government service were in evidence, including a full-length oil painting of himself in full uniform as commander of the U.S. Army's 101st Airborne Division in World War II. "I had received the unique title of military representative of the president, and worked in the White House with him as his advisor on military and also intelligence matters. He knew of my earlier service in the Far East, and Laos was very important when I came on board with him in the summer of 1961. And very shortly he asked me to keep a special eye, from the White House point of view, on Vietnam."

Taylor said that a trigger for his trip was a request from President Diem to increase his own military forces substantially. "I had encountered the president one morning in the White House as I was walking down a corridor. He said, 'I have a letter here from President Diem. Tell me how to answer it.'" Taylor laughed as he said to me, "Well I spent the next 11 years trying to find an answer"—not only at that time but also in his future roles as chairman of the Joint Chiefs of Staff, as ambassador in Saigon in 1964 and 1965, and as chairman of President Lyndon Johnson's Foreign Intelligence Advisory Board until 1969.

Taylor said questions Kennedy asked "really amounted to: 'Was the United States in favor of a major increase in the military effort to achieve the political objectives in Vietnam'—that of an independent pro-Western state? I understood that Diem had asked Ambassador Nolting orally for the commitment of American military forces, so it was likely I would get that request when I got to Saigon." Taylor said that the question of American forces came up in the stopover he made at U.S. Naval headquarters in Honolulu and in Saigon from the civilians in the American embassy and personnel in the military mission. "They were all convinced that South Vietnam could never make it against the increased effort without American aid and American presence," he said.

Taylor suggested a subterfuge that later took on a meaning much more significant than he intended. "At that time, I recommended only that we commit an experimental test force, taking advantage, if you will, of the great flood in the Mekong Delta in 1961, the biggest in history there, and bringing in an American task force largely of engineers and technical people, to help deal with that serious natural crisis. I was quite aware, and the president was aware and all his advisors were aware of the undesirability of our getting into a military presence of any importance in Vietnam before it was necessary. One of the arguments in favor with the task force would be that we are lifting the morale of a country that is deeply depressed by the prolonged guerrilla warfare being waged. Some on our team said, 'Let's make that effort.' The counter argument was if we move in we will be expected to take over. There was truth in both those arguments, although I did recommend the forces, estimated at about 8,000 strong."

President Kennedy postponed indefinitely the question of sending an American task force, but historians later pinpointed Taylor's recommendation as an effort to push open the door for the eventual Americanization of the war. Taylor said Kennedy did approve other recommendations of increased American non-military assistance. "That involved improving the political and economic assistance that did indeed move slowly, but gradually our intelligence system was brought together in some order, and I had the feeling we were getting a more accurate report that year than ever before."

What did the American public think in the early Kennedy years? As an AP reporter covering the emerging commitment in Vietnam primarily for American newspapers, I did not challenge the reasoning of the Kennedy administration that the defense of South Vietnam was essential to our security, even as I and other reporters criticized the effectiveness of that effort.

Most American editors at that time were watching with interest the performance of the young president and his White House team, wanting to believe that taxpayers dollars and the risks to the American lives sent there were worth the effort in South Vietnam. I believed that our stories from ringside would help them in their judgments.

Brian Jenkins, a civilian member of the long-range planning task group advising the command of General Creighton Abrams in Vietnam, and long associated since with the RAND Corporation, a prominent research organization, says that many Americans at that time, according to public opinion polls, were supportive of the effort.

"Take myself," he said in an interview for a television project I was writing in the 1970s. "I went through the university during the Kennedy era, and one only has to recall the rhetoric of that time, and a resurgence of what appears an anachronism today, the words patriotism and duty, and serving of your country. That could be in the form of the Peace Corps, that new invention of the Kennedy era, or of the Army Special Forces, the 'Green Berets,' both the symbol of willingness to become involved in these issues of the world. There was a great fervor at the time of international involvement. The war was in its early period, not at all the unpopular undertaking it later became."

Jenkins went on to join the special forces and served in Vietnam. He said, "The climate of the Kennedy era made war acceptable. It made this particular contest acceptable, it made American involvement in this contest acceptable. We had sent troops into Thailand in 1962, we had intervened in Laos, we were becoming more militarily involved in Southeast Asia. We were demonstrating not only our resolve but our ability to deal with this new form of warfare.

"What was considered an anachronism in the early 1960s, our only military response at that time was massive retaliating, the ability to fight an all-out war with the use of our nuclear weapons. And here we were met with the new kind of warfare in places like Southeast Asia and other places in the Third World, and so this was not only a demonstration of resolve but also a demonstration of capabilities to take on this type of battle and deal with it successfully."

Adam Yarmolinsky, a special assistant to the Secretary of Defense, put it this way: "I might argue that one of the reasons we got onto the tragedy of Vietnam was that the Kennedy administration took a decisive step away from massive retaliation, from the doctrine that the United States would even consider using nuclear weapons at times and places of our choosing, in order to enforce our policy objectives in the world. When it was officially recognized that this was nonsense and still dangerous nonsense, there was a kind of reaction, a swinging of the pendulum almost to a sort of euphoria: Well, now we can get away from the notion of Armageddon and the imaginative quarrels we have with the Soviets and their satellites. And the name of the new doctrine was counter-insurgency."

Roger Hilsman, a foreign policy advisor to President Kennedy, said in an interview after the war, "I'd like to say there were really three

Kennedy policies on Vietnam. He went through these three phases. He was badly shaken, or the word frightened, but that isn't probably quite correct, by Nikita Khrushchev's speech where he said they (the Soviets) would support wars of national liberation, and by President Eisenhower's warning that Laos was the big problem. Ike said to him on inauguration day that 'I think you're going to have to send troops, and if you do I will come up from Gettysburg and stand beside you and support you.' The memory is vivid in my mind of Kennedy's standing before three maps and the TV cameras, marking the progressive incursions of the communists into Laos, and he talked in very strong language, diplomatic language, but it was a threat to intervene. Then came the Bay of Pigs. Kennedy said many times, 'The Bay of Pigs has taught me a number of things; one is not to trust generals or the CIA, and the second is that the American people don't want to use troops to remove communists 90 miles away from our shores. So how can I ask them to use American troops to remove communists 9,000 miles away?'"

Hilsman continued, "So, I think we entered phase two: This is what I call the counter-insurgency phase with American military and aid advisors assisting the Vietnamese. Phase three with Kennedy was 'let's get out.' He then adopted a policy towards the very end which was the same as he adopted towards Laos. I was sent to Saigon early in 1963 to report back to him on the many problems there. I'm not saying my report was the overwhelming piece of evidence that caused him to change. But that report, coupled with the Buddhist crisis of 1963 in Saigon and other cities, I think moved him to phase three, which was to do to Vietnam what he had done to Laos, to neutralize it."

3

THE DAY DIEM DIED

AMERICAN AMBASSADOR HENRY CABOT LODGE visited South Vietnamese President Ngo Dinh Diem at his baroque Gia Long Palace in Saigon in the late morning of November 1, 1963, on the eve of a routine trip back home. It was a courteous but cool meeting. Of the several ambassadors representing the United States assigned to Saigon since Diem had taken presidential power in 1955, Lodge had proven the most critical of him. Their first meeting late summer was a near-disaster as Lodge conveyed the White House demand to have Ngo Dinh Nhu, Diem's brother, removed as his top advisor. Lodge told me in an interview after the war, "He was as unreceptive as I've ever seen a human being to be and he almost said to me, 'Well, what business is it of yours whether I have my brother here to advise me or not?' To which of course there was a good answer. It's my business because the president of the United States has made it my business. I didn't say that, but I thought that. I thought that I was doing my business just as much as he was doing his. There wasn't any doubt that his brother Nhu was quite a sinister influence, I think."

In the months after Lodge's arrival in early August, the weakening American support of Diem had emboldened a group of Vietnamese generals to plan a coup d'état to overthrow the regime. Lodge was privy to the details. The American ambassador had pretty much ignored Diem in the months that followed his first meeting, leaving it to his staff to handle diplomatic business. At this rare gathering at the Gia Long Palace on November 1, he took along General Paul D. Harkins, the commander of U.S. military forces in Vietnam, and the visiting chief of all Pacific forces, Admiral Harry D. Felt.

After a few pleasantries, Lodge recalled, "Diem said to me, 'Every time the American ambassador goes to Washington, there's rumors that there is going to be a coup. And I hear these rumors now, but I don't know who is going to do it or where he's going to do it. The coup planners are much cleverer this time, more than they've ever been before, because there are a number of them and I can't find out which is the real one.' That's what he said; that was noon." Two hours later when he was at his residence, he told me, "We were sitting there having lunch when there was tremendous automatic weapons fire. It sounded like it was right in the next room, and planes flew overhead—you were there, you saw it—and that was the beginning of the overthrow."

Nearly nine years earlier, on April 4, 1955, Ngo Dinh Diem's picture was on the cover of Time magazine, when the threat to his life came from communist Vietcong guerrillas and not from his own generals. The cover-line read, "The hour is late, the odds are great," in reference to the perilous nature of his selection as America's man in South Vietnam, a new nation formed after the failure of the French attempt to restore its Indochinese colonies after World War II.

Diem was known as a nationalist opposed to both the French colonialists and the Vietnamese communists fighting them. He was at one time a high ranking civil servant who had chosen voluntarily to move overseas.

Historian Arthur Schlesinger Jr., who was to become an influential aide to President Kennedy, told me after the war, "When Diem was in exile in the United States he came to us. He was sponsored by such exemplary figures as Bill Douglas of the Supreme Court and Mike Mansfield of the Senate. Jack Kennedy met him then, and when Diem went back to Vietnam Kennedy was one of his supporters." With American help Diem was unexpectedly named prime minister of South Vietnam just before the Geneva agreements of 1954 partitioned Vietnam into north and south. The agreements provided for joint elections on reunification within two years.

French historian Jean Lacouture told me that after having seen the communist victory at the battle of Dien Bien Phu earlier in the year,

"The sentiment at Geneva was that the communists had made a large concession to the French and the West. Almost everybody thought the elections would end in in a victory for the north and the reunification of the country. That was said in the memoirs of (U.S. President Dwight) Eisenhower and it was the opinion of 90 percent of the people after the Geneva conference."

The United States and the Saigon government decided not to sign the agreement, and by June of that year the Eisenhower administration had decided to train and finance a 243,000-man army for South Vietnam. Diem went ahead and held his own elections with CIA help in early 1955, and after a decisive win proclaimed himself president and appointed his younger brother, Ngo Dinh Nhu, as his chief advisor. In the years that followed, the United States poured billions of dollars into preserving the independence of the new state.

But by 1961, when Kennedy took office, serious doubts had arisen over Diem's leadership in the fight against the communist Vietcong guerrillas challenging his rule, and the young president dispatched friends, civilian and military officials, and a new ambassador to assess the situation. The envoy, Frederick Nolting, told me in an interview after the war, "I was sent out by President Kennedy to try and determine if President Diem was the person on whom we could rely, and whom the Vietnamese people could rely on, to lead them in the right ways and the right direction, to treat them well and fairly. And to win the struggle against the Vietcong."

The scholarly Nolting, whose foreign experience had primarily been in Europe, said, "My convictions grew that he was the right man despite opposition to him in some quarters, despite a turning against him in overseas countries, particularly in the United States. I felt then and I still feel that he was the best available leader of the South Vietnamese and that he probably could have succeeded in keeping the country free. There had been no experience of democracy in the sense that you and I know it, so that he was quite aware that it took a number of years of education and of responsible self-government before the constitution of South Vietnam could be really fleshed out and made a living reality."

Nolting became one leg of a triumvirate of senior American officials in Saigon dedicated to the preservation of the Diem regime. The other two were General Harkins, commander of the U.S. military effort, and the Saigon CIA station chief, William Colby. Nolting and Colby in particular cultivated intimate relationships with the ruling family that only became fully apparent after the war. Both became especially close to Ngo Dinh Nhu, President Diem's younger brother, seen by many officials in the Kennedy administration and the American media as an increasingly negative influence on successful policies.

Nolting praised him. "Ngo Dinh Nhu was the inspiration for the Strategic Hamlet program, which in my opinion was a successful way to protect the civilian population from the depredations of the Vietcong. He was also a difficult person to know and gave the impression that he was very devious. I knew him, would see him quite frequently, went shooting with him, hunting with him. On several occasions, I spent the night around the campfire and so forth up in the mountains with him. I never considered him a devious man."

As the CIA man in Saigon, William Colby was allowed far more freedom to interact with the regime than the American diplomats and military advisors. In an interview after the war, he said, "I used to travel with Diem and his brother Nhu and we would go around with them, and I became very close to them both. I think I was probably the very first person who had any depth of relationship with the brother at all."

Colby described Nhu as "a very theoretical person. He had been trained in French schools. He was a Cartesian musician, you might say. He would analyze anything down to the nth degree, and we would go at this for three, four and five hours, together, spending the whole afternoon discussing the fine points of some problem. He was convinced that his mission and his brother's mission were to bring Vietnam into new kind of world, a Vietnamese world, not an American one and not a French one; to do away with the old French heritage, but not to become an American puppet either. This was his mission to the very end."

Colby said he also had a unique relationship with Nhu's wife, Tran Le Xuan, popularly known as Madame Nhu and notorious during the Kennedy years for criticizing the nature of the American effort. As an AP reporter in Saigon at the time, I, like other journalists, sometimes mocked Madame Nhu's outrageous flaunting of power, and we were subject to her frequent ridicule, particularly at her public events when she appeared with her female supporters and verbally trounced the attending press.

Colby said, "I knew Mrs. Nhu, of course, as Nhu's wife. But I also had a particular relationship with her which gave me a slightly different view than most people have of the so-called Dragon Lady, who really acted as the Empress of Vietnam at that time, no doubt about it. Unfortunately, she was not gifted with the gift of tact. She never really had any tact, but she was a very determined woman, a forceful and very imaginative one.

"My first connection with her was to help her translate into American legalese a law that she had forced through the legislature to give women rights. The previous situation which she was very indignant about was that when a woman married, all her property, all, became her husband's, and that her husband had practically no obligation to her and she had all the obligations to him. She was particularly incensed, I know, about one point. A husband could go off and have a liaison with some other woman and if a child was produced the husband could bring the child into the family and nominate him as an heir of the husband, displacing the legitimate wife's own children. One can imagine the effect of this in a Confucian society, let alone Western morality."

Colby was also sympathetic to Madame Nhu's strident demands that dancing be banned in Saigon's bars and dance halls, upsetting those who enjoyed the hedonistic lifestyle of a city often described as "the Paris of the East."

Colby said, "She took the position that people were dying in the countryside and that it was inappropriate for people in Saigon, who were supposedly leading the war effort, to be dancing. It was a rather puritanical way to make a point, and there was a certain amount of surreptitious dancing going on from time to time. But I think it showed both her feeling of the importance of the whole nation getting together in the struggle and not just leaving it to the poor peasants to suffer the deaths, and that the higher levels should make some sense of obligation, some sense of participation."

Colby also observed, "It showed her lack of tact because it wasn't a practical thing to do. So, we get the two sides of the woman, and I know that she is generally considered as some terrible dragon, but I have to say that I had enormous respect for a number of her positions."

Colby said he also drew close to Diem. "He was a rather rotund and very short gentleman and had a lot of presence, a lot of humanism. He was a mandarin, and he made no secret that he thought that as a mandarin, his function as a kind of monk almost was to bring Vietnam into a modern world, to develop its economy, improve its social structures, social service, health, education, public works, roads, all those things. These were his passion. The political, the more intangible problems. were taken over by his brother, whereby he was very much a practical man. He loved to take out to the map and show you where the road would be put through so he could establish a new village in some areas that were just jungle at that point."

There were others within the ruling family who drew the attention of critics including two brothers, the Roman Catholic Archbishop of Hue, Ngo Dinh Thuc, eventually involved in an emerging Buddhist crisis, and Ngo Duc Can, the autocratic governor of the important central Vietnam region.

Both Diem and Nhu had a reputation among visiting Americans as being long-winded, with courtesy calls lasting into the hours. "This was a family characteristic," Colby said. "They liked to spend a long time talking to you and . . . their objective, quite obviously with an American, was to maintain support for their American-backed efforts to modernize and protect South Vietnam. And therefore, when they got hold of an American with any influence at the local embassy, or a visitor, they would make the mistake of overstating their position."

And there was another issue, Colby said. "Sometimes you would go in there at 3 o'clock and wouldn't get out until 7:30, and this sometimes was rather a test on your bladder, quite frankly. The servants would come in and pour more tea for us and after a while you learned not to take it, and just keep the tea sitting there, because that was the only way you could get through to the end of the session."

Colby indicated that dealing with Ngo Dinh Nhu was a delicate conversational minuet demanding great patience. "In a rather Socratic way of asking the right question in the middle of these kinds of discussions, you could begin to get not only other facets of the issues you needed to bring out, you could actually make them think of some of these other things you needed to bring up. And that is what I used to do, just occasionally ask a question which would raise a kind of a problem with them. I wouldn't test them and say, 'No, you're wrong,' because they really wouldn't have accepted that. That is not the way you do your business in that kind of society. You just rather humbly ask the question that causes your conversation to run in another way. And in that way, you are able to get a great deal across just as Socrates was able to so many years ago."

Visiting officials traded pointers on handling the long sit-downs with Diem. General Maxwell Taylor, at that time the military advisor to President Kennedy and a key figure in the growing American involvement in South Vietnam, told me, "It was always a bit of an ordeal to call on the president, and I came to appreciate the problem. My procedure when I came to Saigon was to go and get my briefing from my ambassador and my military mission. And then call on the president.

"And after the usual amenities, I would say, 'Mr. President, I have just received an excellent discussion of the current situation from the Americans, and I would like it if you would be good enough to give me your observations on the current situation.' And it never turned out that way. Diem insisted on going back nearly two centuries, earlier sometimes, to trace the Chinese influence on his country and more historical background. Eventually, he would bring it forward to the current time. He was very learned, and I think that I profited somewhat from it, but it was conducted in French and he was constantly smoking a cigarette. He would get a sort of glassy look in his eyes, as if he were dozing off. I would have specific questions that I wanted to ask. Usually in the last half hour I could probably bring him back again to those things that I would like to carry home to Washington. It was hard going, but nonetheless I had a high regard for the little man. He was certainly an intense patriot, a deeply religious man. He believed that he was serving God and country in what he was doing. And considering the resources that he had available to him in terms of administrative government talent, I always felt that he did a very good job."

Criticism of the Diem regime coalesced in the summer of 1963 with a Buddhist uprising that made headlines around the world when my AP colleague Malcolm Browne photographed an elderly monk committing suicide by fire on a street in the center of Saigon in opposition to government policies. William Colby, back home in the United States as chief of the CIA's Far East Division described the crisis this way:

"Leaders of the Buddhist movement took the view that Diem was favorable to the Catholic population and this blew up into an incident that occurred in Hue when several Buddhists demonstrators were killed. And then the Diem regime began to suppress the Buddhist opposition. There were a few people in jail. Some were killed. Now this kind of thing created an uproar among the Buddhists, and I think this led to the final overthrow of Diem. The thing that did as much as anything to lead to the overthrow was that photograph of the bonze burning himself in the street in Saigon. Now the fact was that that bonze was on protest against Diem. The fact also was that his fellow bonzes had alerted the press to ensure that they would be there, and get those photographs. That was a rather cynical maneuver by the Buddhists, making sure they got the greatest possible coverage of that event. Now this made the position of the American government almost impossible for President Kennedy, who said that he was a liberal and wanted to fight for freedom. And here were those shocking photographs and the regular news coverage of the opposition to Diem's mandarin regime."

Kennedy's impatience with the Diem regime was quickly made evident to Henry Cabot Lodge who called on him at the White House prior to leaving for Saigon on his assignment as the new American ambassador to South Vietnam.

"I remember going into the Oval Office and there on the president's table was a picture of that old man sitting cross-legged and burning himself to death. President Kennedy said to me, 'Look at that. Look at what things have come to in Vietnam. Now, I want you, I have confidence in you, to go out there and see if we can't get that government to behave better,'" Lodge told me. He added: "You see, up to that time the embassy was uncritically supporting the Vietnamese government. Well, President Kennedy didn't want to continue with that policy. He wanted American influence to be actively used, and he wanted it used to improve the behavior of the Vietnamese government, and that's what we tried to do."

William Colby said, "In August of 1963, our government sent a telegram out to our mission in Vietnam, which the ambassador (Lodge) interpreted as 'go out and see if there is a coup,' and he sent a CIA operative out to see if there was a coup. We frightened an awful lot of generals by asking then, because they were horrified it would get back to the government and lead to their incarceration, at least. So, they said no at that time. But they said if we get interested we will give you a call sometime and we will maintain these friendships.

"At the end of October, the CIA got a call from one of the generals who said, 'Come over to our office and join us, as we are having a meeting,' and when we got there we discovered the coup was on. Now this was a Vietnamese generals' coup, yes, but I think the fundamentals of it were decided in our White House because a few weeks before, the president said publicly it was essential to contemplate new people in the Vietnamese government, and that could only be interpreted as a final warning signal to the president and his brother.

"We also announced the cut-off of the commercial import program. And the generals obviously saw that America was going to cut down on its support for the regime. We cut off the support the CIA was giving to a particular unit in the Vietnamese army, and the interpretation of that was that if we were dissatisfied with the leadership we would cut off the assistance there and to the army. Now these were green lights to the generals to go ahead, reinforced by a question asked by one of them, that if the Diem regime was replaced, would the United States continue to support his successor? Answer from the White House: Yes."

As the Buddhist crisis built up momentum, General Maxell Taylor, a member of the National Security Council, would attend regular sessions at the White House. He told me in an interview after the war, "We'd have meetings. We'd see these dramatic and terrible impressive pictures of Buddhist monks burning themselves, presumably in protest to the tyrannical rule of Diem. The impression was very vivid in Washington. This results in really a split between the president's advisors on where do we go from here, because there was a strong group that picked up the slogan, 'You can't win with Diem.' The other group, to which I belonged, said maybe we can't win with Diem but if not Diem, who? And the answer was always complete silence."

Taylor said, "So we really did not get our hands on the situation in Vietnam at our end in Washington, because during this period we ourselves did not make up our minds. President Kennedy was hoping that it would work itself out, and he became sympathetic to the idea of a coup if the Americans were not responsible or not involved in it. Well, the record shows to what extent we were involved in the coup, at least to the extent of the open knowledge that we were discouraged with Diem, that we disapproved of his dealings with the Buddhists as being unduly harsh. Those facts were out, and the word was around Saigon that certainly that if any of the generals decided that this was a good time for a coup, then they would probably get American support."

Colby, a CIA member of the National Security Council, who went on to become director of the CIA in the early 1970s, mirrored Taylor's view in an interview after the war.

"The period of 1963 was one of the most agonizing and intensive periods of debate that I ever experienced inside our government. I was a middle grade officer in the CIA but having come from Vietnam in 1962, I was one of the people in Washington who knew quite a lot about Vietnam and had dealt with the people there. There was a very intense division of opinion in the government. And both sides in good faith, both trying to do the very best for the country. One was the State Department group that looked upon the problems in Vietnam as essentially political. That translated into a belief that if the Diem regime could be pressured into democratizing he would become less of a mandarin, he would be better appreciated by his people, and better able to support himself against the appeal of the communists.

"The other side of the argument made by the military, was simply there is a war on. This viewed the alternative to the Diem regime as much more dictatorial, much more dangerous, not only to our interests as Americans but to Vietnam as a whole. And that therefore we would not want to weaken — should not weaken — the Diem government by pressing or attacking it. We should support it as we build up our strength to meet the external opponent. And these were the two ends of the agreement. I was convinced that Vietnam would democratize a little bit. But there was no use in weakening the only leader that you have in Vietnam, which is the Diem regime."

"My position was very plain, "Colby said. "We should support Diem, that he was the best leader we could get at that time, and the problems were correctable if we could put down the real threat to Vietnam and American interests in the form of a potential for a Vietcong victory."

Roger Hilsman, at that time director of the bureau of intelligence and research at the State Department, commented, "It was very interesting to watch the two Brahmins, you know, the Boston Brahmin Lodge and the Vietnamese mandarin Diem, at odds with each other. Lodge very quickly made up his mind, I believe, that the South Vietnamese had no chance of winning so long as Diem and Nhu were around and that therefore either Nhu had to be removed to Paris as ambassador and Diem persuaded to get in a whole new set of advisors or we should wash our hands of it. So, I think Lodge made up his mind to that and I think to some extent he pursued an independent policy along those lines."

I was one of a team of AP reporters covering the coup d'état, and we were as surprised as most of Saigon's population as the tanks began rolling towards the Gia Long Palace in the afternoon of November 1, 1963. Lodge did not share with us his advance knowledge of the coup, and confusion raged in the city as fighting continued against the few security units still loyal to President Diem.

In an interview with me after the war, Ambassador Lodge revealed that at 4 p.m. on the day of the coup, President Diem telephoned him saying that the coup had begun and he wanted to know what he would do. "I said the obvious truth that I had no instructions and that it was 4 in the morning in Washington, and I had no opportunity to do it. 'Oh well,' he said, 'you must know what the policy is.' 'Well,' I said, 'I don't know what the policy is for every circumstance.' I told him I was worried about his safety and that I've made arrangements to get you out of the country so as to protect your safety. I said if you don't want to do that, I've made arrangements that would authorize your becoming titular head of state, and you can stay here in a position of honor and you will be relatively safe. He said, 'I want to restore order,' and he hung up. I've left out a few details, but that's roughly what happened."

Lodge said, "That's the only conversation we had. I had reports of him, culminating, of course, in the horrible tragic report of his assassination, terrible thing, terrible thing. And I don't believe we know now whether that assassination was done in response to private initiatives or in response to government initiatives."

General Taylor was at a meeting with President Kennedy and other members of the National Security Council at the White House when details of the coup began coming in. "Well, strangely enough, and it seems strange on retrospect, we were all surprised when those events of November 1 occurred. I think it was because there were so many rumors of coups about to take place, and that created a background clutter, so to speak, of a certain incredulity on our part when a new report came in. General Harkins had cabled about 48 hours in advance indicating that a coup might be about to take place. Well, it had been said before, so we were relatively relaxed until the cables came in that there had been this coup."

The generals' coup d'état had proceeded smoothly, with rebel Vietnamese marines wearing red arm bands taking control of the buildings housing the National Police and the Interior Ministry in a mid-afternoon attack. Diem and Nhu had plans of their own, and were initially complacent when they received reports of unscheduled troop movements because this was the day when they had planned the start of a fake counter-coup designed to smoke out the generals they believed were plotting against them. By late evening after once loyal senior officers were won over by the coup-making generals, only the Presidential Guard was left to fight for the survival of the regime. Without informing their loyal defenders, Diem and Nhu escaped from the palace in the middle of the night, probably through one of the three "coup" tunnels built just for that eventuality and leading to the streets outside. They spent the night in at the home of a friendly Chinese merchant in the suburb of Cholon, and moved to the nearby St. Francis Xavier Catholic Church in the morning where they surrendered. The military convoy sent to pick them up forced the brothers, under protest, into an armored personnel carrier. They were assured it was for their own safety, but en route to military headquarters the convoy stopped at a railway intersection where two army officers, one of them the bodyguard of the coup leader, General Duong Van Minh, shot them at close range and stabbed them repeatedly, according to an official investigation of the murders.

Kennedy was caught unawares by the assassination of Diem and his brother. Taylor said, "This was indeed a shock to all of us, but I think perhaps to the president more than any of us. He didn't realize that we were all playing with fire when we were at least giving tacit encouragement to the overthrow of the regime."

"When the news came in, and I recall it was brought to him from the outside by one of his aides and put in front of him, he read it. Nobody said a word, and there was silence around the table. The president was obviously shaken by the news. He sprang to his feet and walked out of the room, saying nothing to anybody, and stayed out the room for some minutes. He eventually came back in and took his chair, collected his thoughts, and then discussed — as we all did — the consequences and the causes and what would we do about it."

William Colby was attending a meeting of the National Security Council at the White House that Saturday morning. "I reported what I knew about the movement of troops and the way that the event had transpired. And after the meeting my boss, Mr. McCone (CIA director John McCone), asked me to come to the Oval Office because he wanted to suggest to the president that I be sent over to Vietnam to see what we would be doing from here on. With President Diem gone, with the generals in command, we were suddenly realizing that we really didn't know much about the successor government that was apt to appear over there. The president seemed pale and distraught when I met him, and I think he felt a sense of responsibility for it. Certainly he hadn't anticipated it — whether he should have or not is another matter — but he was very upset by it. Obviously.

"Mr. McCone told the president that he was sending me there to check into it because I knew a lot of the generals from previous service, and I knew quite a lot about Vietnam, having lived there and traveled all over it. And the president wished me well."

Colby said, "It really sounds incredible today that we made those decisions about getting rid of Diem without careful consideration of what kind of government would replace him."

John Kenneth Galbraith, a close friend of Kennedy, had a contrary argument to Colby's in an interview with me after the war. He said, "I would like to say a word about the dynamics of revolution. This is something that we need to understand, certainly in relation to Ngo Dinh Diem, to the whole problem of Vietnam. There is never in revolution a good calculation as to the alternatives. If one has a regressive leader such as Diem, the pressure will develop to eliminate him, even though it is quite possible that what takes his place will be weaker, or more oppressive or more inefficient or worse.

"The calculation is always on the poor quality of the particular leader as against the dream. And the dream, of course, will always win. And so, we should never make the mistake of thinking that we can hang on to a regressive, a Somoza (deposed Nicaraguan President Anastasio Somoza), a Diem or perhaps even the shah (Iran's overthrown leader), on the assumption that the alternative will be less good or worse. This is not the way the calculation works. And if you have a bad enough leader he will be thrown out quite without regard to the alternatives."

The dream for the Americans in South Vietnam was victory.

4

LBJ DISCOVERS VIETNAM

NEWLY INSTALLED AS VICE PRESIDENT of the United States, Lyndon Baines Johnson made his first visit to South Vietnam in May 1961, and when I arrived on assignment in Saigon for The Associated Press a year later the locals were still talking about it.

As American Ambassador Frederick Nolting recalled in a later interview with me, "It was a whirlwind visit, and Johnson with his usual vigor went around and shook hands with many, many people. It was rather difficult because most Vietnamese at that time would rather press their hands together in front and bow, but some of those that did organized a club later on called 'The Shake the Hand of Lyndon Johnson Club' that was in vogue for a while."

The vice president was in South Vietnam primarily because President John F. Kennedy needed him to glad-hand the monastic President Ngo Dinh Diem, whose relations with the United States were deteriorating. The trip was a windfall for Johnson because Kennedy was finding little real use for him in his major legislative efforts, and had decided, as he remarked to a political friend, "to use Johnson's finesse in handling people on an international level."

The vice president would eventually make 11 international trips, with an ostentatious traveling style. It included transporting his seven-foot-long bed and his personal pillows all over the world, along with his special shower attachment, a case of his preferred Scotch whisky, and boxes of cigarette lighters and engraved ballpoint pens that he handed out to crowds. It drew some criticism and ridicule, but concerns in the State Department about his garrulous conduct drew this response from Johnson:

"We cannot demonstrate the essence and spirit of the American political system unless we get out of our limousines abroad as we would at home. After all, what dignity are we trying to prove — that of the office of the vice president or that of the human race."

The cigarette lighters and the engraved ballpoint pens were very much in evidence in Saigon, South Vietnam's capital, during the four-day visit, the first by an American official of such importance since Vice President Richard Nixon visited in 1957.

"An amusing aspect," remembered Ambassador Nolting who was at Johnson's side, "was how it developed into vigorous campaigning on behalf of Vietnamese democracy, shaking hands and greeting people, much as he might have done during a political campaign in Johnson City, Texas. So, as we toured Saigon and its environs, crowds — some of which I am sure were drummed up by the government — would gather where he was going to stop. Mr. Johnson would plunge into the crowd greeting people. Some were soon reaching out to him, and even holding out their babies. Between stops the vice president, sweating profusely in the very hot climate, would change his shirt in the back of our car. Of course, when we arrived at the next stop he would appear to be wet again."

The Kennedy administration was hoping that Johnson would do more in Vietnam than just entertain the crowds, and that his amiability would rub off on President Diem who in the six years of his American-supported administration seemed to be losing against a communist-backed insurgency. "The main motivation for American policy in South Vietnam at that time was always two-fold," according to William Bundy, then a deputy assistant secretary of defense. In an interview after the war he told me, "The first was to enable South Vietnam to preserve itself in the face of what clearly seemed from 1961 onward a determined effort by North Vietnam, with the aid, of course, of some sympathetic elements in the South, to take over the South.

"And second, to deal with the wider aspects of that threat. In 1961, it appeared that a victory for North Vietnam would have considerable significance in appearing to indicate that the wave of communism was sweeping over the area, perhaps in Soviet form," Bundy said.

A speech by Soviet premier Nikita Khrushchev on January 6, 1961, just days before the Kennedy administration took office, shocked the Americans into believing that, as Bundy said, "What was going on in Vietnam seemed the clearest possible case of what Khrushchev had said in January was 'wars of liberation.'" In the text if his speech, Khrushchev said, "Liberation wars will continue to exist for as long as imperialism continues to exist, so long as colonialism continues to exist. These are revolutionary wars. Such wars are not only admissible but inevitable since the colonialists do not grant independence voluntary. What is the attitude of Marxists towards such uprisings? A most positive one."

Kennedy White House aide Arthur Schlesinger Jr. has written that the president-elect was so concerned by the Soviet leader's remarks that it prompted him to take a more hawkish approach in his inauguration speech, including a soon-to-be famous line, "Let every nation know, whether it wishes us well or ill, that we shall pay any price, bear any burden, meet any hardship, support any friend, oppose any foe, to assure the survival and success of liberty."

Just a few days prior to his vice president's visit to Vietnam, Kennedy approved the top-secret National Security Action Memorandum No. 52 that called for 12 immediate steps "to prevent communist domination of South Vietnam, to create in that country a viable and increasingly democratic society, and to initiate. on an accelerated basis, a series of mutually supporting actions of a military, political, economic, psychological and covert character designed to achieve this objective."

Vice President Johnson waded into his political task in South Vietnam with enthusiasm and superlatives, referring at a press briefing to Diem as "the Churchill of Asia" and at another time likening him "to Andrew Jackson and Woodrow Wilson." Ambassador Nolting was amused and impressed by Johnson, stating. "Both publicly and privately, he was forthright in his dealings with President Diem, his family, and his government. As a participant, I was impressed by Mr. Johnson's drive and energy, by President Diem's calm determination and inner force. And especially the enormous difference of approach to political leadership between the two men — the one occidental the other oriental, the one outgoing and the other reserved, the one seeking popular approval and the one seeking to deserve respect, the one democratic in our sense, the other paternalistic in his attitude toward his people in the accepted mandarin tradition. Yet there was evident rapport between them."

The vice president had one more opportunity to flatter the Vietnamese leader, at a farewell dinner in the presidential quarters that was also attended by two of Johnson's entourage, Jean Kennedy Smith and her husband Stephen Smith. That was "a touch not lost on the Ngo family that the Kennedy administration favored strong family ties," recalled Ambassador Nolting. A persistent criticism of President Diem was that he gave too much governing authority to his brother Ngo Dinh Nhu and his brother's wife, Madame Nhu.

At the dinner, Johnson delivered an all-embracing endorsement of his host, praising him for his "strong and unwavering resolve to protect his hard-pressed country from communist domination," and promising increasing American moral and material support. Johnson touched on a more familiar subject, elections, won by Diem several weeks earlier. "Your people, Mr. President, returned you to office with 91 percent of the vote. You are not only George Washington, the father of your country, but the Franklin Roosevelt as well." Ambassador Nolting said, "At the conclusion of this extraordinary eulogy, on a signal from Mr. Johnson, we all rose and drank a toast in warm champagne to the president of South Vietnam."

In a lengthy May 23 report to President Kennedy on his return home, Johnson wrote that "the situation in Vietnam is more stable than is indicated in newspaper and other reports reaching Washington in recent weeks. The picture we received at home has been colored by journalistic sensationalism. It may also be distorted by these other factors:

1. An obsessive concern with security on the part of many of our mission people and a tendency to incorporate this concern into interpretations of its general situation. After all, occasional murders

in Rock Creek Park (in Washington), deplorable as they may be, do not mean that the United States is about to fall apart.

2. A conscious or unconscious desire in various quarters to stimulate the flow of United States aid.

3. An excessive reliance by our mission on the evaluations of the situation by Vietnamese government officials, often checked only against other government sources or discontented Vietnamese intellectuals who are in opposition to the present government. This reliance stems in part at least from the government's discouraging of travel by Americans outside Saigon on grounds of security.

4. An assumption that because conditions have turned bad in Laos they must inevitably turn bad in Vietnam."

Johnson concluded his report to the President with this admonition: "There is a chance for success in Vietnam but there is not a moment to lose. We need to move along the above lines and we need to begin now, today, to move."

Ambassador Nolting told me that inefficiency was the major weakness of the Diem government. "A very weak bureaucracy comprised of people poorly trained for jobs throughout the government. Secondly, I would say the inability of the Vietnamese people to grasp even the fundamentals of democratic self-rule, that resulted from a lack of education, a tradition of thousands of years of authoritarian government, and 75 years of French control. It was unrealistic to expect, in my opinion, that they should suddenly bloom into a democracy that the United States or some of our newspapers and some of our government officials felt that they should."

What impact did the visit of Lyndon Johnson have on President Diem? Ambassador Nolting said he raised the matter with Diem when he got to know him better. "While he showed good humor and a certain curiosity about American politicians' practices, he concluded with a serious remark, 'There are profound differences between the Vietnamese and American people in customs, outlook, political training and philosophy. I hope we can find a bridge between Eastern and Western cultures.' But Diem did not miss the opportunity to remind me of Johnson's remark about his getting 91 percent of the vote."

Of the vice president's visit, Ambassador Nolting told me, "I think it was very influential on President Johnson. For example, he was one of those — I want to put this in now, if I may — one of those who opposed the Kennedy administration's backing or encouraging or, to use the least damaging word, conniving, in the overthrow of the Diem government." Nolting himself was to quit the State Department when his own strenuous efforts to prevent the November 1 coup d'état failed.

Johnson's memorable visit to Saigon, a city 12,000 miles distant from Washington, D.C., but much further apart in terms of culture and history, and his style of friendly familiarity, would come to typify the U.S government's public relationship with the small Asian country, even as behind the scenes the discussions, the desperate debates and the decisions would soon embroil both countries in an embittered, tortuous relationship that that would bring mounting sacrifice on both sides.

5

LBJ TAKES OVER

LYNDON BAINES JOHNSON WAS SWORN INTO OFFICE on Air Force One flying from Dallas, Texas, to Washington, D.C., on the afternoon of November 22, 1963, his wife Lady Bird and Jackie Kennedy, in a blood-stained dress, standing beside him. The body of the slain president, John F. Kennedy, lay in a casket in the cargo hold.

In Johnson's first words to the nation, he pledged to heal the wounds of Kennedy's assassination, and to build a society based on impartial civil rights. Vietnam was not at the top of his agenda, but two days after taking office he convened a meeting with his top advisors to discuss the war with the visiting American Ambassador Henry Cabot Lodge.

Hearing contradictory viewpoints, Johnson expressed his serious misgivings about the overthrow of the Diem regime earlier in the month saying, "It is not important to reform every Asian into our own image." And he demanded immediate results in the war. "I am not going to lose Vietnam. I am not going to be the president who saw Southeast Asia go the way China went," he told his assembled top advisors.

Within a few days, Johnson publicly pledged "to keep our commitments from South Vietnam to West Berlin." And he privately signed off on National Security Action Memorandum (NSAM) 273, a top-secret document drawn up at a Honolulu conference by Kennedy's top Vietnam advisors that began the day before the president's assassination in Dallas.

In his autobiography, "The Vantage Point," Johnson wrote that his approval of the secret document "was my first important decision on Vietnam as president, not because it required any new actions but it signaled our determination to persevere in the policies and actions in which we were already engaged."

The memorandum preserved the decision of President Kennedy, made early the previous October, to withdraw 1,000 American servicemen. But paragraph 7 suggested future possible escalation of the effort. It read, "Planning should include different levels of possible increased activity, and in each instance, there should be estimates of such factors as resulting damage to North Vietnam, the plausibility of denial, possible North Vietnamese retaliation, and other international reaction." One of the attendees at the Honolulu conference was McGeorge Bundy, a top national security advisor to Kennedy, who offered an addition to paragraph 7. It read: "With respect to action against North Vietnam, there should be a detailed plan for the development of additional Government of Vietnam resources, especially for sea-going activity, and such planning should indicate the time and investment necessary to achieve a whole new level of effectiveness in this field of action."

Bundy's paragraph did not make it to the official document, but he was retained by Johnson as a top advisor on the war, and the clandestine sabotage attacks on North Vietnamese coastal facilities and shipping that emerged in the next six months led directly to an engagement with American warships and communist forces in the Gulf of Tonkin, and the first American bombing of North Vietnam.

Johnson was well aware of the pitfalls that lay ahead. He told his biographer Doris Kearns Goodwin that he knew "better than any" the choices he faced. In an interview with me after the war, Kearns Goodwin quoted Johnson as saying, "'If we get involved in that bitch of a war over there my great society is going to be dead.' And yet if he let the war go and let the South Vietnamese lose, he was afraid that all the traditional anti-Democratic party feeling—you lost China, you lost Vietnam—was going to come screeching at him."

Johnson's abrupt assumption of power turned out to be a major turning point in America's approach to Vietnam. As vice president, he had been kept ignorant of higher policy and had taken little part in previous decision making. In ascending to the top job, he pushed ahead with an aggressive program to resolve issues that had left his predecessor with growing frustration toward achieving America's promised goals of creating an independent pro-Western South Vietnam.

Kennedy was already tiring of the effort when he was assassinated in Dallas. Roger Hilsman, director of State Department planning in the Kennedy years, said in an interview after the war, "The first member of the administration who said openly that perhaps the time has come for us to withdraw from Vietnam was Robert Kennedy, sometime after the beat-up of the pagodas when various alternatives were discussed. Robert Kennedy openly said this at a national security council meeting and this became one of the options that we thereafter examined very carefully.

"After this we began actively in my office as assistant secretary for Far Eastern affairs to begin seeking ways to withdraw. We began to look for a neutralist leader in Vietnam as we had in Souvanna Phouma in Vientiane (Laos), where we could build a Geneva accord neutralizing the country. You will recall a few weeks later Jack Kennedy ordered the withdrawal of the first 1,000 people. When he died there were only 16,500 Americans in Vietnam and a 1,000 were under orders to withdraw."

President Kennedy reaffirmed his desire to change policy in Vietnam on the eve of his assassination, telling Michael Forrestal, a senior member of the National Security Council, in an Oval Office meeting that, "I want to start a complete and very profound review of how we got into this country, and what we thought we were doing, and what we now think we can do. I even want to think about whether or not we should be there."

He told Forrestal the upcoming 1964 election campaign precluded any "drastic changes of policy quickly, but he wanted to consider how to bring some kind of gradual shift in our presence in Vietnam." Forrestal would leave the Johnson administration within a year, as did some other senior Kennedy officials disappointed with Johnson's rush to confrontation with the communist Vietnamese.

Roger Hilsman went to work with the new president. "I had decided that Johnson had made up his mind about Vietnam as least as far back as his visit in 1961 and there was nothing we were going to do to change it. Kennedy is on the public record several times as saying, this is an almost exact quote, that 'it is their war, the South Vietnamese. We may give them aid and advisors but they must win it or lose it.' I became convinced before Kennedy's death that Johnson did not believe in those the last three words.

"But I didn't see that Johnson was plotting to escalate the war from the moment Kennedy died. I think that if in the next six months if the counterinsurgency policy of giving them aid and advisors had worked he would have been content. But I think that he had already made up his mind that he would not permit the loss of Vietnam, and during those months he did not change the policy but what he did do, he removed the people who were obstacles to it."

William Colby, the CIA representative on the National Security Council, said in an interview after the war that the new president had little room to maneuver on Vietnam. "By then this chaos and anarchy that afflicted the Vietnamese government at that time caused everything to sort of fall apart. The assessments were very clear that the situation was going downhill very fast in 1964. And our assessment was clear that the communists would probably win the war by about the end of 1965. They began to send their military units, not just their infiltrators, but their military units down the Ho Chi Minh trail in the fall of 1964. They began to build their military forces to give the coup de grace to the South Vietnamese."

Colby added, "Now President Johnson, who was in charge at that time, was of course a very tenacious Texan, a very tough fellow, and he wasn't about to have that happen and he took the only step that he saw available at that time and sent in military forces, combat forces, to Vietnam to stem the tide, to prevent the victory of the North Vietnamese at that time. It is the only thing that prevented it. But I don't think it was all that great; it wasn't the right strategy," Colby said.

The strategies that Colby's CIA had been working on were counterinsurgency and pacification programs. "I firmly believed in the necessity for strengthening the participation of the rural peasantry in the battle. They were the important programs that we should keep our eye on, the building of strength in the countryside."

But the previous year's Buddhist crisis and the Diem regime's destruction had wreaked havoc on the principal element in the CIA efforts, the Strategic Hamlet program, a nationwide attempt to protect the population against the local communist insurgents.

While he lived, President Kennedy kept his musing about changing America's course in Vietnam to himself, his brother Robert and a few trusted aides. In the years since, many have pondered whether he would have avoided committing American ground troops to the effort and settling for a negotiated solution. We'll never know for sure, but what is now clear is that many of his critical decisions were made in secret with little consultation offered to Congress and less to the public. President Johnson seemed to be set on a similar course.

Doris Kearns Goodwin observed, "What happened as decisions on the war concentrated on the White House is part of what happened to the American government in the 20th century. More and more policy decisions became concentrated in the White House rather than in Congress. And his power was such that dissenters had a very hard time staying within the framework of dissent within the White House. He really didn't have to listen to anybody."

Many initially tried to influence President Johnson as he settled into office, particularly those whom he had befriended in his years in the Senate and in liberal Democratic Party politics. One of them was John Kenneth Galbraith, a prominent economist and diplomat, who recounted his experiences in an interview with me after the war.

"I was in New York when I heard of the president's murder, and I went down and was recruited along with others to help with the arrangements over the next days. I was passing from the West Wing of the White House over to the Executive Office Building when I ran head-on into President Johnson. We were the same age, came to Washington at the same time, but that I think it is fair to say that Vietnam broke us apart, we were not close but good friends.

"And he grabbed me by the arm and led me off to his room in the EOB Building, his office, and he wanted to talk about domestic policy, about civil rights and he wanted to assure me as a professional liberal the liberal policies of the past would be safe in his hands. I was easily reassured in a way because the instincts of Johnson in many respects were deep as my own.

"I wanted to talk about foreign policy and I was very anxious that day to press my feelings that there was an adventuresome and grandiloquent quality about our policy in that part of the world, in Vietnam, which I thought was potentially dangerous and would be potentially his greatest problem. I didn't make much of an impression on him on that particular occasion, and I didn't take it too seriously. It wasn't the time for a lengthy talk.

"But in the ensuing months, again I saw President Johnson a number of times on this — in '64,'65 and into '66 — when one could still talk with him. He would try to persuade you that what he was doing was necessary, the minimum necessary. And he made a persuasive case that what he was trying to do was to restrain the military and constrain the Cold War warriors in the State Department.

"And I remember him saying once, 'Ah, Ken, do you have any idea what Curtis LeMay (chief of staff of the U.S. Air Force) would be doing if I wasn't here to restrain him?' And I would say, 'Well, ah ...' One always came out of the meetings with the feeling that President Johnson was trying to follow a moderate conciliatory policy. Or would like to have done so, if the weight of the military and those dynamics of military involvement weren't pressing him in the other direction.

"But also, I have no doubt that the dynamics of the involvement, and under the great pressure that has built up eventually swept him along and took him. In my own case and for what it is worth, it became no longer possible to talk on these matters" Galbraith said.

William Fulbright, the influential senator from Arkansas and the chairman of the Foreign Relations committee, eventually became one of Johnson's most prominent critics but tried in the beginning to be useful.

In an interview after the war, he said, "In 1964, I was very friendly with President Johnson and I had cooperated during his period in the Senate. I considered myself a close political friend. And when he was running for office that year I made speeches in support of him in Arkansas — a man of principal, a man who would keep peace all around the world. He made speeches himself to the effect that he was not going to send American boys to Asia to do the fighting that Asian boys would do.

Senator Goldwater (Barry Goldwater, the Republican presidential candidate) was considered the war monger, I mean he was going to threaten them, use nuclear weapons and so on. I made speeches on the Senate floor criticizing Goldwater and supporting Johnson.

"And I used to see him rather often, and we used to argue about this. I did not believe this was a place where we should have a war. I gave him a memorandum, I believe about that time, that it would be better to have a strong communist country than a weak so-called democratic country like we were having," Fulbright said.

But the drums of war were steadily beating, as revealed in Johnson's reaction to events early in August when communist attacks were reported on three American destroyers. The first, on the American destroyer Maddox on patrol in the Gulf of Tonkin on August 2, was confirmed. Three North Vietnamese navy torpedo boats, later learned to be from the North Vietnamese 135th torpedo squadron, approached the Maddox, and there were exchanges of fire. Crusader jet fighters from the aircraft carrier USS Ticonderoga attacked the torpedo boats with their 20mm canons, damaging all three.

While the White House was considering a response, there were disputed reports of a second attack in the Tonkin Gulf on August 4, again by torpedo boats, this time against the Maddox and another destroyer, the Turner Joy. In 2005 an internal National Security Agency historical study was declassified that concluded that the Maddox had engaged the North Vietnamese navy on August 2, but that there may not have been any North Vietnamese naval vessels present during the engagement of August 4. The report stated, "It is not simply that there is a different story as to what happened; it is that no attack happened that night."

In a television address to the nation on the evening of the second alleged attack, President Johnson denounced the communist actions, and said that retaliatory airstrikes were being launched on the North Vietnamese torpedo boat bases. He called for a congressional resolution to express support "for all the necessary action to protect our armed forces" but promising "no wider war."

Unknown to the public, the destroyer Maddox, at the time of the incidents, had been on an electronic intelligence mission in the Tonkin

Gulf on a program known as DESOTO. And that during that same period an unrelated series of clandestine raids on communist targets along the North Vietnamese coast, called Operation Plan 34A, were being undertaken by South Vietnamese commandos under the control of a special operations unit of the U.S. military assistance command in Saigon.

President Johnson wrote in his autobiography that his seeking of a congressional war resolution in support of his Southeast Asian policy of retaliation against North Vietnam after the Tonkin Gulf incidents "was my second major Vietnam decision." His initial support of Kennedy's policies the previous November was the first.

It was a willing Senator Fulbright who helped President Johnson push the resolution through both houses of Congress on August 10, 1964. It authorized the president "to take all necessary steps, including the use of the armed forces, to assist any member or protocol states of Southeast Asia Collective Defense Treaty requesting assistance in the defense of its freedom." President Johnson viewed America's membership in the treaty as a rationale for defending South Vietnam, even though that country was not a member.

The war resolution was historically significant because it gave President Johnson authorization, without a formal declaration of war by Congress, for the use of conventional military force in Southeast Asia.

"On the decision to bomb North Vietnam because of the Tonkin Gulf incident, the president made it very important that that he wanted it passed quickly that he was most urgent about this, that it would create a mood on the North Vietnamese to settle war," Fulbright said.

"He sold it as a means to prevent any widening of the war—which I believe is the language that he used. That we were going to face this little country of 17 million people with the great might of the United States, they would clearly be inclined to settle and to compromise and have a peaceful settlement, and that there wouldn't be any war.

"In other words, if we acted together and showed our united strength, this was the way to prevent a major war. And that was the way it was sold to us — it was never sold as a declaration of war. Not we are getting ready to go out there and mount a major land war.

"Nearly everyone in the course of speeches on the floor and else-where — and I made speeches — were demanding that there be no intention to send ground troops to Vietnam. General MacArthur, I think, had made public speech saying that it would be insanity to mount a land war against Asian land masses. And so on. There were a lot of people who said such things. I said that in the course of the debate.

"Then the resolution came to a vote in the Senate. I put the record straight. It wasn't my resolution. The president had submitted the resolu-tion, which first went onto the House of Representatives and then came to us. The House passed it unanimously, and we had it in committee for an hour or so and there was one vote against it.

"When it passed in the Senate there were two dissenting votes. I do not think anyone declared it a declaration of war. I don't think anyone thought of it as an authorization to wage the kind of war that Johnson waged. They believed — and I believed — that with a show of strength the South Vietnamese would win the war."

The two senators who opposed the resolution, Wayne Morse of Oregon and Ernest Gruening of Alaska, objected to "sending our American boys into combat in a war in which we have no business, which is not our war into which we have been misguidedly drawn, and which is steadily being escalated."

The Johnson administration continued to rely on the war resolu-tion to justify its rapid escalation of American military forces in South Vietnam that soon turned into open war between the United States and North Vietnam.

Seven years after its passage, in 1971, the Nixon administration agreed to the repeal of the war resolution, arguing that its own conduct of operations in Southeast Asia was based not on the resolution but was a constitutional exercise of presidential power.

6

THE ELEVENTH HOUR

ON MAY 28, 1964, SIX MONTHS after he assumed the presidency of the United States, Lyndon Johnson met privately with Canadian Prime Minister Lester Pearson at the New York Hilton hotel at 53rd Street and 6th Avenue. The meeting remained a secret for nine years, until the subject matter was revealed in the 1973 federal trial of Daniel Ellsberg on espionage charges, ultimately dismissed, for his leaking of the secret "Pentagon Papers" on the Vietnam War.

The American president, it was learned, was seeking a credible interlocutor to travel to Hanoi to deliver an ultimatum to Ho Chi Minh and the North Vietnamese leadership. The message: to end their support of the communist guerrillas fighting in South Vietnam or face an overwhelming onslaught of American military power. But the Americans would offer a carrot with this stick.

"The carrot was that the United States had no interest in overthrowing the regime in the north. It didn't want to change them, and that history would show that the United States could live perfectly amicably with communists, the example being Europe, where it traded with the communist states," said James Blair Seaborn, the Canadian official who made several trips to the communist capital, in an interview for a television program I was writing after the war. He added that the U.S. could even foresee "bringing some aid to assist the North Vietnamese economy."

The Hilton hotel meeting was an early gambit by the Johnson administration to secure an alternative strategy to all-out war, according to Ellsberg, who at the time was Assistant Secretary of Defense for Security Affairs. "I was given to understand that the Canadian connection was the most sensitive secret that I learned during that period, that Canada was being used for what amounted to an ultimatum — an undated ultimatum — to the North, and that the threats had to be made convincingly."

The elaborate secrecy surrounding such diplomacy was essential, according to Gareth Porter, a co-director of the Indochina Research Center. "You had in South Vietnam at the time a political situation which was nothing short of disastrous in the view of Washington policy makers. And the idea of initiating open or serious negotiations to end the war was almost unthinkable because it would have immediately provoked at the very least a very strong movement towards neutralism and settling the war on terms which the South Vietnamese officials themselves would find in their interest, rather than in terms of American interests.

"And at worst it could have, of course, caused a complete disintegration of the regime in Saigon. Then we would have nothing to work with. So, the main concern during that period was not to have that platform collapse on us. And any serious negotiations, anything that would have been acknowledged publicly, would have risked that outcome and thereby would have been ruled out."

Seaborn, the Canadian chosen as messenger, was an experienced diplomat primarily interested in East European affairs, who had been newly appointed as the chief of the Canadian delegation at the International Control Commission, a three-nation group formed in 1954 to observe and report on the implementation of the Geneva Agreements in North and South Vietnam. India and Poland were the other two members.

"On my first trip to Hanoi, I was to convey to Prime Minister Pham Van Dong, or to Ho Chi Minh if he was available, the essential elements of the message which the American government wanted to get across. I think they had been trying to signal that message in public statements but they were not at all sure whether it was getting through. It was my job to carry that as accurately and as dispassionately as I could and report back to my government a response which premier Pham Van

Dong might make and at the same time to try to size up, to analyze if you will, the political, moral and economic situation in North Vietnam, how they were doing, how were they surviving, the situation in which they found themselves."

Seaborn reiterated that he was carrying a carrot-and-stick message. "The stick was a rather generally-worded statement, as I recall, to the effect that the United States could not just let South Vietnam fall by default, to collapse, for any reasons of political instability or by the inadequacies of the South Vietnamese army, and would therefore feel obliged to bring in such military support as might be necessary to shore up the regime in the south. Behind the words lay a faint implication that if things got even worse there is a possibility that the war would be carried to the north, and there was a lot of talk at that time in the South Vietnamese press about it from the military leadership there.

"So, the most specific thing was to convey a message the details of which you probably know: We in the United States have no desire to overthrow the North Vietnamese government; we don't want to have permanent bases in South Vietnam. All we're really looking for is South Vietnam to be left alone, not subject to the amount of infiltration from the North, subversion and so on, which it is now subjected to. And if this could be brought about, in effect a return to the ceasefire agreement of 1954, then it's quite within the realm of possibility that the United States could foster trade with North Vietnam and it was hinted that might even be able to send a bit of aid, because it was not an advanced economy and had been suffering from concentration on the war."

On his arrival in Hanoi in mid-June on one of the twice-weekly ICC flights from Vientiane, Laos, Seaborn noticed that the communist capital was in better shape that he'd read about in the Western press.

"Hanoi had been a rather charming old French colonial city. It seemed strangely quiet rather than the hustle and bustle of Saigon, which was crammed with people because so many had come in from the countryside. And noisy little Hondas and motorbikes and what have you were all over the place.

"Hanoi was soundless, not a happy place. It was looking rather rundown at that time. But the individual people we saw on the street didn't look particularly depressed. While they had a rather thin time of it, there was food to be bought, not a great abundance of it, but no one was going hungry as far as I could see.

"It was not an overly depressing place, not the sort of place you would like to go for a holiday, at least not under these circumstances, but it looked as though people had come to terms with a pretty meager life, but one which was probably not intolerable."

Seaborn met Pham Van Dong late in the afternoon of June 18 in a large reception room filled with deep chairs and Asian antiques in the former governor general's palace. Also present was the ICC deputy liaison officer, Colonel Mai Lam.

"We carried on the conversation in French. The premier's French was impeccable. It was our first meeting. He was an impressive person. I've met a certain number of communist leaders through serving previously in the Soviet Union and having a lot to do with Eastern Europe. I rated Pham Van Dong as an impressive leader by any standard at that time. He listened pretty impassively to the message which I was conveying to him. I emphasized that I was there on behalf of the Canadian government and that it wasn't just my bright idea personally. In my hour-and-a-half conversation with Pham Van Dong he didn't make much comment on the message itself but he took note of it very carefully, and then we got into a broader discussion as to how things were likely to unfurl, and he gave me his view of what was required to restore peace to Vietnam. And I suppose it was pretty simple: If the Americans could just pull out and let the Vietnamese people settle the matter themselves.

"As I mentioned, I conveyed the elements of the message from the United States and waited for his response to that. There was no substantive response. He would think about it and convey any message back if they had a return message at any future time. He appreciated that we had agreed to establish this channel at the American request and thought it was valuable to have that channel itself.

"And then we had a good bit of discussion about the events in the South and what was happening there and his version about what was needed to bring about a solution to the war as opposed to American versions as to what was required to bring peace back to the Indochina peninsula.

"Pham Van Dong gave a great sense of self-assurance, of confidence in the ability of himself and his fellow leaders and his country to withstand whatever rigors might come to North Vietnam in the event there should be an escalation of the war. We certainly talked about that as a possible eventuality," Seaborn said. "He seemed tough, resilient and on the whole rather intransigent in his position. He didn't give any indications of looking for compromises. He did not seem to think that any compromises were necessary, that his country and his leadership could hang in there longer than the South Vietnamese government and probably longer than the Americans could.

"When the talk turned to the possible enlargement of the war, the possibility of that kind of war being carried to the North, Pham Van Dong said to me, 'Don't forget we're members of the socialist camp, and the socialist camp will come to help us if we're in danger.' It was that kind of solidarity, with the Soviet Union and China."

In a top-secret telegram he sent to the U.S. government through his Canadian contacts, Seaborn's tentative conclusion was that it would be unwise at this stage, in June 1964, to count on war weariness or factionalism within the communist leadership or of possible material advantages to North Vietnam as to cause the north to jump at the chance of reaching an accommodation with the U.S.

"I detected no evidence to suggest, as some columnists have been doing, that starvation or war weariness or political discontent are bringing the regime close to collapse, and that they would therefore grasp any straw which might enable them to save something before the country falls apart.

"I reported that it was quite to the contrary. It was confident, strong determined, in no way inclined to give in at this stage. And I know of course that this was conveyed through to the Americans by my government. The North Vietnamese did not seem threatened by the stick and didn't seem interested in the carrot at all.

"There was a repeat of the assertion that all that needed to be done was for the Americans to withdraw from Vietnam to let the Vietnamese settle their own affairs, to let the National Liberation Front, which is what they called the anti-government forces in Vietnam, have its rightful place as representative of the whole population of Vietnam.

"I do not think there was any flexibility in the North Vietnamese side. They saw no reason to be flexible. They were quite confident if they hung tough and hung in there long enough they would eventually have things the way they wanted them, and I suppose a large measure of history has proven them to be right.

"I can't remember them, at least during the time I was there, giving an indication of any willingness at all to come to any sort of compromise. That didn't appear till much later as things had gotten to a far bigger scale in the late '60s and early '70s, I guess when the real negotiations got under way."

Seaborn said, "I know that my messages had a rather sobering effect on Washington, particularly my analysis of the determination of the North to keep going. There had been some feeling, I believe, in some corners of Washington that they were on the ropes or close to it in North Vietnam, and everything I reported indicated quite the opposite to that.

"There was disappointment but perhaps no surprise that Pham Van Dong had not picked up on this tentative offer of getting into negotiations. The Americans were hoping that a little probe of that sort might give a glimmer of hope that there was a willingness to find some compromise arrangement from the North. So there was that disappointment."

When President Johnson sent American warplanes to bomb the North Vietnamese coastal city of Vinh on August 5, 1964, after publicly denouncing the Tonkin Gulf incident to a late night American television audience, he used the "hot line" to assure the Soviet Union that the United States had no intention of opening a broader war. He also ordered a second secret visit to the North Vietnamese leadership by Seaborn, but this time with a message with a tougher tone.

"I was asked to go back to Hanoi with, I suppose, in many ways a repeat of the previous message but this time with a slightly stronger tone to it, saying: Look, on behalf of the Americans, we find it pretty hard to take this sort of thing, attacks on our warships, and if it continues there may indeed be escalation. There was a little more firmness than I conveyed the first time, certainly."

When Seaborn met with Pham Van Dong again in Hanoi and delivered the new message, "he became quite visibly angry and I felt that his mask did drop, and it was not just contrived anger at all. And for a moment I thought he was just going to get up and say, 'That's the end of the interview, Seaborn. On your way.'

"But knowing that I had to do more conversation than that, I interposed rather quickly, and I said, 'Mr. Prime Minister, I appreciate that you don't enjoy receiving a message of this sort. Whether I enjoy transmitting it is another question, but can I use an old phrase about not shooting the messenger? I think you told me the last time we met that you found this a useful channel to have open whether or not you liked the messages that were carried across it. And I hope I may be able to continue this conversation with you and get your reaction so that I will be in the position to report back as faithfully as I can what you are saying and as far as I can tell what you are thinking to my government which will in turn transmit it to the American side.

"I told him that it is important that they should know what's on your mind as well. And then he calmed down a bit and he laughed and he said, 'Well, yes, yes, I appreciate that and I still think that the channel is important. I count on you. I have confidence that Canada will play its role well, and let's continue the conversation.'

"There was a toughness in his response which was disappointing to the Americans. They were hoping that perhaps the North Vietnamese government was getting concerned about where the gradual escalation was likely to lead, that perhaps the war might be extended to North Vietnam, and concerned that it might completely undercut and ruin the attempts which they had been making to build up their economy and restore their economy after the longish war with the French. But in fact, there was no such indication of a willingness to seek compromise in anything which Pham Van Dong said. I was aware that my fellow Canadians who had joined the commission before, had told me, 'They're a tough bunch up there. They're determined, and they're not going to be dissuaded.'"

Seaborn said, "I made six trips to North Vietnam in my year and a half in the ICC. Only on the first two did I carry messages to the leadership. After the first two trips, there was no further interest by the North in what I represented."

Brian Jenkins, a Rand Corporation researcher who was in Vietnam for several years, said the Johnson threats were doomed to fail because he did not understand the dedication of the communist leadership to achieve their goal of reunifying Vietnam.

"We were trying to get people to change their minds, when the pursuit of certain goals had been taken up their entire adult lives. The notion that one could change the minds of a number of people 60 and 70 years old in that politburo in Hanoi, I think was being farfetched. There was no changing of minds.

"Not at any time during the entire Vietnam war, even at the height of the bombing, was there any threat to the stability of that leadership. There may have been discussion and debate as to tactics, methods, timing. But as to the pursuit of that contest, that was a given that those members shared.

"I think, to be fair, that losing the war, to them, would be an issue of national survival but also beyond it. Let's say the political leadership would be losing what they regarded clearly as a moral crusade they saw as right in their eyes. Perhaps it was arrogant, perhaps operating from presumption of moral superiority, but they had to pursue that. It would have been immoral of them to quit fighting. It was never seen that way in the United States; the issues were never at that level in the United States."

GALLERY

THE TET OFFENSIVE

South Vietnamese forces fire on enemy positions in the Saigon area during the Tet Offensive. (AP Photo/Nick Ut)

With dead American soldiers in the foreground, U.S. military police take cover behind a wall at the entrance to the U.S. Consulate in Saigon on the first day of the Tet Offensive, January 31, 1968. (AP Photo/Hong Seong-Chan)

Soldiers flush out Viet Cong fighters in an abandoned hotel in Saigon near the South Vietnamese presidential palace, January 31, 1968. (AP Photo)

Two U.S. military policemen aid a wounded fellow MP during fighting in the U.S. Embassy compound in Saigon at the beginning of the Tet Offensive, January 31, 1968. (AP Photo/Hong Seong-Chan)

A South Vietnamese soldier takes a position on a Saigon street during the Tet Offensive. (AP Photo/Nick Ut)

South Vietnamese Gen. Nguyen Ngoc Loan fires his pistol into the head of suspected Viet Cong officer Nguyen Van Lem (also known as Bay Lop) on a Saigon street during the Tet Offensive, February 1, 1968. (AP Photo/ Eddie Adams)

U.S. Marines take cover behind a tree near the southern bridgehead on the Perfume River in Hue as they fight North Vietnamese troops, February 4, 1968. (AP Photo)

A large section of rubble is all that remains in this one block square area of Saigon after fierce Tet Offensive fighting, February 5, 1968. (AP Photo)

South Vietnamese Rangers and Police fire automatic weapons at trucks and people in the streets of Cholon, the Chinese sector of Saigon, during the Tet Offensive, February 7, 1968. (AP Photo/Dang Van Phuoc)

Senior U.S. advisor Capt. Robert A. Reitz, center, carries a wounded South Vietnamese Ranger to an ambulance after an intense battle with the Viet Cong during the Tet Offensive, February 6, 1968. (AP Photo/Dang Van Phuoc)

Most of the provincial Delta capital of Ben Tre was left in ruins and an estimated 1,000 civilians killed during fighting in this central market hall, February 7, 1968. (AP Photo/Peter Arnett)

U.S. troops of the 199th Light Infantry Brigade march toward the grandstand after they were lifted to the Phu Tho racetrack in Saigon during the Tet Offensive, February 9, 1968. (AP Photo)

A unit of the 1st Battalion, 5th Regiment U.S. Marines, rests alongside a battered wall of Hue's imperial palace after a battle for the Citadel during the Tet Offensive. (AP Photo)

The Vietnam flag flies atop a tower of the main fortified structure in the old citadel as a jeep crosses a bridge over a moat in Hue during the Tet Offensive. (AP Photo)

Vietnamese national policeman crawls through a tunnel and bunker network leading from pagoda grounds to an outside entrance in the Gia Dinh province on the outskirts of Saigon used by the Viet Cong to infiltrate men into the area during the Tet Offensive, March 3, 1968. (AP Photo/Le Ngoc Cung)

7

WESTMORELAND

LIEUTENANT GENERAL WILLIAM C. WESTMORELAND arrived at Saigon's Tan Son Nhut airport mid-afternoon on January 17, 1964, the commander-in-chief in-waiting of a ramped-up U.S. military effort in South Vietnam. American officials were on hand to greet him, as were Vietnamese government and military representatives. I was among the dozen or so journalists gathered under an overcast sky to watch the brief welcoming ceremony for the impeccably dressed officer, a tall man, with ramrod-straight bearing and a confident smile. Word was out in Saigon before he arrived that Westmoreland, a veteran of World War II and the Korean War and a former superintendent at the U.S. Military Academy at West Point, was chosen over more savvy general officers by President Johnson because he personified in appearance and in trusted demeanor an Eagle Scout, a rank he had in fact earned in his youth.

As a reporter for The Associated Press, I wrote much about Westmoreland during the war years, how his tactical decisions played out in the battlefield, his sometimes-stormy relationships with his fellow officers, and his questionable optimism about eventual victory. I did run into him from time to time, and was present when he departed from Tan Son Nhut airport at the end of his tour in June 1968. He was on his way home with a major promotion in hand, as Chief of Staff of the Army. At the airport, shaking the hands of Vietnamese generals who he'd worked with over the years, he was pale and thin, apparently

69

because of a recurrent intestinal upset that he had delayed treating until he returned home.

Military historians have not been kind to General Westmoreland. They blame him for what some see as "his arrogant demeanor." Or for his by-the-book adherence to traditional thinking in a political-military conflict that required new perspectives on the use of American force. They criticize his indifference to the use of the South Vietnamese armed forces in a significant role, preferring the more manageable American and allied forces brought in to do the fighting. And they lay at his door the intelligence failure that led to the near-complete surprise of the communist Tet Offensive in 1968 that shocked the Johnson administration into reversing course on the war.

Yet President Johnson retained Westmoreland as commander-in-chief in Vietnam for the four most critical years of the war, a record that the general remained proud of, comparing his tenure to the four successive American military commanders appointed during the three-year Korean War. The president was well aware of the controversies and the difficulties surrounding Westmoreland's military leadership, but wrote in his autobiography, "I had much greater confidence in Westmoreland and his staff in Vietnam than many people in Washington, including Pentagon civilians." The apogee of criticism of Westmoreland came in a biography written by a prominent military historian, Lewis Sorley, and published in 2013. It was titled, "Westmoreland: The General Who Lost Vietnam." The author, who served as an officer during the war, asserts that "military failure in Vietnam could have been avoided were it not for one man, General Westmoreland." I read his book, and was even quoted a couple of times on my comments critical of the general. But as a reporter who covered the war from beginning to end, I found that the book was much too harsh. I'm reminded of the John F. Kennedy quote, "Victory has a thousand fathers but defeat is an orphan." Vietnam was indeed "lost" to America, but Westmoreland was hardly alone with the responsibility.

President Johnson was asking a lot of the 50-year-old Westmoreland when he sent him to Vietnam to take over the war early in 1964. The general was tasked with implementing U.S. policies that had not changed in 30 years, to preserve Southeast Asia from communism, a vow that now applied to the southern half of a country that was all that remained of the Indochinese colonies of France.

In a television interview with me three years after the war in his comfortable Charleston, South Carolina, home with his wife Kitsy present, I asked General Westmoreland if he knew what he was getting into when he took the job. He said, "I read all I could about the country before I arrived. I don't say that I was necessarily a student of it because I had demanding jobs. I did reflect on it. I was very conscious that it was a very complicated country. I was quite aware of the fact that our nation had no experience of it. I was quite aware of the program of instruction at Fort Bragg, at the counterinsurgency school, that was set up during the John F. Kennedy presidential years. But I was rather surprised to determine from my field trips that this was a formidable task that our nation had undertaken. It was a rather large piece of real estate, much bigger than what the average person perceives on the map. And it was quite obvious that there were many divisive groups in the society, and not just the Vietcong. It was far from being a heterogeneous group."

I asked what were his first impressions of Saigon. "It was during the political crisis that followed the overthrow of President Diem. I had the impression that the South Vietnamese military sometimes just called off the war. The pace was rather slow, taking off on weekends, extended holidays. They were far from diligent in their pursuit of the war; it was somewhat business as usual. Of course, you must realize that things were in a very uncertain state in Vietnam at that time. There had been coups and countercoups. It was very difficult to determine who was running the country from day to day. The political leadership was weak and in many cases, there was uncertainty. This brought about a feeling of insecurity. Now as a result of this, there was the general attitude that you had greater security — that is, you had greater job security — if you did nothing rather than if you did something. That attitude generally prevailed."

Within a few months of his arrival, Westmoreland, as planned, replaced General Paul D. Harkins as the American military commander-in-chief in Vietnam. Harkins had watched helplessly as the Diem regime that he supported was overthrown by Vietnamese generals the previous November.

The coup threw American policies in Vietnam into a tailspin. Asked how he got along with his predecessor, Westmoreland said, "General Harkins would sometimes express his frustrations with the state of affairs by quoting to me a stanza from Rudyard Kipling's early 20th century poem 'The Naulahka,' about British colonial struggles against Indian nationalists. Of course, I have read Kipling and I am very fond of him because he is a kind of soldier poet, and this was a rather apt poem that Bill Harkins would quote."

At my request, Westmoreland spoke Kipling's immortal lines to our television camera:

"The end of the fight is a tombstone white with the name of the late deceased,

"And the epitaph drear, 'A Fool lies here, who tried to hustle the East.'"

He added, "I didn't take it quite to heart to the same degree that Harkins did. And I did my best later on to try to move the South Vietnamese out of lethargy, with, I would say, some success."

I asked Westmoreland about the American military situation that he found when he arrived. "There had been a dramatic change in our involvement in the war. When Mr. Kennedy became President, I believe there were only five hundred military advisors in Vietnam. Kennedy increased it to about 15,000 over a period of approximately eighteen months, but in addition to that he authorized the moving in of helicopters flown by American pilots and fighter bombers flown in the main by Americans. There was an effort to increase advisors down to a lower level of command. Initially they were at division, then they went to regiment, and then they were moved to battalion. In addition to that there were a number of Special Forces troops dealing with the Civilian Indigenous Defense Corps that grew rather rapidly during that time frame, the '62, '63, '64. The American presence grew very rapidly. And the instrument of war, manned by Americans, increased substantially."

Westmoreland said he was concerned about the low profile of Vietnam in the United States. "There was a tendency by the Johnson administration to low-key the war. They wanted to avoid getting the American public aroused. In 1964, I suggested to (Defense) Secretary McNamara that this was going to be a long drawn out affair that was going to test the patience of the American people and there should be some sort of people-to-people program between the American people and the Vietnamese people to get the American people more emotionally involved, and more appreciative of what was going on. This suggestion was not accepted. In subsequent discussions I had with people associated with the administration there was a real fear that if such was set up and the war was given inordinate visibility and was not kept at a low key, then the hawks would be stirred up and that could encourage a confrontation with China. I suppose that was the rationale behind the low-key approach. But I think in retrospect it was a mistake."

Westmoreland's Pentagon briefers assured him prior to his assignment that the capital of Saigon would be a comfortable post, that he could safely take his family with him to join the many hundreds of America dependents living there. For a while that was OK. Westmoreland's wife Kitsy and two of his three children, Rip, aged 10, and Margaret, 9, soon joined him. Their third child Stevie arrived in June from boarding school. "We had a comfortable house," the general said. "Most Americans in Saigon did. It was a very attractive town, and there were a number of very nice houses there. And of course, they had been built and previously occupied by the French. There was an independent school for American children, which went all the way from the fifth grade to high school. And there was an amount of social life, most of it was involving the diplomatic community. I tried avoid getting involved in that, but sometimes I was forced to attend their affairs."

But then the picture changed as President Johnson moved towards a war footing late in 1964, which raised the profile of South Vietnam within the United States and generated a renewed campaign of terrorism against the American community in Saigon. The safety of his own family and of the American dependents in Saigon became a major concern. "There were any number of efforts categorically initiated by the Vietcong designed to bring about fear among our dependents and the heads of households," Westmoreland said. "Explosives were put under the stands at the softball field, with women and children in the stands. Two Americans were killed and 25 wounded there. Explosives were found in the flower pots around the swimming pool that was available to Americans. There were incidents where motorcyclists would fire at Americans or throw grenades and scamper away. It was a rather hazardous existence."

When comedian Bob Hope arrived in Saigon on one of his annual armed forces tours the day before Christmas 1964, Vietcong guerrillas, in a daring attack, detonated a car bomb in the parking area under the Brinks Bachelor Officers Quarters. The six-story building housed American army officers, and two were killed and approximately 60 Americans and Vietnamese wounded in the blast. The American ambassador at the time, General Maxwell Taylor, told me in an interview after the war, "This occurred late in the afternoon, if I recall, and Bob Hope was landing about that time out at the airport. I met him near the scene, in the main square. His hotel was just across from where the Brinks was burning, with flames flaring up and fire engines whizzing past, and all sorts of activities going on. I greeted Bob as he came out and he said, 'Thank you, this is the warmest welcome I've ever had.' And then he proceeded and gave us his usual entertainment to the troops in the days thereafter."

America's top officials in Saigon would soon learn of President Johnson's growing personal interest in the war. Both Westmoreland and the ambassador had resisted calls from Washington for the removal of the 1,610 American dependents resident in Saigon on the grounds that it might panic the nervous governing authorities, who might infer that the United States was beginning a feared general military withdrawal from Vietnam. That threat was hinted at in early December 1965, when hostile senior Vietnamese officers suggested that Taylor be declared persona non grata for criticizing the continuing political uncertainty in the city.

But the Vietcong destruction of much of the Brinks officers' quarters in the heart of Saigon revealed to President Johnson just how poor the security had become. In a personal message to Taylor on December 30, 1964, Johnson said, "I feel very strongly that we ought not be widening the battle until we get our dependents out of South Vietnam. I know you have not agreed with this view in the past, and I realize that there may be some agencies that might face recruiting difficulties if dependents are removed. But no argument I have yet heard overrides the fact that we are facing a war in South Vietnam, and we are considering actions that may bring strong communist reaction by a concentrated effort against

Americans; this last is estimated by the intelligence community as the very likely enemy reaction to an air attack on target 36 (an installation in North Vietnam). In this situation, I do not understand why it is helpful to have women and children in the battle zone, and my own readiness to authorize larger actions will be very much greater if we can remove the dependents and get ourselves into real fighting trim. Neither this nor any part of this message is intended as an order, but I do want you to understand the depth of my feeling, and that the fact that I have not been persuaded by arguments I have heard on the other side."

Westmoreland received a message the next day from General Earle Wheeler, chairman of the Joint Chiefs of Staff, supporting the president. It read, "This has been a matter of continuing concern to higher authority (the president) and was specifically referred by Secretary Rush at our meeting on 28 December. There is concern in Washington, amounting to almost conviction, that our dependents are liable to attack as VC/DVR (North Vietnam) reprisal for a U.S. attack against the DVR. While our dependents remain in South Vietnam, I consider that forceful action by the U.S., outside the borders of South Vietnam is practically precluded."

In a memorandum for the record in files held by the U.S. State Department, President Johnson, at a White House meeting on February 7, 1965, "indicated considerable impatience with Ambassador Taylor 'for suggesting a 15- to 30-day evacuation on a deliberate scale in order not to create any feeling of panic.' The 15-day type of operation has been going on for 15 months and he wished it to move. Secretary McNamara indicated that he preferred a rapid evacuation."

Ambassador Taylor and Westmoreland finally delivered. In a telegram to the State Department on February 16, 1965, a few days after a series of airstrikes against North Vietnam, Taylor wrote, "These air attacks have been greeted with enthusiasm by all of my military contacts, and indeed all articulate, urban Vietnamese opinion appears to be favorable to them, and to sense a turning point of some kind in the long war. Excitement generated by them has allowed our dependents' evacuation to proceed with little public comment and a degree of public understanding. As of noon today, February 16, we have evacuated 1,456 of our total of 1,610, We can easily complete the evacuation within the 10 days which you authorized except for a few medical cases which cannot be moved, and the alien wives of U.S. government personnel who have passport problems; the evacuation has gone very smoothly with minimum discomfort to the evacuees. We are all very grateful to you for having allowed us to follow this orderly pattern."

As Westmoreland grappled with terrorism in the city, he was also responsible for strengthening the South Vietnamese army that was increasingly ineffective in the political chaos following the coup d'état against President Ngo Dinh Diem. Resurgent communist Vietcong guerrillas were scoring spectacular military victories. Secretary of Defense McNamara and the Joint Chiefs of Staff persuaded President Johnson to launch Operation Rolling Thunder, a graduated, intensive bombing campaign against North Vietnam to force it to cease its aid to the southern insurgents, a move Westmoreland opposed.

The predicted communist reprisal terrorist attack quickly followed. A Renault sedan, packed with 250 pounds of plastic explosives on its back seat, slammed into the curb alongside the American embassy mid-morning on March 30, and a gunfight erupted between the driver and armed Vietnamese guards. Most of the staff in the embassy, then located in an office building near the Saigon River, dropped to the floor. Then came a huge blast as the car exploded, throwing a mass of metal window frames and glass shards into the faces of those who had gone to see. The CIA station chief, Peer de Silva, looked out his window and saw the car driver lighting a fuse stuck in the explosive, but before he could react safely he was caught in the explosion and was nearly blinded in both eyes. The view of the outside street from the window of the office of the deputy ambassador, U. Alexis Johnson, was obstructed by a concrete ledge. As he was opening the door of his secretary's office which had a better view, the blast shattered the window and blew the frame across his desk where he had been sitting, enough to have seriously injured or to have killed him if he hadn't moved.

Associated Press photographer Horst Faas and I heard the loud blast and ran the several blocks from our office. It was a terrible scene of wreckage and blood covering the streets. The body of an embassy secretary lay on a stretcher, her face entirely obliterated, and she was still clutching a ballpoint pen. The explosion had demolished a Chinese restaurant across the street, which was burning furiously. The bodies of customers and staffers littered the ground. Fire trucks, ambulances and military police were just beginning to arrive, as was General Westmoreland who was on his way to the embassy for an 11 o'clock appointment with the deputy ambassador. Twenty people died in the terror attack, including two Americans, one of whom was a female CIA employee, Barbara Robbins. There were 183 people injured. A new embassy, an eight-story fortress, was built near the presidential palace and opened in 1967. In the Tet Offensive, the following year the new embassy was attacked by the Vietcong, another strike against the heart of American power in South Vietnam.

General Westmoreland told me that he had opposed the air campaign against the North over two concerns. "One was that I was afraid that bombing could encourage Hanoi to send more of its troops south because they did not have the capability of retaliating in kind. My second concern was that I did not want to provoke them until we were prepared to cope with them in the South. It seemed to me that the graduated bombing response would allow the politburo in Hanoi to adapt themselves to a particular level of bombing. I always considered the enemy a pretty tough group. The message that Washington was trying to submit, specifically that they couldn't win, would not come through by virtue of the on-and-off frequency of the bombing."

Secretary of the Navy Paul Nitze was also doubtful at the time that Operation Rolling Thunder would bring the North to its knees. He visited South Vietnam in mid-1965 to assess the situation. He said in an interview, "I was involved in the U.S. strategic bombing survey, which did the assessment of strategic air warfare during World War II, both in the Atlantic and the Pacific, and from those studies it was clear it is a very difficult thing for strategic air attack to be effective. It can be very effective, but the preconditions for effectiveness are very precise. What is most difficult is to interdict successfully, to stop the movement of supplies from one place to another, because there are lots and lots of ways which one material can be transported: by road or rail or back of bicycle or some other way. To keep people from moving material from here to there is a most difficult job. We had the experience in Korea of trying to interdict the movement of material in North Korea, and there again we found that this was a very difficult thing to do. So, there was no reason to believe that it wouldn't be a very difficult thing to do the same in North Vietnam, along the routes of infiltration from North Vietnam down to South Vietnam and particularly through Laos and Cambodia."

Nitze added, "There was no opportunity to cut off the supply at the source because most of the material came from either China or communist Russia, so you couldn't interdict the factories, you couldn't destroy the factories that produced the material. It was clear that you could cause the North Vietnamese a great deal of difficulty where they'd have to put substantial resources, men and time and effort, into rebuilding those railroads and freight cars or trucks or this and that. It didn't look as though it would be feasible to bring decisive pressure on the North Vietnamese through air attack. It did bring some pressure, and it could have some influence in bringing them to the negotiating table. But (it was) hard to foresee how it could be decisive."

Westmoreland also had a quarrel with the concept of "limited war," the brainchild of Secretary of Defense McNamara, which was being adopted by the Johnson administration as the underlying strategy of the developing war. "It was an unprecedented strategy," he told me. "I know of no other war where that has taken place. It was a theory that grew up in the 1950s when scholars and others were writing books and papers on the subject. President Kennedy was very sensitive to the prospect of 'limited war.' And the concept was that you would put pressure on gradually, hoping that the destruction could be minimized and the use of our resources could be minimized, and that the objective could be accomplished. It was new; no other war where that air tactic had been used. Frankly, it just didn't work. They could have received quite a different message if we had prepared ourselves to deliver a big blow. It would have hurt them severely."

I asked Westmoreland what he had in mind. "To knock out their ability to wage war, military targets, inhibiting their means of moving supplies which were coming from China and Russia in the main. To mainly concentrate on the ports, the destruction of docks. the petroleum storage areas which at that time were well concentrated rather than dispersed. One of the impacts in the North of this graduated response was when they realized what was taking place they removed the petroleum, moved it around in little packages, they immediately dispersed the targets. And instead of having their petroleum concentrated in one place they moved it around the country. A tactical effort involving a surprise effort, a massive effort after studying these targets, which were essential for the waging of war, could have produced an entirely different result."

Westmoreland began sensing early in 1965 that the Johnson administration, newly elected to a four-year term, might be more responsive to his tough war strategy. He asked that the United States commit American ground troops to Vietnam early in 1965, arguing that, "The South Vietnamese Army was losing a battalion of troops a week, battalion after battalion were being destroyed by virtue of the infiltrating North Vietnamese troops, the so-called main force troops along the border in base camps in the jungle areas. Either by ambush or by direct attack they were gradually eroding the morale of the Southern troops. If that had continued, it could have led to a disastrous outcome. The security situation was of concern because the Rolling Thunder air attacks against the North were primarily being launched out of the Danang Air Base in the northern area of South Vietnam. Since the strategy that had been initiated by Washington at that time — through the use of air power, a graduated response — it was essential that our airfields be secure. We had sufficient convincing instances to show that we could not totally depend on the South Vietnamese military to defend them."

U.S. Marines began landing in Danang on February 8, 1965, in answer to Westmoreland's request. He told me, "It made no sense at all to have them dig in and go strictly on the defensive. I had visualized that they would be able to operate and pre-empt any attack on the base because that is nothing but prudent action associated with a tactical defense. When we committed those troops of course, there was pressure put on that airfield and others being developed, and there was threat to those airfields from North Vietnamese main force troops in the environs. I did request authority to pre-empt any attacks, not only using our troops but coordinating them with the Vietnamese efforts."

A month or so later, Westmoreland asked for an additional two divisions of Americans combat troops. "It was because of the intelligence that we were receiving on the movements of North Vietnamese troops from north to south. And the general buildup of the enemy forces. From the standpoint of myself, as military commander responsible on the scene, if we had not responded to that buildup we would have found ourselves fighting with the odds against us, where we could have been overwhelmed by a buildup from the North."

On July 28, 1965, President Johnson announced his decision to go ahead with the limited war. He told a press conference at the White House, "I have asked the commanding general, General Westmoreland, what more he needs to meet the mounting aggression. He has told me. We will meet his needs. I have today ordered to Vietnam the Air Mobile Division and certain other forces, which will raise our fighting strength from 75,000 to 125,000 men almost immediately, Additional forces will be needed later, and they will be sent as requested."

A senior American official involved in that decision at the time, William Bundy, a foreign affairs advisor to President Johnson, told me in an interview after the war, "I would suggest that was the second truly big decision that the president made, alongside his decision to start the bombing in February. I did favor that second decision on the basis that at that stage the North Vietnamese were clearly involved with large units of their own, in addition to all that they had been doing over a long period to help the insurgency in the South.

"There was no question, no possible doubt, that this was approaching the level of conventional aggression. And that the South Vietnamese were so weakened politically, not particularly militarily but there were several attacks in June in which they really came apart. It was thought that South Vietnam might collapse. And it seemed at this stage that only an infusion of American combat units, divisions and all the rest could stop the rot and level things off and make progress.

"I did hope during that decision-making period that we could have limited the commitment and in effect keep it smaller and try to revive the South Vietnamese and keep it more limited. But I was persuaded by late July that the situation was so serious that we had to go, as it were, all the way. So, I thought it was the right decision, and I never had any doubt of it at the time," Bundy said.

An expert on the war, Brian Jenkins of the RAND Corporation, said, "One of the major difficulties in the war was that while there was a military commander in Vietnam, his powers in some cases were quite limited. In fact, in terms of the formal military relationships, the top commander in charge was another commander, commander in chief of the Pacific at Honolulu, who was an admiral. The American military commander further had to deal with the fact that there was an American ambassador who, in a sense, was really the figure who guided American activities. And there was a tremendous amount of interference at very low levels in both the conduct of the war militarily as well as the political course of events by various entities in Washington. Whether one talks about the White House, the Pentagon, or the military side of the Pentagon versus the civilian side of the Pentagon. Here was good number of people running the war. There was no American pro-consul. I guess the closest we came to having one was when General Maxwell Taylor was appointed ambassador (in 1964-65). Here we had a man who had enormous military experience and who was closely tied to the administration. One would suspect he carried a political clout, at the same time being appointed ambassador. And for a moment there, one would think that all these things had converged in this single individual. But Taylor did not operate that way. He basically left General Westmoreland, who was the military commander when he was there, to do the military thing and that caused a difficulty."

I asked Jenkins his assessment of Westmoreland. "The American army occasionally produces people like George Marshall, who I think was a soldier-statesman of the first caliber. Or like Eisenhower who may not have been much of a general but who has this marvelous capacity, through his warm personality, to lead allied forces and get them to work together. After all, you know the British General Montgomery was not easy to work with. Eisenhower's great talent was that he could pull that talented group together. General (Matthew) Ridgway was a soldier statesman. Westmoreland is a soldier's soldier, in my judgment. I would compare him to General (Joseph) Stilwell, who was a good combat general but when brought into the job where policies and international affairs were at issue, he was limited. I think that Westmoreland was probably a very good combat soldier but this was not a war, this was a political revolution; and he never, I think, had the feeling for international politics or for another culture that was required. I think he will go to his death not understanding what went wrong in Vietnam."

General Westmoreland asserted that he was trying to achieve under difficult circumstances the mission given him by the Johnson administration. "Our mission was never changed," he told me. "Our mission was to protect South Vietnam from being overwhelmed by aggressive forces from the North. I was told by Mr. McNamara on innumerable occasions that I should ask for the troops that I felt needed to bring about that end result. He said I should not worry about public opinion, I should not worry about the economy, I should not even concern myself about the availability of the troops."

Westmoreland was made "Man of the Year" by Time magazine at the end of 1965. The president had done his best to try to force the North Vietnamese to the conference table with airstrikes and peace initiatives. He had failed. It would be now up to Westmoreland to win the "limited war" on the battlefield.

8

CHOOSING WAR

WHEN THE FIRST SOLDIERS FROM two U.S. Marine battalion landing teams began wading ashore on March 8, 1965, on the sandy coastline of South Vietnam's Danang Bay, a place military planners had designated Red Beach One, they were met not with the Vietcong sniper fire they had been warned to expect. Gathered to welcome these first American combat troops to ever arrive on their shores were 100 Vietnamese high school girls dressed in traditional white, silken Ao Dai dresses and bearing garlands of flowers that they draped around the wet necks of the surprised arrivals.

A score or so of wire service and newspaper reporters, news photographers, and cameramen from the three American television networks, were on hand to speed the word in print, pictures and in TV film that the Americans had arrived. And with this burst of news, his nation and the world would begin questioning Lyndon Johnson's frequent promises that there would be "no wider war" in Vietnam.

The American ambassador to Saigon at the time, General Maxwell Taylor, told me in an interview after the war: "There had always been a tremendous amount of debate about sending American ground troops to Vietnam. It was really starting in 1961 when President Ngo Dinh Diem asked for troops, and then progressively there were elements of the United States, extremists on the right, who were urging closer military support to include the use of our ground forces."

Taylor, who had made several official visits to South Vietnam to assess the situation on behalf of President Kennedy, said, "Personally, I realized the undesirability of doing this. And the longer I was in Vietnam the more I thought of the danger of our taking over too much of the war from the Vietnamese. And once we brought any troops in, that was the nose of the camel. It would be very difficult to know how much was enough."

Taylor, famous for his military service in World War II and as the military advisor to President Kennedy and then as chairman of the Joint Chiefs of Staff, was a formidable military thinker. He believed that American air power shrewdly used could achieve Johnson's goals of forcing North Vietnam to cease aiding the southern Communist guerrillas.

He told me, "I had no illusion that the use of air power would be decisive and win the war, having seen in Korea how complete mastery of the air did not prevent the Chinese from moving forces and accomplishing a lot. That was evidence of the fact that you can't win a ground war by air alone. But I was convinced that we could get at least three advantages in the use of our air.

"First, morale in South Vietnam. For years they had been receiving and suffering from the atrocities committed by the Vietcong, sent out of North Vietnam against the south. And to give them the feeling of striking back would certainly mean a great deal to them.

"Secondly, we had become aware of the Ho Chi Minh trail and that a great deal of war equipment and manpower was being sent in. I had no impression that we could stop that but that we could inflict, impose losses that would slow it down.

"But the final thing was that I felt the air arm gave us a device by which we could progressively and decisively convince Hanoi that the price was too great to pay. I visualized that eventually there could be a progressive movement of air strikes of increasing intensity toward Hanoi until they were faced with the obliteration of their capital. That is, if they didn't come to the negotiating table and seek a solution.

"I thought that those were three compelling arguments to me, and that was the base of my argument to the president in December 1965."

Taylor's tactics dovetailed to some degree with the Joint Chiefs of Staff that had been lobbying the White House for some time to maximize the American bombing of the north. When two successful Vietcong attacks in February 1965 on American military advisory bases, one at the highlands city of Pleiku, the other at the coastal port of Qui Nhon, caused nearly two dozen deaths, the White House responded by ordering repeated bombing of the North. The air attacks known as Operation Rolling Thunder lasted through much of the war.

Ambassador Taylor was disappointed at the early results of Rolling Thunder. He said, "It was used not the way I visualized it. It was gradual; that meant long pauses in decisive use of the air power. My thought was that we could go in phases, even to announce the duration. But we started out just picking away. I had no objection to the early, highly conservative use of air power to see the reaction in China and the Soviet Union. Bear in mind we didn't know how tightly united Hanoi was by treaty understandings with their two communist supporters. Just to do it early, and to move slowly at the early phases was certainly justified."

William Colby, the CIA's representative on the National Security Council, told me in an interview after the war that the North's continued assistance to the southern guerrillas was the reason for the air campaign. "The purpose of the bombing of the North was to try to convince them that they could not get away with that scot-free. That they couldn't conduct a war of this nature and expect to be immune. And it was also in part to encourage the South Vietnamese to show that something is happening to the other side, to compensate for what was happening to them.

"I never thought that the bombing of the North had much to do with the real issue, which was the war at the village level. To me, it was a kind of diversion from what I considered the real level of the war. . . . And that the more time and effort we spent devoting ourselves to the detailed discussions of targets and putting resources up in the North was time and attention that should be better used against the problems of organizing the villages in the South for their own protection."

In an interview after the war, Senator William Fulbright, chairman of the Foreign Relations Committee, told me that during his visit to the White House early in 1965 to protest the Rolling Thunder air campaign, he was briefed on the theory of "surgical bombing" propounded by the president's influential national security advisor, Walt Rostow.

"I heard him elaborate on this on many occasions, that you would give the North Vietnamese notice that we will bomb plant A tomorrow and take it out. Now we don't want to hurt you, we don't want to kill any civilians, everyone gets away, this is what we are going to do. Now all you have to do is go to a peace conference and settle this matter. If you don't, then after plant A, we go to plant B and just give them notice. And surely at some point you know they would quit because they see we could utterly destroy their country."

Fulbright said, "Rostow insisted that this was reasonable, a natural thing. But I saw that he was interpreting the Vietnamese as probably he or an American would react. Somebody who was able to do that, say Boston, we are going to take this out. Then to Washington to take the Capitol first and then the White House next. Probably, or if they were that much more powerful than we Americans, he thought we would say, 'OK let's have some peace. We don't want to be completely obliterated.'"

Fulbright said, "All of this reflects a big psychological problem for a big country like ours. We completely misapprehend the nature of the world and our relations to it. But this happens to all the big countries when they become very powerful. The get illusions of grandeur and think they can do anything. And they also completely misunderstand other people. We certainly had no conception of what the Vietnamese were like — neither did Johnson."

"If we had any understanding of Vietnam, we would never have gotten into it. It was a perfectly asinine and insane undertaking. Johnson would never have done that if he had any idea about the Vietnamese. Or about the Asians. It wasn't bad motives. He thought he could bring 'the Great Society' there. But they didn't know anything about the Great Society, and I don't think that they wanted the Great Society. Americans just can't get away from the idea that we are big, and therefore God must have out his hand on our shoulder. And we wouldn't be so rich if we weren't so wise. And therefore, we must be wise."

General Taylor's deputy ambassador, U. Alexis Johnson, an experienced diplomat whose previous tour had been in Thailand, wrote in his book "The Right Hand of Power," that "Ironically it was the decision to start bombing the North that led to indirectly deploying the first American ground forces. It started innocently enough, the Air Force conducting its raids of the North from Danang, a base just south of the demilitarized zone from which maximum loads and a maximum number of sorties could be generated. The base was understandably worried that there was no anti-aircraft protection. We considered their concerns legitimate and approved the deployment of a Marine anti-aircraft battalion carrying HAWK missiles".

Because of the lack of protection from the insufficient South Vietnamese forces in the area, the Marines were also concerned about Vietcong attacks as they set up their equipment in the hills around Danang.

Taylor and his deputy advised of the need and Washington responded with an offer of a 5,000-man Marine expeditionary force with its own artillery, tanks and fighter aircraft.

"Max and I were appalled and refused to approve this grandiose scheme," Johnson wrote. "It went beyond anything we envisioned or the military requirements could justify. That night, Washington compromised by approving two battalion landing teams. We replied that we reluctantly concurred on condition that there be no more and that these would be withdrawn as soon as Vietnamese replacements were available.

"The word was hardly out of our mouths when 3,500 Marines, who had been waiting offshore, stormed ashore in full battle dress — to be greeted by smiling Vietnamese girls offering flower leis."

In Washington, several senior Democratic legislators were expressing increasing concern to President Johnson and his aides about what they saw as a rush to war.

Senator Fulbright said, "Johnson always maintained that his purpose, you know, was not to widen the war but to make peace. And I think he may have well thought that. But he changed his views and in early 1965 after the Pleiku incidents and the other incidents, he began to widen the war.

"(Senator Mike) Mansfield and I went to see him on these occasions and we used to talk to him. He used to talk to us — he used to call us occasionally: Come down on my way to the office. So, I went along to see Johnson many times, sometimes with Senator Mansfield, and he would say his purpose was to end the war, that he did not want to enlarge the war, that the North Vietnamese were people who surely should see, that as any rational person could see, that they couldn't prevail, that they ought to surrender and have peace."

Fulbright continued: "Johnson is a very big man, big physically and a powerful intellect, but with no training or experience in foreign affairs. He had been out of the country hardly ever before he became president. But in any event, he had no background in foreign relations and I think that the Texans, and he especially, had a way of feeling that they could do anything. I mean they are powerful people, physically, materially and so on. And I think he thought he could stop the Vietnamese. I think that he sort of believed the theory that if we kill unity (the unification of the North and the South) they will see the hopelessness of their cause and they will quit. And then you will have a settlement. I don't think he had any background about the Geneva Conference, or anything else about that era, and certainly not about the character of the people or the history of Vietnam."

Taylor was not alone in worrying about an expanding U.S. military commitment to a distant Asian land that three previous presidents had vowed to save from communist expansion, but that during the early Johnson administration was beginning to lose its significance to America's national interests.

Historian Arthur Schlesinger Jr, a former presidential advisor to Kennedy and to Johnson, told me in an interview after the war: "Somehow in 1965 the idea still held that the Vietcong were the spearhead, the instruments of a planned system of Chinese expansionism in the Far East." For instance, liberal champion Adlai Stevenson, in a letter released after his death, argued that we were preventing Chinese aggression in Asia. Yet Schlesinger said from what was known at the time about the centuries-old hostility between China and Vietnam, the notion that the Vietcong and the North Vietnamese were undergoing all this sacrifice in order to turn their country over to the Chinese was preposterous.

"The U.S. government needed to believe this because the public had been told it for so long. Johnson in turn had to build the threat, and save the world from the hordes of Red China." Schlesinger said he asked Johnson's people how in the world they came to believe this and was told we are paying the price of the 1950s. Washington could not just argue that it was saving the world from Ho Chi Minh. No one in their right senses expected that if Ho Chi Minh won in Vietnam the next week his legions would appear on Miami Beach."

And a secret memorandum from the Board of Estimates to the Director of the CIA, John McCone, on June 9, 1964, challenged the basis of the "domino theory" that previous American presidents had warned would result in the loss of all of Southeast Asia and other Pacific nations if South Vietnam fell to the communists.

"We do not believe," it said, "that the loss of South Vietnam would be followed by the rapid, successive communization of the other states of the Far East. Instead of a shock wave passing from one nation to the next there would be a simultaneous, direct effect on all Southeast Asian countries. With the possible exception of Cambodia, it is likely that no nation in the area would quickly succumb to communism as the result of the fall of Laos or South Vietnam. Furthermore, a continuation of communism in the area would not be inexorable, and any spread that did occur would take time — time in which the total situation might change in any number of ways unfavorable to the communist side."

Despite the criticisms and the revised intelligent estimates, the White House pushed ahead rapidly with its war plans. Soon after the arrival of Marine reinforcements for those that had landed in Danang in March, General Taylor traveled to Washington to plead restraint, and returned to Saigon believing he had succeeded. But on April 14 in a confidential message to the State Department he expressed worry:

"Recent actions relating to the introduction of U.S. ground forces have tended to create an impression of eagerness in some quarters to deploy forces into SVN which I find difficult to understand. I should think that for both military and political reasons we should all be most reluctant to tie down Army/Marine units in this country, and would do so only after the presentation of the most convincing evidence of the necessity."

He concluded his message by writing, "It is far from an unmitigated advantage to bring in more U.S. forces. A consideration of the disadvantages convinces me that, while logistic preparations should be made now to be able to receive additional forces, the forces themselves should be held just outside of SVN just as long as possible and until their need is incontrovertible. From a purely military point of view it is essentially wasteful of the specialized mobility of Marines and airborne troops to commit them prematurely to restricted land areas. Politically it is undesirable to seek authority for their introduction until a clear and specific need exists, which assured them an unreserved welcome from their GVN hosts."

Deputy Ambassador Alexis Johnson supported Taylor's views, but noted that soon after his return, "We were inundated with plans for putting in more American troops. The Pentagon proposed introducing cadres of American troops into Vietnamese units, placing Army Civil Affairs officers trained for military government duty into the provinces. Our zealous president was obviously whipping Washington into a fury of activity as only he could do."

Johnson believed he had the authority to move ahead with his war plans. Official summary notes of a meeting of the National Security Council on February 8, 1965, state: "The President said that the Congressional Resolution on Vietnam (passed the previous August after the Gulf of Tonkin incident) plus the legal power of the President made it possible for him to carry out at a manageable level an effort to deter, destroy and diminish the strength of the North Vietnamese aggressors and to try to convince them to leave South Vietnam alone. He said that the views of a few Senators could not control his action. He intended to use the Congressional Resolution carefully but effectively."

In an April 18 top-level administration conference in Honolulu, General Taylor gave his reluctant consent to an increase of American troops of up to 82,000. By the end of June, Washington had jacked up the proposed end-of-the year ceiling to nearly twice that.

Deputy Ambassador Johnson wrote, "Neither Max nor I had any enthusiasm for Americans fighting in Vietnam, but once our superiors made the decision we did not continue to resist it."

President Johnson on July 28, 1965, publicly confirmed that he would commit 175,000 troops to the security of South Vietnam by year's end, and that he foresaw the possibility that there would be more to come.

The record shows that on the eve of the announcement at a press conference at the White House, Johnson convened a meeting of his National Security Council for a final consideration of the issues. He reminded those present that "Ike, Kennedy and I have given this commitment" to the security of South Vietnam. Referring to the American soldiers in combat there, and to the additional forces he would send, "You wouldn't want your boy to be out there crying for help and not get it."

In his autobiography Johnson wrote that "when a president faces a decision involving war or peace, he draws back and thinks of the past and of the future in the widest possible terms. A president searches his heart and his mind for the answers. And that is what I did—when I was alone and sleepless at night in the Executive Mansion, away from official cables and advisors. When I was alone in the Aspen Lodge at Camp David, when I walked along the banks of the Pedernales River or looked out over the Texas hill country. In these lonely vigils, I tried to think through what would happen to the nation and to the world if we did not act with courage and stamina—if we let South Vietnam fall to Hanoi." He went on to say, "None of the very few who opposed this decision gave me facts or arguments that broke or even weakened the chain of conclusion."

Ambassador Henry Cabot Lodge, who would soon return to Saigon for his second tour of duty, felt that the president's actions to expand America's efforts to quickly win the war were illusory. Lodge told me, "Well, President Johnson's idea was a very human idea. This was an awful thing, awful thing, and let's get it over with as soon as possible. God knows we could all agree with that. Let's get it over with as fast as we can. But there is such a thing as make haste slowly, and I think he thought he could get it over quickly more than most other people."

According to his biographer Doris Kearns Goodwin, "By this point, Johnson didn't look back until his presidency was destroyed. As he became more committed to actions, he became less and less doubtful."

Paul Nitze, a former top security official in the Kennedy administration serving as Johnson's Secretary of the Navy, warned of what later became known as "mission creep," the need for more resources than initially anticipated.

In an interview after the war, Nitze said, "As Secretary of the Navy I went to South Vietnam in mid-1965, after Johnson announced the major troop buildup, to see how the Marines were doing. And during the course of it, I made a fairly detailed survey of the positions and came to the conclusion it was a most dangerous position.

"The Vietcong controlled the countryside right up to the fence surrounding the airfield at Danang. They controlled the mountains overlooking that airfield, and you couldn't get from the airfield to Danang city at night. You could go only at daytime. And Monkey Mountain, which is between the airfield and the ocean, was totally controlled by the Vietcong.

"And Chulai and Phubai, where the Marines proposed to build airfields, were completed surrounded by the Vietcong. It seemed to me the political structure in the rest of the country was not strong and that the military position of our forces was dangerous indeed. And frankly I didn't see how it would be possible with 200,000 people to turn that thing around and achieve a military success.

"What I did when I got back was to talk with Mr. McNamara and report to him on my impressions from that trip. I did not talk to the president. I can remember Mr. McNamara's reaction was, 'Well, Paul, if we don't reinforce there, what do we do? Do we withdraw our men?'

"I said I would think that's what we will have to do. And McNamara then said, 'If we withdraw from Vietnam, do you think it is likely that the communists will challenge the Western world someplace else afterwards?' And I said I should think it wholly likely.

"And he said, 'Do you think we would necessarily be in a better position geographically and politically to resist at this other place than we are in South Vietnam?' I said, 'I can't guarantee that we would be because I don't know where the Russians would bring pressure some other place.'

"Mr. McNamara's reaction was, 'Well, then you are really not giving me an alternative.' And to that I had to agree. I wasn't giving him an alternative. I couldn't guarantee him that there wouldn't be pressure by the communists someplace else. And that the position there would be better than it was in South Vietnam.

"I thought that there was every reason for us to help the South Vietnamese resist this infiltration and this subversion of their government from the North. But I didn't see how it could be done within a reasonable limit of the resources we could bring to bear upon the problem."

General Taylor had concerns that military planners envisaged assigning American infantry units to particularly difficult areas. "I had misgivings when I saw the extent to which we were dispersing our troops along the frontiers. It would sound very reasonable if we are going to the frontier, seal it off and thereby protect the hinterland from the further depredation and the infiltration of the enemy. The thing is that one forgets the tremendous distances — over 600 miles of the western frontier to cover.

"The business of fighting on the frontier is complicated by the fact that you engaged an enemy just inside our lines and then he retreats across it, and by the ground rules under which we operated we couldn't move into Cambodia, we couldn't move outside South Vietnam. So those aspects make it questionable in my mind whether we should be so diverse in our tactics rather than our strategy.

"My South Vietnamese friends were constantly urging our going into Cambodia and Laos, where the enemy would build up and then at leisure come across the border and strike. There was every military reason to consider it a desirable thing to do. But we didn't have the means. It just meant going into another jungle from which they would fall back. And then we would follow them further into Cambodia and Laos. Meanwhile, we are not able to clean up our own front yard in South Vietnam. So, I constantly opposed that. But it was not because I didn't think it was a desirable thing to do. But that it was simply infeasible to do."

General Tylor departed Vietnam on June 30, 1965, and eventually joined the Foreign Intelligence Advisory Board in Washington, D.C. He told me he was already realizing "that we wasted our efforts in Vietnam by bringing in too many things, by trying to press help too rapidly on a very fragile political structure.

"Our basic decisions that President Kennedy and President Johnson had to take — their greatest mistakes — stemmed, grew from the fact that they were based on inadequate intelligence, for instance, the intelligence about South Vietnam, about our allies. Only by hard experience did we learn what the allies could do and what kind of American aid they could utilize effectively.

"First, we didn't know our allies. Secondly, we knew even less about our enemy. I never knew anybody, I never met anybody, who had ever met any of the senior leaders in Hanoi. We knew only one of two of them by name, but only by name.

"I must say that having fought in the Korean war, I tended to think, 'Well, the North Vietnamese are a lot like the Chinese, who are very tough and very hard fighters.' But I also would say that I expected them to show a recognition of their own national interest, like they were going to pay too high a price for continuing in their course of action. Hence my hope that the air bombardments, the air attacks, properly used, could be a device to accelerate the peace. It didn't turn out that way, proving that we didn't know the enemy and we had no idea of the personalities of the people we were dealing with.

"And of course, the last and most impossible of our mistakes, not knowing our own people, how they would take a limited war, so far away, with vital interests at stake, but very difficult to explain. And where difficulties came not only from the objectives, but the conditions in South Vietnam where there was not one war, but 44 wars — one for every province. So really it was the fact that we went wrong in not having a solid base of knowledge essential to the understanding of our enemy, our friends and ourselves."

The day prior to his departure from Saigon at the end of his ambassadorial tour, General Taylor visited the coastal base of Cam Ranh Bay to greet the arriving brigade of the U.S. Army's 101st Airborne Division that he had commanded in World War II, an outfit that become popularly known as "The Screaming Eagles" for its battlefield exploits.

"My son, a captain in the infantry, was being assigned to it. I had the greatest personal pleasure in meeting my old organization landing there and turning my son over to the Screaming Eagles, hoping that it makes a better man out of him, and I think they did.

"I had trouble convincing all of them that there was a war going on because everything was so quiet there. And they said, 'General, where is that war?' And I told them, 'Wait until after dark, and you go over that hill and you will find out.'"

9

BLACK FLIGHT SUITS AND PURPLE SCARFS

WILLIAM COLBY ARRIVED IN SAIGON as CIA station chief in 1959 as the administration of President Dwight Eisenhower was seeking ways to come to grips with the growing communist insurgency against the government of South Vietnam. Colby quickly sized up the situation. "With infiltration going on from North Vietnam to South Vietnam of military supplies and personnel, some of the potential answers were, 'Well, why don't we return to the North some of the things that they are trying to do in the South?'" he said in an interview after the war.

Colby had useful experience in World War II when, as an agent of the Office of Strategic Services, the predecessor of the CIA, he parachuted into France and Norway to work behind the lines against the Nazi occupations. And he had the tools and the authority given by the U.S. government to his Central Intelligence Agency to undertake clandestine missions against America's enemies, preferably covertly.

"I was in charge of the Saigon station that was preparing these operations, organizing the teams, the training, things of that nature. We would parachute agents into North Vietnam, not dropping Americans but Vietnamese who were courageous enough to want to go. Some of them were coming from villages in North Vietnam and wanting to go back and see what they could do about organizing resistance there. In this process, I ran into the commander of the Transport Command in Vietnam, named Colonel Nguyen Cao Ky, a very courageous pilot."

A quiet-spoken southerner, Nguyen Van Thieu, was another young Vietnamese military man spotted by American officials with the potential to build a stronger base for the war against the communist Vietcong. Like Ky, Thieu joined the Vietnamese military in the mid-1950s and spent four years directing the National Military Academy at Dalat. He was then selected to study at the Command and Staff College at Fort Leavenworth, Kansas, and in weapons training at Fort Bliss, Texas.

These two young men, as rivals, would soon play pivotal roles in the rapidly evolving history of America's Vietnam involvement, with the flamboyant Ky taking over as prime minister in 1965-66 and the conservative Thieu as president from 1967 until the fall of Saigon to the communists in 1975.

The first efforts by Colby and Nguyen Cao Ky against the northern communists did not work out. "It was not a success for a rather fundamental reason," Colby said, "that the communist control structure was a very different thing than" control structures seen elsewhere. "It was easy to drop into the back country of China during World War II and find many people supporting you in the struggle against the Japanese; it was a different thing to drop into North Vietnam and run into the kind of control structure that the Vietnamese communists had established there.

"Finally, when we were prepared to launch our air drop into North Vietnam from C-47 transport planes, Colonel Ky insisted on being the man to fly the first flight. Now this was a violation of the doctrine because he obviously was a significant figure as an officer and an official in the military, and he knew quite a lot about our intentions and our plans, and so in theory he should not have gone.

"But I understand the requirements of the commander in that nature, that he cannot be in the position of sending people into something that he cannot go to himself. So, it made a great deal of sense for him to lead and show his colleagues and his compatriots that he was the leader of this operation, and that he would fly the first flight to the North and then send others on this mission. And when he came back safely, we all had a bottle of champagne together. Unfortunately, the team was not successful in the long run."

Ky later wrote about the fate of "the brave men we had delivered over the North." He said that every last one of them was picked up by the communists, most within a few days of arrival. A few were shot, a few were imprisoned. Some spent over 30 years in confinement before they were released.

"The CIA, which had invested a large effort in the operation, had failed to note that virtually all North Vietnamese wore sandals; the men we dropped in wore shoes. We also failed to realize that after five years in power the communists had so thoroughly indoctrinated the people, and that there were many subtle but telling disparities in the way Northerners and Southerners spoke and acted. There were differences in vocabulary, certain words that Southerners used for example, and in the way that people tendered pleasantries. Northerners even ate differently, used different condiments to season their soup and gripped their spoons with different fingers."

But Ky's involvement in those early clandestine failures cemented his reputation for boldness amongst his military colleagues, and also revealed his flashy style. Graduating from the CIA training program, he flew a C-47 to Singapore and returned with black flight suits, silk scarfs and cigarette lighters for his team.

Ky was born in North Vietnam, and in his youth admired the communist leadership then fighting the French colonialists. He later wrote: "Ho Chi Minh was lucky because he led the fight against the French and foreign domination. So, as you know, as the first man who led the fight for the country he gained some sort of prestige and sympathy from the people. When I was young, and I don't think just for myself but for the majority of Vietnamese at that time, I considered Ho Chi Minh a great patriot. I myself had a great admiration for him."

But he joined the anticommunist Vietnamese Army being trained by the French in the South, and received his early flight training from French military instructors. With the French departure in 1955, he moved up in the newly equipped South Vietnamese air force. It was his command of fighter aircraft in Saigon and neighboring Bien Hoa that made him a key factor in all of the coups d'état that swamped the capital of Saigon in political anarchy from late 1963 to mid-1965.

Ky revealed his usefulness in the brutal overthrow of President Ngo Dinh Diem on November 1, 1963, that led to the murder of Diem and his younger brother Ngo Dinh Nhu. Though not one of the senior Vietnamese generals who planned and carried out the coup d'état, he was a willing participant when it came to administering the coup de grace.

As Ky explains it in his autobiography, a senior general asked for his help in persuading the presidential palace guard to surrender. He scrambled two T-28 trainer aircraft fitted to carry bombs and rockets. "Before they took off," Ky wrote, "I went to the flight line and met with the pilots. 'I need you to go up and fire one or two rockets at the palace guard's base. For now, try not to kill anyone.'"

After the second rocket exploded, Ky wrote, "The officer commanding the gate radioed that he understood the situation. And his men put down their weapons and surrendered. For the first time, I realized that I had power." For his activities on their behalf, the coup generals promoted Ky to air vice-marshal and chief of the Vietnamese Air Force.

Nguyen Van Thieu also played a critical role in the coup. Long thought to be a fervent supporter of Diem, he was won over by the conspiring generals and led a key military unit, the Vietnamese 5th Infantry Division, in the first assaults on the Gia Long palace in the mid-evening of November 1. For his successful efforts, he was promoted to a general officer.

President Kennedy had approved the coup in late 1963 in the hope that a new Vietnamese government would empower leaders more sensitive to American demands to redress grievances of Buddhist protesters who had suffered from the growing brutality by the Diem regime.

As an AP reporter, I covered the coup on the streets of Saigon during the afternoon, and from the security of the American Military Mission building on Pasteur Street overnight. An intelligence officer offered to brief me on what he was learning. Radio traffic revealed the coup was being led by Generals Tran van Don and Duong van Minh, both veterans held in high regard. And it was backed by practically every senior commander in the Vietnamese military. The apparent clockwork precision of the operation led the briefing officer to observe: "It shows that the Vietnamese can run a pretty good war if political considerations are removed."

Kennedy was himself murdered in Dallas, Texas, on November 22, three weeks after the deaths of Diem and his brother, and was not alive to coax the Vietnamese towards better government. But he did see the initial positive impact of the coup. At the beginning, there was celebration on the streets of Saigon by the Buddhist majority who believed a new era was coming. Several of the half-dozen general officers who organized the overthrow were mixing with the locals in bars and nightclubs for several days, enjoying the adulation.

I had been in the country for 30 months during the dark days of Buddhist repression by the old regime. I wrote of the changed scene: "The new era dawning in Saigon seemed to have an element of hope. The air in the city was taking on a strange new quality, an intangible sort of feeling made up of many little things, the most important of which was probably the relative absence of fear. People weren't looking over their shoulder. They didn't stop in mid-sentence to wonder if they were being overheard. People were not scared to talk with Americans anymore. Buddhist monks in brown robes strolled the streets, and Westerners didn't shun them in fear they might be walking Molotov cocktails. Students, professors and politicians told us that another element of fear was gone, the fear of the midnight knocks on the door that in the Diem era filled the Saigon jails to overflowing with opponents of the regime."

The coup makers initially made popular political moves, forming a two-tiered Military Revolution Council headed by General Minh and appointing a civilian prime minister, Nguyen Ngoc Tho, who had been the powerless vice-president under Diem. The generals vowed support for free elections, unhindered political opposition, freedom of the press, freedom of religion and an end to discrimination. They stated that their main purpose was to fight the Vietcong insurgents.

It was an agenda worthy of a healthy democratic state. But South Vietnam was neither democratic or healthy. Over the next 20 months the military leaders squandered the trust of their local supporters and confounded their American backers by launching a series of traumatic internal confrontations and coups d'état that frequently threw the major cities into turmoil and undermined the war effort. The new authorities were clearly failing to live up to the expectations of the slain American president, nor the adoring population that had been so supportive of their actions.

Both Ky and Thieu, now with hero status in the post-Diem era, were actively courting other young officers to challenge the authority of the "old guard" generals who had taken power. These so-called "young Turks," led by the mild-mannered Thieu and by Ky, the charismatic flyboy with the black flight suit, purple scarf and a pretty new wife often seen beside him similarly attired, would be influential in the 18 months of political instability that lay ahead.

Just a day after Lieutenant General William C. Westmoreland arrived in Saigon on January 27, 1964, with the understanding he would take command of the American war effort in a month or so and have the support of a committed pro-American Vietnamese government behind him, there was a coup d'état by General Nguyen Khanh. It overthrew the floundering regime that had grabbed power three months earlier. The political roller coaster ride had begun.

A new American ambassador, General Maxwell Taylor, arrived in Saigon on July 1, 1965. He told me after the war, "When I got there, I started dealing with the post-coup government of General Nguyen Khanh. In the course of my ambassadorship which had been agreed to last just one year, I dealt with five governments, which meant five sets of senior generals, five sets of province chiefs in the 44 provinces. In other words, the house was cleaned, it turned over, five times, with the chaos that one can imagine. And furthermore, from the outset there was no firm government to build on."

In an early confidential memo to the White House, General Taylor wrote: "As the past history of this country shows, there seems to be a national attribute which makes for factionalism and limits the development of a truly national spirit. Whether this tendency is innate or a development growing out of the condition of political repression under which successive generations have lived is hard to determine. But it is an inescapable fact that there is no national tendency toward team play or mutual loyalty to be found among many of the leaders and political groups within South Vietnam. Given time, many of these conditions will undoubtedly change for the better, but we are unfortunately pressed for time and unhappily perceive no short-term solution to the establishment of stable and sound government."

General Taylor, as one of America's most decorated soldier-statesmen, brought enormous talent and prestige to the job of ambassador to South Vietnam. And he was sorely tested from the beginning by the disruptive activities of General Khanh. The attractive, flamboyant Khanh, fluent in French and English, was a media favorite because he was more accessible than other senior officers. He had early won the favor of Taylor's predecessor Henry Cabot Lodge, who had told Washington that he thought Khanh was the best choice for leadership among the Vietnamese officers vying for the top job.

According to U. Alexis Johnson, the deputy American ambassador to Taylor, "On LBJ's orders, Max Taylor and Defense Secretary McNamara, who both liked Khanh at the time, barnstormed the country with him. Frequent joint platform appearances ending with the cheer 'Vietnam muon nam' (Vietnam's thousand years) were intended to signal would-be coup plotters that Washington was tired of instability, and intended to prosecute the war vigorously under Khanh's leadership. LBJ, who had a real genius for pressing the flesh, had unbounded faith that Asian politicians would soar in popularity if they would only follow his example and 'get out with the people'

"But though Khanh was bright and beguiling, he was also mercurial and, as it turned out, utterly devoid of character," Alexis Johnson wrote in his autobiography. "He seemed to delight in plots and trickery. No sooner would he launch one scheme for governmental reorganization than he would abruptly terminate it without as much as a prior hint to his closest associates. He was once described as a man who succeeded in a juggling course but missed the last lesson—able to hurl multitudes of objects in the air but unable to get them down."

Among Khanh's closest supporters were the "Young Turk" conspirators Ky and Thieu who, it turned out, aspired to the top job themselves. The anarchic situation came to a head in December 1964, when they dissolved the High National Council with its civilian leadership, arrested most of the members and flew them to the central highlands city of Pleiku.

As U. Alexis Johnson wrote, "The embassy strenuously tried to get hold of Khanh for details, but he was avoiding us. Instead, four of the Young Turks including Air Vice Marshal Nguyen Cao Ky and General Nguyen Van Thieu called on Max and me at noon to explain their action. We deliberately gave them a frosty reception to underline our deep disappointment. Ky said the demi-coup was aimed at strengthening the council. But Max and I were not impressed. Not only had they broken all their assurances about preserving stability, we told them, but Washington would now have to recalibrate the long-term strategy of support we had so carefully worked out. Max asked them to reconsider what they had done."

Nguyen Khanh fought back, publicly attacking General Taylor, particularly for his suggestion that the common cause would profit if Khanh withdrew from public life. He claimed that the ambassador had insulted his fellow generals, and let it be known that honor could be restored only with Taylor's speedy recall. Rumors circulated widely in Saigon as Christmas approached that General Taylor would be declared persona non grata.

Alexis Johnson wrote, "Even the Young Turks were aghast at Khanh's selfish maneuverings, especially his attack on Max. It was obvious that Washington had no intention of recalling him to please General Khanh. But it also seemed that if he did depart, the American effort would accompany him. Max and I kept our silence while the Young Turks worked out their position."

Their position turned out to be Khanh's ouster, prompted by yet another failed coup attempt by a rival, a year after he had grabbed power with U.S. approval. He had brought political chaos to South Vietnam, but his departure ushered in a relatively calm period under a new civilian prime minister.

On February 8, 1965, at 8 p.m., General Taylor sent a message to President Johnson from the Saigon embassy detailing his relief that it was all over. "This has been the topsy-turviest week since I have come to this post. A new government installed, a coup attempted against the commander-in-chief, the coup suppressed, the commander-in-chief deposed by those who had put down the coup. The coup itself was an ill-considered, ill-timed move against Khanh by a group of officers and former officers, many of whom had been discredited by their earlier unsuccessful attempt against Khanh last September 13. One might have expected General Phat, the coup leader, would have done better on a second go, but he again misjudged the temper of the military commanders having effective military strength in the Saigon area. Phat's effort did have the effect, however, of breaking Khanh's spell over his colleagues in the Armed Forces Council and of bringing them to a decision to unseat him. This action appears to have been successful and Khanh's appointment as ambassador-at-large has just been announced. I understand that he will depart Saigon for Hong Kong on 25 February, but one cannot exclude the possibility of his making a last-minute maneuver to save himself. With Khanh the troublemaker removed from the scene, we hope that the Quat government can get underway with our joint programs."

With Khanh gone, Ambassador Taylor would now look to the Young Turk generals to provide long-sought political stability. Taylor had even informed the State Department, that, "with his hip-shooting tendencies, Ky is likely to continue to take ill-advised actions from time to time, but it is just possible that he will be able to create a new outlook favorable to getting things done."

In the early hours of June 1, 1965, Deputy Ambassador Alexis Johnson was awakened by a phone call from Prime Minister Phan Huy Quat. He went to his office on the second floor of one of the old French government buildings. Ky and Thieu were waiting with Quat. The prime minister told him that his crisis with others in the government could not be resolved by constitutional means. He had concluded that there was no alternative but to dissolve the civilian government by a military coup.

Johnson wrote: "A mutually agreed-upon coup. A diplomatic first! I thought that I had seen just about every permutation of coup possible in the past year, but this was a new twist."

Ky was proud of his achievements. "For the first several months the Americans seemed to expect the cycle of coup and counter-coup to continue," he said. "U.S. Secretary of Defense Robert McNamara privately described my selection as prime minister to his comrades as 'the bottom of the barrel.' French President Charles de Gaulle issued an audaciously sanctimonious statement calling for the neutralization of South Vietnam and the immediate and permanent withdrawal of American troops. Instead I arranged for the immediate (but temporary) withdrawal of all French diplomats from Saigon and the Vietnamese diplomats from Paris. Perhaps I rid myself of a crew of communist sympathizers.

"I was acutely aware of my shortcomings. I was a flyer with no political background and little patience for administrative minutiae. And I had never prepared myself to lead a nation. By that time most of the generals who had overthrown Diem were no longer in uniform. More than half of the top leadership were comparatively junior officers like myself; the others had either been exiled or forced to retire after one coup of another, something that had never happened before. I could get the military leadership to sit down with me and discuss ideas and problems face to face. I could rule less by decree and more by consensus."

The new Vietnamese leaders were invited to meet with President Johnson in Hawaii on February 7, 1966. Ky delivered a speech. "I spoke in a large conference room in CINCPAC (U.S. military Pacific command) headquarters to about 100 people. Americans on one side of the huge table, Vietnamese on the other. I emphasized defeating the Vietcong but also building true democracy and eradicating social injustice. When I finished Mr. Johnson rose from his chair and said to me, 'You talk just like an American boy.' 'Fortunately, I am not an American boy,' I replied as everyone laughed."

Ky said after the war, "You know, Americans are an impatient people. And I told Mr. Johnson and Mr. McNamara many times, if you decide to win the war, go do it fast and quick and get it over. You can't fight an extended war because your people are a very impatient people. You see what happens, after five years, six years, seven years. There's many promises from the American leaders, from the president, from the commander-in-chief of American forces. They told the American people we'll see the light at the end of the tunnel next Christmas, and we'll bring our boys home. The American people waited one, two, three, four, five Christmases, and they didn't see any light at the end of the tunnel. In the end, they became impatient."

America's hopes of having a civilian government in Saigon to help legitimize the regime in the eyes of the world failed. Ky was the sixth prime minister in the 17 months since the overthrow of Ngo Dinh Diem. He held considerable power until the elections of 1967 when he agreed that Thieu would head the military ticket that won easily. His authority would quickly erode, with Thieu remaining chief of state until the communist takeover in 1975.

In an interview after the war, Ky complained, "Most of the time the Americans in Vietnam were trying to do things by themselves, even in the fields of propaganda. They did it for us. Remember at that time, every time the press wanted to know something or to hear something about the war in Vietnam, you go to ask President Johnson or General Westmoreland. But never our opinion. The leaders of South Vietnam did not have any consideration. Now it's very funny but also very tragic that it happened. The other side, the communist side, the Vietnamese communists always treat us as puppets of America

"But then the American people also consider us as puppets of America, not true leaders of the Vietnamese people. At that time, they called me a Johnson man. They said it many times. It was very common at that time, to impress a person that you knew, you would say I'm a CIA man, I'm a Bunker man (U.S. Ambassador Ellsworth Bunker). I work for the U.S. Embassy. In the end, we lost our own identity."

The former South Vietnamese ambassador to Washington, Bui Diem, was to offer similar views in an interview. "From the very beginning, my personal attitude had been always that the Americans should try to help the Vietnamese but they should encourage the Vietnamese to do the job themselves, instead of trying to take over the job. I think the Vietnamese people are a responsible people. A lot of things have been said about corrupt regimes of South Vietnam. Yes, there are from time to time corruptions and there are bad people like everywhere else. But mainly I think there are millions and millions of Vietnamese who were willing to bear their own responsibilities. And if they had been asked, and if you could explain to them what they had to do, I would say they would do the job willingly. But that didn't happen. Isn't that the case?"

Brian Jenkins of the RAND research organization, who spent several years in Vietnam during the war, was asked in an interview after the war if South Vietnam was taken over by the United States. He said, "In part it was and it became increasingly so. The national palace, the political leadership, increasingly reflected a United States imprint both in terms of the form of the institutions as well as in terms of the leadership itself. We tended to create a mirror image but it was really like one of those funhouse mirrors, a very distorted mirror image. But clearly it was, it appeared very much a foreign creation. This caused some difficulties even amongst the South Vietnamese themselves.

"Ngo Dinh Diem had many shortcomings, and I am not advocating his style of rule," Jenkins said. "But he did have some claim to political authority and legitimacy which no subsequent South Vietnamese government was ever able to achieve. The American presence was a major corrupting factor. And we took basically a small country, a traditional society, and it wasn't simply the American military presence, but everything that came with it. We were ubiquitous in every aspect of Vietnamese culture, the air conditioners, the soda pop, the tape recorders, just a massive infusion of American culture came along with the American military presence.

"And also, a tremendous intervention in their own political system to the point that (it was) not just the American military advisors, but American political advisors, American aid advisors, where we were deciding what colors the lights in the fountain should be in downtown Saigon. Whether in the national library and the national museum should we do a Dewey Decimal system or a regularized checking out procedure for the books. We were into every aspect of the culture, whether the trees in Saigon should be cut down to make way for parking meters because that would be a more orderly way.

"This is not to say that there was any shortage of willing Vietnamese accomplices to this corruption of the culture. There was, for sure, in every way that one can imagine, economically, politically and culturally. The net result at least in my view was a leadership that could claim less and less legitimate authority to the Vietnamese."

In September 1965, after the first meeting of the Armed Forces Council appointed him prime minister, Newsweek magazine made Nguyen Cao Ky the subject of a cover story. "Soon afterwards," Ky said, "I received a gift from a man I had yet to meet, one of my childhood heroes, John Wayne. He sent me a pair of ivory-handled John Wayne Commemorative Colt .45 revolvers. I am told that only 150 of this particular model were manufactured, and so I kept one in its original box and wore the other proudly whenever I armed myself. For some reason, however, American newspapers mistakenly reported that my sidearm was 'pearl-handled.' Only a bordello pimp would be seen packing a pearl-handled gun. Nevertheless, the myth that I wore such a firearm was accepted as fact and repeatedly published."

10

THE OTHER SIDE

HE DAY I REPORTED FOR DUTY as a reporter for The Associated Press in Saigon in June 1962, the bureau chief, Malcolm Browne, a tall, bookish young colleague who gave up a career in chemistry for journalism, handed me a thin paperback book with the title "People's War, People's Army." It was published in Hanoi the previous year and contained the military theories of Vo Nguyen Giap, the communist Vietnamese general officer who was a legend in Southeast Asia for his orchestration of the final victory over French colonialism in Asia, the climactic battle of Dien Bien Phu in 1954. Browne said to me, "Read it, understand it, and you'll know what's going on around here."

Giap's book was the intellectual underpinning of a call to arms in the North to assist the growing communist insurgency in the heavily populated countryside of South Vietnam. Giap wrote, "The restoration of peace in Vietnam has created a new situation. The North is entirely liberated but the South is still under the yoke of American imperialists and the Ngo Dinh Diem clique, their lackeys. North Vietnam has entered the stage of socialist revolution while the struggle is going on to free the South from colonial and feudal fetters."

Giap called for the transformation of the primarily guerrilla forces he led to victory over the French into "a regular and modern army, an army that will always remain a revolutionary army, a people's army. That is a fundamental characteristic that makes the people's regular and modern army in the North radically different from Ngo Dinh Diem's army, a regular and modern army, too, but antirevolutionary, unpopular and in the hands of the people's enemies. The People's Army must necessarily see to the strengthening of the leadership of the party and political work. It must work further to consolidate the solidarity between officers and men, between the troops and the people, to raise the spirit of self-conscious discipline, while maintaining internal democracy."

At the time I read "People's War, People's Army," the Kennedy administration had sent 8,000 military advisors to South Vietnam, and the communist insurgency was just getting off the ground. In the years that followed, as a war reporter, I watched it grow just the way Vo Nguyen Giap had planned it, even to the introduction of formidable forces from the "regular and modern army, the revolutionary army, The People's Army" that he had proposed years earlier.

By 1965, President Lyndon Johnson had ordered massive, continuing air strikes against North Vietnam in Operation Rolling Thunder in attempt to force the communists into ceasing support for the southern insurgency. By 1967, more than 500,000 American combat troops were fighting in jungled mountains and populated villages where peasants had watched the French army depart a little more than a decade earlier. And by 1975, with the American forces back home licking their wounds, the South fell to the North in a lightning military campaign that General Giap had helped envisage. In the years since, American military professionals, academics and war veterans have debated the war and its outcome even as America's governmental relations with its former enemy have grown close.

An expert analyst of the Vietnam War for the RAND corporation, Brian Jenkins, explained in an interview after the war that the patience of the North Vietnamese paid off in victory. "If one looks at Vietnamese history — and the communists certainly did — they are able to bite off half-centuries in a gulp whereas we think of five years or 10 years as being a long time. Ho Chi Minh boasted that they were willing to fight 10 years, 20 years, 30 years, or longer if necessary, and that was no idle boast but rather reflective of the Vietnamese view of history. It probably made little difference to them whether ultimately, they would achieve their goals in the year 1969, 1970, or 1975. It could just as easily have been the year 2000 for them. Those gulps of history were really indigestible to Americans; we could not think in terms of that. It was always 'can we get there by Christmas,' 'another two years,' 'the light at the end of the tunnel.'"

Jenkins said, "I think when we talk about the North Vietnamese leadership we are talking about dedicated Marxists who nonetheless are as traditional as the ancient Confucian mandarins that ran the country centuries ago. In fact, its intriguing that some of the leadership traces its origins in terms of its own families, not the proletarian backgrounds but rather to the advisors to the emperors, to court mandarins. But clearly the Marxism, legitimate and true, to those leaders was very much something you could put on top of Vietnamese nationalism.

"Marxism gave them the conviction that ultimately the forces of history would prevail, as all good Marxists believe, that they were aligned with the forces of history and ultimately would win. And Marxism gave them a more international stature in which to portray that struggle. And Marxism also brought them alliances that were essential in terms of providing military support and economic support to achieve these aims. But at the root, I believe they had a drive that would precede that Marxism."

The Australian journalist Wilfred Burchett, sympathetic to the communists, was one of the few Westerners to meet Ho Chi Minh in his jungle headquarters during the French war in the late 1940s and early 1950s. His small group of invited reporters were driven by truck and walked and rode horseback about 70 miles into Vietnam from the Chinese border. "Their headquarters moved around all the time. There were always three headquarters: the one that they moved from, the one they were in, and the one they would move to. The one I was in was covered by very tall jungle completely safe from air observation, and there was a collection of very neat bamboo and thatch huts neatly spaced apart," Burchett said in an interview after the war.

"Ho Chi Minh was dressed in casual brown-colored cottons that the peasants wear in the north. When I met him, he was just coming out of a hut and walking up a jungle path with a windbreaker across his shoulders and a walking stick. He was wearing a sun helmet and rubber tire sandals and with a bit of rope tied around his waist to keep up his trousers. We spoke in French, but every now and then he broke into English, speaking very good English with a very attractive French accent.

"I had heard about the ongoing battle of Dien Bien Phu when I was in China but knew nothing about it. I asked Ho, and he took off his sun helmet and turned it upside down on the table. And he felt around with his hands on the bottom and he said, 'Dien Bien Phu is a valley and it is surrounded by mountains. The cream, the elite cream of the French expeditionary force is down there in that valley, and we are around in the mountains and they will never get out.'"

Burchett also had the opportunity to meet the North Vietnamese prime minister. "I talked to Pham Van Dong in Hanoi after the war. He is a very sensitive, rather poetic person, really. And of course, he and Vo Nguyen Giap were the two closest disciples of Ho Chi Minh. They were the two who carried on when Ho had to be away. I asked him, 'Look, people are now interested. They realize what great fighters you are. Why are the Vietnamese like what you are? What makes you tick?' And he laughed and said, 'Well, you know, what is our history? There is nothing else in our history except struggle. Struggle against foreign invaders, always more powerful than ourselves. Struggle against nature. We had nowhere else to go; we had to stay where we were and fight things out where we were. And this — the result of 2,000 years of struggle– it has created a very stable nervous system in our people. We never panic, and whatever situation arises we think: Well, here we go again. There is nothing else in our history except struggle. And this has developed a very special psychology and mentality in our people, and we can count on them in any situation. This is a wonderful thing for our leadership — we can count on them, in any situation at all. And there is one thing we understand and that is mobilizing people. Our people have confidence in their leadership and that is a tremendous asset."

Burchett also met the legendary Vo Nguyen Giap several times. "He is an extraordinary, intelligent man, an extraordinary, relaxed man. When you ask him awkward questions, he always has sort of an ironic smile. He has a great sense of irony, not only in his smiles but in his remarks.

I asked him—that I had heard on the radio that the war is going to be won in the South by bombing the North. Now what do you think about that? And he says, 'Well, there are all sorts of theories about this war. The main theory is that they can never win in the South by bombing in the North. I mean the main truth is that they can never win in the South by bombing in the North.'

Burchett said, "Giap is one of the most unflappable men I have ever met. I remember Prince Sihanouk (Cambodian leader Norodom Sihanouk) telling me a story about when he was in Hanoi in May of 1971 at the time of the South Vietnamese invasion of southern Laos. He and Giap had a leisurely dinner, just the two of them alone. Afterwards Giap put on some music and they had some coffee and cognac, and finally, Sihanouk says, 'I couldn't restrain myself any longer. I had to say, "Mon general, I am taking up too much of your time. I heard the radio this morning. There is a terrible battle campaign in Laos. I heard that Nguyen Cao Ky (the South Vietnamese vice president) was saying that they are going to stay there through the rainy season." Giap said to me, "Ah, that. We have been expecting that for a long time. The boys down there, they don't need, there is no reason for me to interfere." And he laughed.'"

Burchett said, "Giap is the supreme sort of military strategist, although in the final offensive that captured Saigon it was General Van Tien Dung who was the field commander. But it was a strategy essentially devised by Giap, and they were in touch all the time, almost hourly. They had been together right at the very earliest activities. A military committee was set up and Giap was the head and General Dung was No. 2. They knew each other's minds, and Giap directed the whole thing."

American air power was directed against the North from early 1965 to early 1968, intensive bombing mainly by the U.S. 7th Air Force and U.S. Navy jets. A total of 864,000 tons of bombs were dropped on the small country, nearly twice the amount of tonnage used in the Pacific area in World War II. Losses of warplanes and pilots were high.

Researcher Brian Jenkins said of the communist defenders, "They had the most elaborate measures to deal with the bombing in terms of relocation of their industries, in terms of rerouting of transportation. I don't mean to say that the bombing was not hurting them. No country can be bombed and take it complacently. But bombing was something they had dealt with before, that they were prepared to deal with. I'm sure they desired it to stop, but I don't think that they would have been willing to make concessions had the bombing continued.

"I think they would have continued to fight. For how long the bombing continued, it would not really become a matter of how long they could stomach it, but rather how much destruction would be brought against the country. I suppose that the cumulative effect of the bombing could have reduced North Vietnam to rubble, but even amidst that rubble I believe that the North Vietnamese would still have had the stomach to fight."

Wilfred Burchett made several visits to the North during the war. "I was in Hanoi in April 1966, and there had been a lot of air raids in the general area. A lot of the population had been evacuated by then, especially people who had children and old people who had no particular reason to be in the city. The authorities built this fantastic system of individual air-raid shelters on the principle of three cylindrical one-person shelters dug onto the ground. And the authorities said they had three for every person remaining in the city: one shelter close to home, one close to the place of work, and one along the road in between so the person could jump into it in case of being caught between home and work. The people had great confidence in the system. They were well informed. Loudspeakers would warn that aircraft were approaching, say, from the southeast, in the direction of Hanoi. The order: Get ready. They are presently 60 kilometers away, say. And they would sound a sharp red alert if it would be time to jump into the shelters. And there would be a last one, if necessary, to pull the covers over, because each shelter had a thick concrete cover. The minute the bombs had been dropped or when the planes had flown away, the all-clear would be sounded. The people knew what was going on, and the casualties were light because of this very effective system. I did not see a panic. People would run, however, when they had to.

"I remember one attack when I was staying at the Metropole Hotel in Hanoi, and there was a little group of women on the staff who were the antiaircraft or air-raid wardens. I remember there was an alert and they trotted out with their guns. I remember one stopping in front of a mirror in the lobby and straightening it before running out to join the rest of them. That is rather typical of the calm way the Vietnamese handled the whole thing."

Burchett recalled visits he made to the countryside during the war. "The Northerners were masters of camouflage. Children heading to school in the countryside were required to wear clothing that approximated the color of the vegetation they were passing so they could more easily hide in an emergency. I remember driving one day near the coast and to my astonishment a whole field of maize suddenly got to its feet and charged across the road. These were the local peasant militia in camouflage uniforms going through their maneuvers aimed at repelling any attacking commandos or invasion attempts in their area.

"I was told that when communist soldiers were preparing to attack the French fortifications at Dien Bien Phu in 1954, they built a primitive road through the jungle that French surveillance planes never detected because it was constructed during the night and disguised with trees, bamboo and brush before each dawn. When completed, the road was used by military convoys at night and concealed during the day.

"To better combat America's air war, there were also artfully-made bridges in North Vietnam that crossed the many rivers and spanned ravines and other obstacles along the transportation routes to the South, that wound across the coastal countryside and over the border mountains. Bamboo bridges that would be lowered into the water at dawn by winches and then raised at night for the supply convoys to use. Pontoon bridges with one half hidden on one side of the river and the other on the other side during the day, but pulled together each evening for the trucks to pass.

"They also had specially trained teams, with beams and replacement parts on hand, to repair the many permanent bridges which were the frequent targets of American warplanes. They also had alternative routes over less-used bridges that would allow truck traffic to proceed while repairs over the main roads could be made. Communist officials asserted that no bridge crossings could be delayed for more than three or four hours through the whole course of the war.

"All land routes from the North led down the legendary Ho Chi Minh trail that wound along the Annamese mountain chain for 700 miles through eastern North and South Vietnam and the western borders of Laos and Cambodia. At a meeting I had with him during a reporting trip in Hanoi in 1994, General Vo Nguyen Giap told me that the Ho Chi Minh trail was essential to the North Vietnamese war effort: 'Without our access to the South through the trail, we could not have sent down the troops and supplies necessary for our military campaigns. Without the trail, we could not have conducted the war in a manner that would have given us victory.'"

Wilfred Burchett traveled the arduous Ho Chi Minh Trail route during the early years of the war. "I think some think of it as just a single trail, and much of it was originally. It took me close to six months to get from the 17th parallel border to anywhere near Saigon. It went through rugged and very mountainous country, with hair-raising moments, like having to cross swinging little bamboo bridges. But as the war progressed there were many improvements. Multitudes of parallel paths and interwoven trails were developed. Parts of the trail were becoming surfaced for truck traffic, along with necessary pit-stop places, rest areas and medical centers for the injured or ill soldiers, and even entertainment troupes.

"American warplanes ceaselessly dropped bombs on both sides of the Vietnam-Laos border in an unsuccessful effort to close the trail. All sorts of electronic monitoring devices were dropped to detect traffic movements within the jungle vastness where the trail existed, some of the devices shaped like little trees or shrubs to blend in with the natural landscape," Burchett said.

By the closing days of the war in 1975, a gasoline pipeline stretched along the trail to a border area about 60 miles from Saigon. Some senior communist officials were using motorcycles to drive along the improved trail from Hanoi to the Saigon area in just a few days.

Burchett spent some reporting time on the communist side in South Vietnam during the war. "My first visits were before the big bombings in the South by the Americans that began in mid-1965. In the Vietcong 'liberated' areas life went on fairly normally. I moved around mainly on a bicycle. In those days, there was plenty of vegetation along the roadside almost right up to Saigon. There were rubber plantations and patches of jungle and we moved mainly at night on quite narrow winding tracks. For security, if daytime travel was necessary, we had one sentry on a bicycle ahead and one was left behind. If one or the other fired a shot we knew we had to scramble. I tried to make myself as inconspicuous as possible by wearing the same sort of black pajamas that the Vietcong wore, plus the conical straw hat and the Ho Chi Minh sandals made out of recycled tires which in any case were absolutely indispensable for the kind of travel we were engaged in.

"At the time of my first visits in 1963 and 1964 I found quite extensive tunnel systems around Cu Chi, for instance. I had to drop into a tunnel system once, and it was quite narrow. A Vietnamese could walk doubled up, but as a bulky Caucasian I had to crawl around on my hands and knees. There was not much air and with the excitement of the occasion — a battle was going on outside with automatic weapons firing and explosions — it very uncomfortable. There were a number of us in the tunnel that was only about 10 meters long. We got to an earthen wall and waited for a while, and I thought: How can we all manage now? Then somebody pulled a plug out from the other side of the wall, a rectangular plug, and I was invited to pass through it. I got stuck and somebody had to push me through.

"I found myself in a small village, and my guide told me that if things got hot again we could get in another tunnel and come up to another village. He said that particular tunnel was about 20 kilometers long and was started during the war against the French, and there were branches to the left and right. You could move underground according to the moves of the enemy above, and there was nothing to worry about. Afterwards, of course, these were very much extended. They were deepened, and had proper airholes and ventilation systems."

Researcher Brian Jenkins said little was known on the American side about the North Vietnamese soldier. "I think many of the things we did in Vietnam with regard to psychological operations were naïve, or were irrelevant. We really did not have a picture, until quite late, a portrait of the enemy soldier until a major study done by the RAND Corporation in the mid-'60s, which involved thousands of interviews with Vietcong and North Vietnamese soldiers, which ultimately began to provide us with information. This began to provide a portrait of this fighting machine which had previously been addressed in terms of the names of the units or the American designations of the units. As soldiers go, the North Vietnamese soldier was not unlike a soldier in any other army. He is not a robot in search of an ideology. He had the same problems with morale and motivation that all armies have.

"What they did have, however, was a unique system within their armed forces for dealing with the problems of motivation, of continued dedication to the cause, for constantly reinforcing each other. That was what came out of communist ideology and in part out of their own experience of fighting wars of this type. It was extremely effective, and perhaps provided them with better psychological defenses against the great military power they were faced with. An opponent that did not have some of these internal structures that are constantly addressing that question, their state of mind and their dedication to the cause, might have been strained by being up against an opponent, the United States army, that was clearly and vastly superior in technology and in terms of the application and the ability to apply brute force.

"The main motivation of the peasantry to support the government was the American bombing. The Northern peasant was motivated by a great deal of hate. There was bombing all over the North that provided ample cause for many people to hate the U.S. We are also talking about a society that is enormously disciplined, that historically was well disciplined. During the course of the war, every aspect of that society was geared to fighting the war."

Jenkins said the history of Vietnamese resistance to foreign rule was not understood by U.S. policymakers when they drew up their war plans. "The tradition of the historical background of the war itself, the conflict between North and South. The tradition of resistance in general, particularly to foreign rule, to which the communists successfully attached themselves and exploited, even to the extent of naming some of their military offensives after ancient battles against Chinese invaders or other foreign invaders, using names that were readily apparent even to Vietnamese schoolboys.

"The communists had managed to capture Vietnamese history. They successfully attached themselves to these powerful traditions," he said. "They made history work for them, and psychologically and politically this put the South Vietnamese and the Americans as foreign intruders very much at a disadvantage, in that the North was able to portray themselves as fighting the foreign invaders. They were able to take advantage of this powerful tradition of resistance, that in some cases had lasted in their history for decades, for example their centuries-long resistance to Chinese rule."

In an interview after the war, I asked General William C. Westmoreland, the American commander-in-chief during the height of the war, his appraisal of the communist side. "They were a very dedicated group," he said. "The training of the North Vietnamese soldier involved more propaganda and indoctrination than military training. They were tough; their commanders were well trained but they were ruthless in demanding strict obedience by the men under them, the men in the ranks. They had a fatalistic attitude when they moved south — many of them had a statement tattooed on their arms, 'Born in the North to die in the South.' They were very persevering, and this characteristic was typical all the way from the politburo in Hanoi down to the lower ranks. However, there was a great deal of discontent in the lower ranks, particularly among the very young and the very old. There were old men and young men drafted into service. Previous to and after the Tet Offensive, we would find 15- and 16-year-olds, but we would also find men in their mid-30s. They were controlled to a major degree by fear.

"To me, it was unbelievable the way that they would throw waves and waves of men into a situation that was inevitable that they were going to be killed. That was the way they attacked our well-defended positions. An American commander who lost casualties of the magnitude of Giap's would have been axed in a matter of days. The American people would never have stood for it, and the officials in Washington would never have stood for it."

What about the Vietnamese soldiers on his side? Westmoreland said, "The South Vietnamese soldier performed very well when he had good leadership. The problem with the South Vietnamese army was the shortage of good leadership. They had inherited from the French a policy of taking their leaders from the educated group, young men who had a chance to go to high school. In most cases they were city boys. Few sons of peasants in the early days were officers. Now, one of the things that I did as advisor to the army, from the very beginning, was to encourage more promotions from the ranks and more promotions from the peasant class. That did take effect and was helpful, but nevertheless the problem of small unit leadership and company-level leadership and even battalion, divisional leadership always fell short of what was required. But when the South Vietnamese soldier had a good leader, then he fought and he fought well. The problem from the very beginning was to select those leaders."

When American combat soldiers began arriving in South Vietnam in 1965, some began using the pejorative term "gook" for the Vietcong soldiers they fought against. Within a year the nickname "Charlie" had caught on, from the abbreviation of Vietcong, VC, (Victor Charlie in military terminology). By late 1967, after the brutal battles in the Central Highlands and south of the 17th Parallel demilitarized zone, I started hearing the more respectful "Mr. Charles" by the American combat troops who were facing off against an enemy that was proving its mettle.

11

EARLY VICTORIES, EARLY CONCERNS

PRESIDENT LYNDON JOHNSON AND HIS closest advisors planned the air war against North Vietnam and the ground war in South Vietnam while revealing little of their intentions to the American public and members of Congress. And some of the president's actions remained under wraps for years, such as his early-morning trips to the situation room in the White House to personally pick many of the bombing targets of the day, and poring over the classified tickers and reports that indicated the results.

But from the moment the first U.S. Marine combat troops hit the beaches of Danang on March 8, 1965, revealing America's entry into a new war in Asia, to the time when desperate Marines clambered into a rescue helicopter on the roof of the American embassy in Saigon on the last day of the war, April 30, 1975, the actions in Vietnam ordered by President Johnson and later President Richard Nixon were under intense scrutiny by Congress and a media that were determined to question the impact of the decisions.

As American combat forces moved into action against the Vietcong from their newly-established base camps, their progress was recorded by journalists from America's major wire services, newspapers and television networks. This was the first modern American war without censorship, a situation brought about by the Johnson administration's unwillingness to seek a declaration of war from Congress that would have permitted censorship and other extraordinary actions. But the media did agree to withhold security information from publication, including troop movements, upcoming operations, casualty figures and the identification of victims until families were notified. These agreements were rarely violated.

Washington had protectively set up a well-staffed public relations program in Saigon in 1964 headed by Barry Zorthian, a former Marine officer and a veteran of programming on the government's Voice of America. Zorthian was a genial, witty official, he played a clever hand of after-hours poker, and he was popular with reporters. But he was hard-pressed to persuade the ever-growing international press corps that the war was a necessary one and that victory for the United States was inevitable.

The perception problems quickly mounted. An emotional TV news report by CBS correspondent Morley Safer on the burning of Cam Ne village near Danang by U.S. Marines on August 5, 1965, enraged President Johnson so much that the morning after the broadcast he phoned the president of CBS, Frank Stanton, and accused him of desecrating the flag. Coverage by myself of controversial stories such as the weaponizing of enhanced riot control gas by the South Vietnamese Army, and criticism leveled against the administration by commentator John Chancellor of NBC and columnist Joseph Kraft of the Washington Post in 1965 prompted the president to launch an FBI investigation of the three of us, revealed in congressional hearings on the war in the early 1970s.

General William Westmoreland was expected by the Johnson administration to limit the media's access to the battlefield. He told me, expressing a viewpoint I've heard expressed by other senior military officers: "A new dimension for warfare evolved in the course of the Vietnam conflict. This is the first time in history that Americans or, I think, any other country have fought a war with no censorship. And it was the first war fought on the television tube. And the American people received in their living rooms and their bedrooms the gory part of the war. The criteria for news on the home front is: something that is unusual or unexpected. Criteria for news on the home front is different from what I believe should be for covering a war. When reporters covering the home front found themselves traveling overseas — specifically to

Vietnam — they conducted themselves as a group, as a profession, the same as they had done in the United States."

Westmoreland continued, "There was at one time an understanding that criticism of national policy stops at the water's edge. And here we had a group of professional people that serve our nation, and serve it well, and are basic to our type of democracy, who continue to practice their profession overseas while young American men have been sent to war in order to accomplish the objective that was decided by political authority. They were portraying the seamy side of the war just as they covered the home front, like the police beat, where the offbeat and the unusual on TV news were displayed several times daily, and large and in color."

Westmoreland's media problems were enhanced by the arriving army infantry divisions' officers' eagerness for news coverage of their biggest battles. UPI's Joseph Galloway, Neil Sheehan of the New York Times and myself were allowed to fly into Landing Zone X Ray, the center point of the storied U.S. 1st Cavalry Division's battle in Ia Drang Valley in November 1965. The news stories that followed cited the heroism of the embattled battalion of American soldiers and their success in holding off the North Vietnamese 5th Infantry Division in the first major battle of the war. But we also reported on the devastating communist ambush of a sister infantry battalion two days later as it was attempting to exit the area, an action that caused many fatalities and was initially concealed by the division brigade commander. In an angry phone call to the Associated Press Saigon bureau editor Ed White, General Westmoreland protested the use of graphic quotes from the American soldiers involved in the ambush, declaring, "What do these young men know of responsible commentary. Why, they were interviewed by your people even before we could talk to them."

Major General Lewis Walt, the commander of U.S. Marine forces in Danang, quickly ordered the renovation of a decrepit French motel alongside the Danang River, turning it into to a flourishing press center staffed with Marines. They were under orders to get along with journalists and do all that was needed to get them out to cover Marine military field operations, and make them comfortable when they returned. The

Marines came into Vietnam with the reputation of being friendly to the press, and General Walt's growing antagonism to Westmoreland and the Army officers around him at command headquarters in Saigon only strengthened his interest in publicizing his men.

As senior commander in Vietnam, Westmoreland also had to respond to criticism that the vast military power of the United States used against the enemy forces in South Vietnam was causing considerable casualties to civilians. He told me, "We took extraordinary steps in that regard, contrary to some of the reports given to the American public and the perceptions that were created. These perceptions were very unfair, and as one who has fought in three wars I can say categorically that never in the history of the use of Americans arms has more attention been given to the avoidance of civilian casualties than we did in Vietnam. Extraordinary attention was given to avoiding the destruction of villages or the killing of civilian population associated with our efforts to destroy the armed enemy.

"There was the famous case of burning a village by the Marines outside of Danang. But that village had been a place where the enemy was harbored by the local population, and where they moved out from time to time to attack the Danang Air Base. The village was destroyed by the commander at that time based on the fact that he believed, and I think properly so, that this was a liability to the safety of his command and a liability to the safety of the airfield. But before those villages were burned the people living in those villages were humanely relocated, which was the general practice. It was the policy of the command that if the enemy developed offensive positions in and chose to fight in a village, we would, over the public-address system, or by leaflet, urge the civilians to move out and give them ample opportunity to move before we attacked the village. There were cases when additional jeopardy was imposed on our own troops by virtue of efforts to avoid civilian casualties."

I asked Westmoreland about the use of indirect fire by artillery and air bombing. "There were any number of cases where artillery rounds were off target," he replied. "Any number of cases where a pilot dropping a bomb misread the target, and there were cases when bombs went astray. And this happens in every war, but these were accidents and not the destruction of civilian property by design."

Westmoreland said that he endeavored to instill in all his soldiers respect for the people of Vietnam and their cultures, and to avoid them misbehaving. He said, "A little card was issued in 1965 and thereafter to every American soldier, known as the rules of conduct. And I have those rules right here. The first one was, 'Remember, we are guests here, we make no demand and seek no special treatment. Join with the people. Understand their lives. Use phrases from their language, and honor their customs and laws. Treat women with politeness and respect. Make personal friends among the soldiers and the common people. Always give the Vietnamese the right of way.'

He continued: "Be alert to security, be ready to act with your military skills. Don't attract attention with loud or unusual behavior. Avoid separating yourself from the people with a display of wealth or privilege. Above all else you are members of the United States Military Forces on a difficult mission. Responsible for all your official and personal actions. Reflect honor upon yourself and the United States of America."

Westmoreland said every man carried the card in his pocket, along with a second card explaining how he would treat prisoners in his hands, in accordance with the Geneva Conventions.

The increased flow of hard news from the Vietnam battlefields encouraged Senator William Fulbright to hold public hearings on the war in his Foreign Relations committee. The senator had firmly supported the 1964 Tonkin Gulf resolution that authorized the retaliation bombing of the North, but he felt President Johnson was illegally using that authority for his military buildup in Vietnam. In an interview after the war, Fulbright said about his Senate hearings: "I tried to use them as a means to inform the public and thereby to bring pressure upon the president and hopefully upon the Congress to stop the war. That was the purpose of it. There were two levels of hearings. I also had a hearing on the psychological aspects of the international relations which I think were very important and relate to the subject, and those hearings I thought were maybe more significant than the hearings directly on Vietnam."

Fulbright said, "I had made speeches before that didn't have any effect on the administration. And I thought that the committee could serve as a forum to publicize the facts about this war and make it clear that it was not in our interest and ought to be stopped. And that was the purpose — my purpose was to try to bring pressure upon the administration to stop. During this period, there were efforts in Congress being made to restrict or stop it, but we didn't get anywhere. The clear majority of both houses wouldn't support us. They didn't know anything about it, but they always supported the president.

"Underneath all this, and this is very important, there was a real obsession with communism. See, it wasn't very long before this that we had the McCarthy period when the country went crazy — just lost their minds, over an obsession with communism. This was a very biased period, during Stalin's period. They developed this almost paranoid fear of communism. And we over-reacted." (Senator Joseph McCarthy led hearings that he said were to root out communist influence in the U.S.) And of course, McCarthyism was a disgraceful period and afterwards there seemed to be improvement. Then (Soviet leader Nikita) Khrushchev visited here, then you had the Bay of Pigs under JFK, and then the Cuban missile crisis and then you had a revival of that communist fear. It goes and comes."

By 1966, Senator Fulbright was one of the lone voices against the war in the United States. He said, "You have to pay a big price for that. I was conscious of it. When I got to make my first speech in 1965 against the administration my administrative assistant responsible for my relations in Arkansas, Lee Williams, said, 'You shouldn't make such a speech. You will be ruined politically, the president and the administration will not approve, they will punish you every way they can. That is the way our system works. You ought not do it, leave that to the Secretary of State.' The other side, Carl Massey, said: 'Well, you are chairman of this committee, and if you don't do it, who will? Whose responsibility is it if you believe this? If this is what you believe is true, who is going to do it?' We delayed the speech and argued about it for two weeks, on the very question as to whether you should take the punishment for speaking what you believed to be the truth, although it is critical of the president, or you lay back and let nature take its course."

Fulbright said there were attempts by the administration to discredit him "any way they could. The president of course makes pubic speeches.

I was here one day out at the armory when I wasn't further from him than I am to you. So that was when he used the phrase 'the nervous nellies and the sunshine patriots' with all of them standing up and supporting the president, and everybody hoots and hollers. And you were made to look like a traitor, in effect. Then there was the Gridiron group dinner in Washington, where I used to be invited. The president of the Gridiron that year was the editor of the Washington Post, and they had a special skit devoted to me with a big white dove, you know, which they had picked all the feathers out of the tail. Really killing me, really killing my role, you might say. Wherever you would go. And that rather irritated me. I mean to be put on public ridicule for a position I knew that wasn't very pleasant but that I knew was important. But I went to a great deal of trouble to try to inform myself. This is way beyond the experience of most Americans."

Fulbright said he had support from Senator Mike Mansfield "and a few other members of the Senate, I would say eight or ten members in there; they gradually grew. They supported me. You understand, most of the people in the country did not have any idea of Vietnam—I don't think they do yet. And I didn't know prior to that. I didn't play the game. I wasn't on the team. I am only commenting that this is what happens in this society. It is not healthy. It is not beneficial to take issue with the government or the conventional wisdom. It is sometime referred to as the tyranny of the majority. If you disagree in this country with the majority views they don't put you in jail and kill you, as they do in many countries, or incarcerate you. They just ostracize you and you become a pariah within the society. And that is about what they do. This is nothing new."

The Johnson administration, even as transport planes and shiploads of combat soldiers were arriving in Vietnam late in 1965, still hoped that this show of military strength would persuade the North Vietnamese to reconsider their war policy. Presidential advisor William Bundy said, "After the Ia Drang battle in November, many of us came to feel that this was a time worth testing, whether the North Vietnamese could be persuaded that they wouldn't be able to achieve their ends, and would pull back. We never thought that they would abandon their ambition; we thought they could accept a pullback and a restoration of the situation. We had a 28-day bombing pause that ran from just after Christmas in 1965 to late January in 1966. But we had a definite no from the North Vietnamese, a Hanoi statement from Ho Chi Minh, and everything we heard thereafter confirmed that they simply weren't ready to move toward peace at that time."

By early 1966, Westmoreland was being pressed by Washington to come up with a positive assessment of the war situation, and to implement the controversial body count of enemy dead. He told me, "There was a meeting in Honolulu in February 1966, attended by the president and senior members of his staff, military commanders and Vietnamese leaders. It was called to talk about the tactics and the strategy of the war. When I left I was given a memorandum that included body counting in certain required statistical reporting. Mr. McNamara was very strong on statistics as a businessman; that was his main tool. On the other hand, in fairness to Mr. McNamara, you could not measure progress of the war on the ground as we were able to do in World War II and even in Korea, because neither of those had the guerrilla aspect of war to be considered. And since we did not have enough troops in South Vietnam in order to form a line and sweep the whole country, we had to deal with area warfare. Therefore, it was a very fluid type of field operation. It was not unreasonable to try to setup some rules of measurement as to progress, and we had to do this, to count the bodies, to report them on a weekly basis. Although this was the only way that progress could be measured I think it was somewhat overdone."

RAND Corporation researcher Brian Jenkins said, "The body count served to promote the continuing of the war because it indicated we were winning. There was a factor to it, and as long as you could demonstrate a favorable kill rate, sure, the notion is the enemy will run out of people before we run out of bullets. When we talk about body count we talk about attrition. One can dress it up in various euphemisms, or tactically elegant terms, but that is what it comes down to. It comes down to, 'Can we kill them faster than they can be replaced. Do we have more bullets than they have people?' The inflated body counts, I think, often suggested to us that we were doing better than we were. Also, I think there was an inherent flaw in the sense that heavy casualties, if we were inflicting heavy casualties, it would have a deterrent effect. In other words, there might have been some justification for it if the opponent was playing by the same rules. And that simply was not the case. Then we could talk about inaccuracies. But it was not the same currency of exchange."

Westmoreland's strategy of seeking victory through the attrition of communist forces began to be criticized. He explained, "My strategy was not one of attrition per se. One can make the point that every war is a war of attrition, either attrition of forces or attrition of will. Certainly, the Civil War was fought until the South just ran out of men and the ability to wage war. In World War I, Germany was defeated because they just did not have the manpower or the resources to carry on. And you can say the same thing in World War II. So, in any war you would try to attrite the enemy's ability to wage war. And that is in terms of manpower, in terms of material, in terms of supplies, and in terms of national will. You try to break down that national will. So, the word attrition is a very broad word to use. And during that time, yes, we were doing our best to attrite the enemy. But we did not have the ability to do that the way we would have liked.... We did not have the ability to exercise the mobility that we acquired in 1966 and well into early 1969. We didn't have the political authority to extend the battlefield into Cambodia and Laos and north of the DMZ. We had the capability but we did not have the authority to do that by virtue of national policy."

Westmoreland did not quarrel with the objectives of the Johnson administration to win the war. He said, "Before coming to Saigon I had a long talk with General MacArthur, and he had served for many years in the Orient himself. His theme song was, 'There is no substitute for victory'. And the sense of my discussion with him was that we would commit whatever forces we needed to carry out our objectives. General McArthur was very conscious of the national objective being the overriding consideration, and you commit whatever forces are needed to accomplish that objective."

Close advisors to the Defense Department were already having misgivings about the Americanization of the war. William Bundy told me, "In April of 1966 at a meeting at the White House, I presented a paper that suggested that Vietnam could possibly become an albatross around America's neck. I could remember all too vividly that when we did get involved in the Korean War, and that the war dragged on inconclusively, a very great tide grew up against this politically. By using the word albatross, I was suggesting that the war would drag on, that it would be difficult in domestic, political terms if the communists failed to pull back, as we had hoped, because they wouldn't be able to achieve their military ends. We never thought that they would abandon their ambition, we thought they could accept a pullback and a restoration of the situation."

At the same time Secretary of Defense Robert McNamara was having second thoughts. He had played a major role in escalating America's involvement in Vietnam. In a memorandum to President Johnson on July 20, 1965, he wrote, "I recommend that the deployment of US ground troops in Vietnam be increased by October to 34 maneuver battalions. The battalions — together with increases in helicopter lift, air squadrons, naval units, air defense, combat support and miscellaneous logistic support—would bring the total of U.S. personnel in Vietnam to approximately 175,000. It should be understood that the deployment of more men (an additional perhaps 100,000) may be necessary early in 1966, and that the deployment of additional forces thereafter is possible but will depend on developments." It was a recommendation that President Johnson publicly acted upon several days later in a press conference that alerted the American public to the emergence of a war policy that would eventually cost the lives of 58,000 of their sons, husbands and fathers.

Adam Yarmolinsky worked in the Pentagon for a year from late summer of 1965 as McNamara's assistant for international security affairs. He said in an interview, "McNamara is an extraordinarily powerful personality and in any matter on which he is engaged he tends to be perhaps the most influential or, one might say, the most logical and forceful person, after the president. I would think that in any issue involving national security, Mr. McNamara was the most influential figure, and on all matters involving national defense, which of course would include Vietnam."

Diplomat George Ball said in an interview, "Toward the end of the time I was in the department, I got a sense from Bob of real anxiety. 'We've got to settle this thing. Let's get the diplomatic machinery going and get it settled,' he would say. His idea of diplomacy was, as I had gathered, was just to send a lot of people out to talk to a lot of people. Well, I don't think we had any absence of channels, any lack of channels. The problem was we were not prepared to say anything that could be a basis for settlement. So that is why I felt his anxiety, I knew it was genuine. I don't think that there were genuine efforts to get discussions going. They were foredoomed efforts, because we were not prepared to make any real concessions. Negotiations at that time still consisted pretty much of saying to Hanoi, 'Look, let's work out a deal under which you will capitulate.' And therefore, I never had much optimism about any of these things. But I thought it was useful to keep things going, But the problem was that while people said they desperately wanted to negotiate, they never were prepared to make any real concessions."

Presidential advisor Roger Hilsman said, "McNamara was an extraordinarily intelligent man in terms of sheer IQ. So, by the way, was Lyndon Johnson — one of the most powerful IQs I had ever met. Eric Goldman, his intellectual in residence, said that Johnson's was an empty mind, that is, an uneducated mind, and though very high in IQ had nothing to chew on, you see? McNamara's was an almost computer-like mind, but he had no feel for history. I would say that always his gut feeling would be wrong, but if given time to think about it he would come around. Indeed, he eventually became a dove on Vietnam."

McNamara's doubts came too late to contain the war. William Bundy said, "He was a very central figure in Vietnam policy from 1961 onwards. In strategic terms, he fully supported the major decisions to commit American forces to the successive decisions of presidents Kennedy and Johnson. At the same time, he became more skeptical from 1966 onwards that we could in fact carry this through, that we should keep going with the costs in terms of divisions at home, in terms of extended warfare and all its costs, in the most important dimension the lives lost. He had believed in the war's purposes. He also believed that the costs were outrunning the purposes at a certain point."

An internal CIA review of McNamara's book, "In Retrospect: The Tragedy and Lessons of Vietnam," written 20 years after the end of the war, noted that, "Mr. McNamara's accounting of history is ambiguous, debatable, and above all, selective. It does illuminate certain facets of policymaking and intelligence, but it does not dispel many of the frustrations that have long clouded our comprehension of the war. McNamara's troubled conscience tells us repeatedly that he and his colleagues were wrong, terribly wrong. They should not have tried to fight a guerrilla war with conventional military tactics against a foe willing to absorb enormous casualties… in a country lacking the fundamental political stability necessary to conduct military and pacification operations. It could not be done. And it was not done. They did not adequately level with the public. There were many occasions they were considering a withdrawal from Vietnam. And so on."

McNamara took 20 years to write his confessional mea culpa about his involvement in planning and conducting the Vietnam war. But the mistakes he much later admitted making were becoming all-too obvious as the war mounted in fury in 1966.

12

THE AMERICAN WAY OF WAR

I WAS RIDING IN A U.S. ARMY UH1B Huey helicopter 5,000 feet above an immense green jungle, while beside me an American two-star general was shouting instructions into his radio. I peered out over the door gunner's shoulder and saw a hundred more helicopters flying behind us in a vast inverted V-shape, like Canadian geese in perfect formation heading south to escape the winter. A battalion from the U.S. 1st Infantry Division was on its way to begin a major "search and destroy" operation against North Vietnamese forces believed to be operating in the forbidding landscape below. It was summer 1966.

Looking over the pilot's shoulder I saw flashes of bright orange fire bursting from the jungle ahead of us. "Artillery," the door gunner shouted to me. "We're prepping the LZ (landing zone)." As our helicopter dipped lower, I noticed the aircraft behind us dutifully following suit. Major General William DePuy grinned at me, leaned over and handed me some headphones so I could tune into his conversation. He was giving instructions to the artillery gunners back at their Lai Khe base to lift the barrage in thirty seconds because we were coming within their range. But even as the artillery men were following his orders, DePuy was ordering into action American warplanes from the Bien Hoa airbase to provide the last few minutes of covering fire before we landed.

Above the roar of the rotor blades I shouted to the general, "Aren't we cutting it a bit fine?" — because I could see airstrikes begin pounding on and around a large open place in the jungle not too far ahead that was designated the landing zone for the air armada, the LZ. DePuy turned and said into his radio mike, "The trick, Arnett, is all in the timing." And indeed, as the warplanes made their final passes, the hundred transport helicopters soared in, one after the other, to disgorge their loads without incident.

In mid-March 1966, General DePuy, a talented unit commander in World War II who had previously served in Saigon as General Westmoreland's operations officer, had taken command of the 1st Infantry Division, also known as the Big Red One for the red numeral on the uniforms the soldiers wore. He had developed some unique ideas on the use of helicopters in jungle warfare, and on the day I joined him he was putting them into practice.

And the U.S. high command was looking for new tactical ideas in Vietnam. American troops were landing on beaches and moving along roads and scrambling though jungles that French troops had used in the late 1940s and early 1950s when they were fighting to retain their Vietnamese possession. They fought well for nearly a decade, but ultimately lost the war. Researcher Brian Jenkins of the RAND Corporation, in an interview after the war, said, "There was a strong inclination to feel we had nothing to learn from the French because the amount of resources we could bring to bear were so much more enormous than the French had been able to muster. Indochina was at least to us not the same war at all, our experience, our historical experience in World War II was, we knew how to win wars."

Jenkins added, "The other thing is even when it was recognized by some that our military operations, that our style of fighting, was not particularly suitable either to the political situation in Indochina or to the military situation in Indochina, there were institutional obstacles to change our own military establishment. A prerequisite for change is the realization that what you are doing now is not working; in other words, the perception of failure. There was never in Vietnam on the part of the American view, the official American view at least along with the military view, that we were failing. We were succeeding, so why did we have to change or why did we have to do anything? Why would we have to learn anything from anyone else?"

General DePuy, who had come up with some unique small unit tactical maneuvers that limited his soldiers' exposure to surprise attack, told me in an interview after the war, "The tactical game in Vietnam as always, is the spoils of victory go to the side that can concentrate its forces at a critical place at a critical time on the battlefield. In Vietnam in the guerrilla war, this is a cardinal principle on which the communists based their actions. Their guerrillas moving in the jungle never attack unless they can be able to concentrate superior forces on whatever he picks. In this case in a country trying to defend itself with many district towns, province capitals, railroads, industries and so on, the helicopter didn't turn that around entirely but went a long way toward turning that around. We were able to put very small unit platoons and companies into the jungles. And then from the time the first shot was fired and every minute thereafter the advantages turned because the VC or NVA were seldom able to factor in reinforcements. They started the battle with whatever they had. In a minute, we would be able to bring in fighter bombers, artillery, attack helicopters and additional troops by troop-carrying helicopters so it reversed what was an exclusive advantage of the guerrilla. When used well, it resulted in frustration for the guerrilla and victory for either the South Vietnamese or us."

General DePuy's tactical innovations depended on the availability of combat helicopters that were distributed to the three U.S. combat divisions working adjoining areas in the critical communist-threatened regions in the vicinity of Saigon. His close association with General Westmoreland allowed him to assemble unusually large formations of helicopters for his operations, often to the chagrin of other commanders whose own plans were sometimes disrupted. DePuy told me after the war, "Our most revolutionary new technology in Vietnam was the helicopter from the Army standpoint. And even though the helicopter got its start in Korea in medical evacuations, it came into full flower in Vietnam. Use of the helicopter gave us advantages that the French never had."

General DePuy detailed how he used them. "Of course, it depended on how many helicopters were available. I think that we must have used at any one time during my time there about 90 lift helicopters supported by about 30 or 40 gunships. That was not an extravagant use, but a rich mixture. It was enough to lift a battalion with all of its support equipment literally at one time and put it on the ground simultaneously. And that meant within a matter of minutes you could bring another battalion in at 90 miles an hour. This is an advantage the French, who were subject to many ambushes during their war here, did not have. Most battles in South Vietnam were short: maybe an hour, an hour and a half usually the longest. But within that very restricted amount of time we could bring in maybe two or three battalions, in addition to the Air Force fighters, the artillery and the attack helicopters. And for each specific battle you were able to do this, the chances were you would win that fight."

A slim, compact officer, DePuy could be personable or pugnacious with associates but had an amiable relationship with the press. The hawkish columnist Joseph Alsop called him "the fighting general" and wrote several favorable columns about his abilities. I was often out with his troops on combat operations, and in one story for the Associated Press about his relentless determination to "search and destroy" the communist forces I described him as "a genius . . . he'll kill all the Vietcong in his division area north of Saigon or they'll kill him." But DePuy was also getting criticized for his unforgiving attitude to combat officers who in his opinion did not measure up to the task.

General Alexander Haig, later President Richard Nixon's top military aide and Secretary of State under President Ronald Reagan, wrote in his book, "Inner Circles," that when he served with DePuy in Vietnam he had a free hand as a battalion commander, "as long as I did the job right in his eyes. If he had not been satisfied he almost certainly would have fired me. DePuy, the personification of a fighting general, was known to have little use for officers who came to Vietnam from soft billets in the Pentagon with the idea of getting their ticket punched for future promotion by spending a few months in the war zone before going back to another desk job. When I arrived, he had fired no fewer than 13 lieutenant colonels from the 1st Infantry Division. Some who left under the cloud of DePuy's stern judgment were officers straight from the Pentagon whose political skills were greater than their leadership abilities and had been the protégés of very important generals back home who believed, and openly said, that DePuy was ruthlessly destroying the reputations and careers of some of the most promising young officers in the service."

The growing antagonism to DePuy's actions reached General Harold Johnson, the Army chief of staff, according to DePuy biographer Henry G. Gole. He wrote that General Bruce Palmer recalled Johnson calling him and General Creighton Abrams into his Pentagon office one day and saying, "'Goddamn it, what am I going to do with DePuy? If every division commander relieved people like DePuy, I'd soon be out of lieutenant colonels and majors. He just eats them up like peanuts.' Abe grunted, 'You want me to call him?' 'No,' Johnny said, 'Let me tell him.' So, he wrote DePuy a back channel and said just that. He said 'Your utilization of people is not very good at all. I can't afford division commanders like you.'" General DePuy had the last laugh. When Westmoreland became chief of staff in 1968, he hired DePuy to assist him in rebuilding a U.S. Army that was in a state of collapse after the Vietnam War. He would take over TRADOC, the military's Training and Doctrine Command. His success in revitalizing the American army after Vietnam would make him one of the most influential American generals in modern military history.

Researcher Brian Jenkins said that General DePuy's insistence on superior performance from his field officers in Vietnam was not the norm. "The war was often used more as a field training exercise. People were rotated through command positions, particularly battalion or brigade level, in order to give a great number of commanders opportunity of command. . . . So that a military officer in Vietnam might find himself doing in a year's tour perhaps three or four different jobs, meaning he held these jobs for no more than a few months, and there was very little opportunity to learn. The battalion commander would be rotated and there was a tendency to use the war to get tickets punched. If you're a battalion commander it put you higher on the promotion list."

Jenkins continued: "We have to step back and see how the American military perceived the war in Vietnam. And what happens in all military institutions, they tend to fight the last war. It just so happens that our last wars, particularly our experiences in World War II, were not altered much by our experience in Korea. And they were not appropriate for the requirements of the situation in the Vietnam war.

"Another difficulty we had here was that the Vietnam war was not really seen as a war that really did count, nor really should count. Many people in the American military had the attitude that somehow the war in Vietnam was the exotic interlude between the wars that really count, World War II in the past and World War III in the future — which, if one looked at the doctrine and the training of the U.S. military establishment, was to look very much like a rerun of World War II with the exception of having more sophisticated weapons and a different opponent. So, there was a tendency to say that Vietnam was not worth it — to put it in the words of one senior military commander, who said, 'I'll be damned if I see the U.S. Army, its history, its doctrine, its institutions changed, altered, just to win this lousy war.'

"And that attitude, of course, was a tremendous impediment to making the kinds of changes that some thought necessary. Now I'm talking about doctrinal changes in the style of fighting. There were, of course, broader issues that had to do with whether it was even in the interests of the U.S. government to commit the level of resources we did to achieve whatever objectives we were trying to achieve. I'm being somewhat vague about objectives here because the objectives were vague. The other marked difference between Vietnam and World War II is that in World War II what was victory and what was defeat is something that could be readily defined. In Vietnam, even near the end of the American war, people were still grappling with the question of what victory meant, what did defeat mean. There was no clear-cut objective."

DePuy took a different view: "I would say that although there were a small number of small-unit defeats in the jungles and in the cities by platoons and companies, that the American Army walked away from Vietnam with no defeat — no tactical defeats. And yet the interpretation is that there was an overall defeat. My feeling therefore is that it was not a tactical defeat. It was a strategic political defeat, and I don't think that the tactical soldiers could or should have that particular label put on them, the label of defeat. To the contrary, they did well. I don't believe that armies are designed for anything but large battles. It was the large battles in Vietnam that they did well in. The man who invented the army, and the architect of the army, probably didn't have in mind low level subversive and guerrilla war, as confronted by the American army in Vietnam."

DePuy added, "When you send an army, you get big battles. If you send a Marine Corps, you get amphibious landings. If you send an air force you get strafing and bombing. And if that is not what you want, if that is not what is called for, then you mustn't send any of those." He said he had one more thought, about the time when "the American army was withdrawn and the thought was that the battle would be turned over to the Vietnamese. Now, whether this country was fair to the Vietnamese in terms of the support we gave it is a question that only history will decide. In my opinion, we did not."

Brian Jenkins said, "The fact is the war was not seen as a succession of failures. Here we go back again to the criteria of success. In the absence of geographically measured criteria, that is approaching the capture of the enemy capital, we substitute these qualitative criteria, counting this and counting that. The career incentives combined with a fervent desire to achieve progress, in terms of what could not readily be checked. I mean, there were no auditors in the system. It led to perversions, the body counts were enormously inflated, terribly; I don't think at all an accurate indicator. And according to that criteria we were always succeeding. We may not have won but we were always, in a sense, winning. These successes were in turn rewarded or at least there were damn few visible failures that were punished. Generals who achieved high body counts were likely to be promoted and given expanded responsibilities. The criteria did not permit a clear judgment."

I asked General DePuy what he felt would constitute a win in a guerrilla war. He said, "I would say that in the event the enemy were attacking for example a district town, a province capital, a beleaguered or small unit, victory would be the survival defense of the unit or the town. The other measure is of course based on which side had the most casualties. That has since become very controversial, the so-called body count. Soldiers who fight all over the country and don't hold territory because they can't, as was the case in Vietnam, tend to automatically do that. And in those kinds of wars people always develop a distaste for it. I guess it is because it is a bit gruesome and there is always the suspicion of exaggeration which applies to both sides."

Reflecting on some of the same issues concerning Vietnam, Jenkins said: "In terms of doctrine, it still was very much World War II and battalions in line, two companies up and one back. There are only so many ways you can conjure major military organizations. To me, at times it almost struck me not as World War II but 18th century. Battalions of soldiers, quite brave to stand out there and to walk in line across rice paddies or across open terrain until one of them was picked off by a sniper or until he ran into an ambush or when he was blown up by a mine. A very ponderous, slow moving, heavy, again I would almost say an 18th century campaign. That was belied by the technology—helicopters to be sure, hundreds of helicopters if necessary, jets that flew at hundreds of miles an hour, but on the ground, it was that very ponderous thing,

"Insofar as the other technology and things like aircraft, I think that the unfortunate thing in our technology, some mentioned that our technology was too advanced. We could fly at 500 miles an hour; we dealt with an enemy that walked at 2 or 3 miles an hour. We could bomb at 30,000 feet; they were just five feet off the ground. Technology did not readily translate into things that gave a real measure of military effectiveness.

"In a battle to be sure, when the enemy would give battle, ultimately the superiority of weapons would prevail, and hard-fought battles ultimately were won. But that was the whole point of the war... The other part of it, of course, is that the military success, when there was military success, measured even in geographic terms, occupying something or defeating something, did not translate into political success. People fought over and many died taking hills that meant nothing three days later. It wasn't success in the sense of occupying terrain that had great meaning."

DePuy's take: "We fought many large-scale engagements in the fall of 1966, and at the end of this the VC and the NVA went into one of their rather traditional and cyclical retreats from the battlefield. Of course, we interpreted it very hopefully because we had some tactical victories. It was having some effect on the long-term prospects of the war. I would say that at the end of that period I was personally quite optimistic, at least that campaign. It turns out, of course, that they came back again. And the war cycled that way. There would be a heavy series of engagements and then they would slack off and withdraw into their war zones. Or sometimes into Cambodia to refit, train and have at it again. The war did go in cycles. One of the peaks was Tet. There were many Tets after that. Then there were the big campaigns that finally defeated the South Vietnamese army.

"One thing that characterized each of these cycles was that it went to a higher plane. In other words, each time the peak was higher than before, meaning more troops were involved. I think many people don't understand that the last peak at the very end of the war, there were 22 North Vietnamese divisions involved. That is larger by far than the current United States Army. So those who think that it was a sophisticated guerrilla war fought for the hearts and minds of people in the villages and hamlets were only partly right. It was all that, but at the same time a very large, vicious, tough war."

Jenkins said: "I would say that the first major point would be whatever our objectives were, our political and military objectives in Vietnam, that our mode of our military operations, our style of fighting, was not in my view likely to achieve those objectives. Any notions we might have had about persuading the North Vietnamese to desist from continuing the struggle were unfounded. They would continue to fight for the foreseeable future, decades if necessary. There was no notion of dissuading them from continuing this contest in some form, and that we should have no illusions about that. That if we wanted to get into a contest of wills, then one had to be prepared for perhaps the only military strategy that might have worked, and that would be a low-cost sit-in, and prepared to sit in the place for half a century. In regard to the strategy I did advocate, the sit-in if you will, the cheap long-term, low-cost sit in, to me it became unrealistic because the international political environment scene wouldn't find it acceptable. The American public would find it unacceptable. We are not a colonial power; simply, we have no patience for that."

DePuy commented, "I am confident that the problems of troop leadership increased as the war went on, for several reasons. One was that the non-commissioned officer corps was gradually decimated. . . . For example, when I commanded the division we had a full complement of non-commissioned officers. And when I went back to visit Vietnam in subsequent years I found each time that there were fewer and fewer non-commissioned officers. And fewer and fewer lieutenants who had ever served in a unit before they went into action in Vietnam.

"And I think it made it more difficult to — for subsequent division and corps commanders — to achieve a high level of performance. And then toward the end of the war, when there was disaffection in the United Sates, there was some reflection of that, I think, in the lack of enthusiasm in Vietnam as well. Although I think that the fact that the units continued to fight and that the tactical integrity was maintained was miraculous, and a great tribute to the leaders of the army who served there at that time, both at the level of the sergeants, the lieutenants and all the way up to the high command."

Could America have won the war? I asked General DePuy. He said, "Obviously, it would have taken more time than the United States was willing to devote to it. And I think that's the key, in terms of national wealth and in terms of the young people in America. And also, I think in terms of being jaded by being weary, by having too much war, and too many commenting on too many television sets for too many years. All that finally broke some tolerance point that we had never experienced before."

GALLERY

PETER ARNETT REPORTING

Peter Arnett with a South Vietnamese Army Captain near Can Tho, 1964. (Peter Arnett Collection)

Arnett meets with Colonel Markey, Senior American Advisor for the 7th Division where fight in Kien Phuong province took place, 1964. (AP Photo)

AP's Horst Faas and Peter Arnett, at typewriter, in the Saigon Associated Press office, 1964. (AP Photo)

Arnett inspects a severely damaged aircraft, 1965. (AP Photo)

Arnett during coverage of the aftermath of battle between troops of the 1st U.S. Infantry Division and a Vietcong battalion near plantation town of Bau Bang, 1965. (AP Photo)

Arnett standing beside the burned out hulk of a A1 Skyraider, 1965. (AP Photo)

Arnett holding a captured Chinesed flamethrower, 1965. (AP Photo)

Arnett moves cautiously through heavy grass during the fighting at La Drang Valley, 1965. (AP Photo)

Peter Arnett accepts congratulations at the Saigon bureau from fellow Pulitzer winners Malcolm Browne, left, and Horst Faas upon learning that he has won the 1966 Pulitzer Prize for International Reporting. (AP Photo)

Arnett meets with soldiers of the U.S. 1st Infantry Division before a military operation, 1966. (Peter Arnett Collection)

Arnett wearing gas mask while reporting on U.S. effort to penetrate enemy tunnel systems, 1966. (Peter Arnett Collection)

Arnett accompanied by tank, 1967. (AP Photo)

13

THE SOLDIERS' WAR

JIM WEBB, A YOUNG MARINE officer flown to the Vietnam War in 1969 in a chartered commercial jet packed with American soldiers, remembers his first days as being like nothing he was trained for. "I guess one of the real shocks to me, and something which the people in the rest of our civilized world have for some reason been unable to comprehend, is how quickly you come to be debased, degraded, physically in that environment," he said in an interview after the war for a documentary I was writing. "One of the hardest things to adjust in my mind was to step off an air-conditioned plane, where I had just watched a first-run movie, (and) have this German stewardess say, 'You have a nice war,' just as somebody mentioned to me that she was getting combat pay to touch down in Danang. And within a space of three days to literally make a hooch out of a poncho with boot strings, and that is the way I lived for nine months. I had three hot meals in nine months in the field. And it was so primitive. And yet in this deus ex machina world, the helicopter would come in and get you out of that environment if you were lucky enough to get the right kind of wound, a sickness or R and R (rest and recuperation), or something. It was very strange."

Tim O'Brien, drafted soon after he graduated from a Minnesota college in 1968, arrived in Vietnam expecting violence but entered instead something he felt was like a fool's paradise. "I had been bred and raised on World War II movies and that was my image of war, lots of battle,"

O'Brien told me in an interview after the war. "And I was surprised when I was assigned to an infantry company helping secure the U.S. Marine Air Base at Chu La along the northern coast. We began going out in operations in what seemed like a kind of vacation land; it reminded me of what Miami Beach must be like without the hotels. Beautiful clean sands, and in the distance green sloping hills. Beautiful.

"And as we would go from position to position along the beach we would be followed by maybe 100, 150 Vietnamese villagers who I supposed lived nearby. There were prostitutes, there were young kids, there were girls peddling cocaine at a dollar whack or 50 cents a whack. They were making a killing on us. And we had our own personal mascots or valets, a little kid of 7 or 8 who would hook up with a soldier and wash his socks for him and clean his rifle for him, and sometimes carry his rifle for him if we were exceptionally tired that day, and they'd dig our foxholes at night. In a way, it was a symbiotic relationship in that we were feeding off them and they were feeding off us. There was a sense of familiarity and almost love. It was like a circus in some sense—going through town, going across the beach where us soldiers would be lined up and heading off, and behind us like the tail of a kite would be a hundred or so Vietnamese, kind of coming along for the ride."

Tim O'Brien and Jim Webb both became successful novelists after the war, channeling their experiences into insightful stories of bravery, brutality and naivete that established them as important literary figures and insightful commentators on the military experience in Vietnam. The American combat soldiers sent there were faced with defeating a determined enemy in an unfamiliar environment in a war that was governed more by political objectives than military ones. Of the 2,700,000 American soldiers who served in South Vietnam during the war years, 1965–1972, there were nearly half a million who were assigned to infantry combat battalions that bore the brunt of the battle against the Vietcong and the North Vietnamese. A third of those soldiers were draftees, recruited straight out of high school or college, and sent the many thousands of miles across the Pacific Ocean to a distant Southeast Asia that most knew little or almost nothing about.

A noted researcher for the RAND Corporation, Brian Jenkins, who spent several years in Vietnam, said in an interview about the American combat soldiers: "In terms just of appearances, they carried an enormous amount of equipment, ammunition, canteens. In fact, it was burdensome in the environment and the climate even to move. They moved slowly. They were frightened. Anything could set them off—a pig running across the road, a chicken running out of a door could have set them off. In areas where they knew the people, there was a certain amount of joshing. The little children who would shout OK Salem for cigarette, or for Coca-Cola or something like that. But the minute they got beyond their very tightly circumscribed circle of familiarity it was foreign, alien, and I just don't mean alien in terms of somebody who speaks another language. I mean alien in the sense of other world of culture to them."

Jenkins said, "There was certainly a fear operating against an enemy that they seldom saw, taking in some cases dreadful casualties from mines and booby traps. seeing their comrades die or being maimed as the result of these things but not having any outlet in the sense of being able to shoot back, in the sense of being able to give it back to the enemy. In some cases, I think it led to outlets of violence against people who could not, by any standards of warfare, be called the enemy but just the population in general. And it was a reaction of fear and the frustration of dealing with an unseen enemy. It would be a greater satisfaction if somebody could see someone to shoot at."

Both Jim Webb and Tim O'Brien gave interviews in 1979 for a television documentary I was writing, their memories still vividly fresh from the war. Webb was interviewed soon after the publication of his successful novel "Fields of Fire" in 1978, the first of several books on his military experience. He was Secretary of the Navy in the Reagan administration and a U.S. senator from Virginia for a term during the presidency of Barack Obama. He said, "Some of my real frustration is trying to explain to somebody what exactly the Marine infantry went through. When you look at World War II operations, you saw a guy with a pack on his back and going through things. You can relate to it as a Marine. In World War II, we saw some of the finest hours of the United States Marine Corps. But you never stop to think that those battles were so bloody, because you never stop to think that those battles were over very quickly. All I carried in my pack was a poncho, a poncho liner, a toothbrush, letter-writing gear — and that was it. That is all I carried for nine months. We moved our positions, like, every two days. There was no barbed wire. If you were going to make a call of nature you just got off the trail, or you dig a straddle trench if you are in a perimeter, and stand in front of everybody.

"You don't have a bath for months, literally months. Maybe you wash off in a stream, or find a well. And we ate C-rations continually. I know that some Army units were guaranteed a hot meal a day because they have so much better helicopter support. Virtually every single person in my unit got either ringworm, hookworm, dysentery or yaws (a tropical infectious disease) one time or other. And some of us had all of them. And malaria as well. We did saturation patrolling. We set up a company and platoon operating base, which we would patrol out of, hoping to make contact with the enemy. If you moved as a platoon or even a reinforced squad, it was almost seducing the enemy into attacking you. Then you could fix the position and bring in other units and supporting arms to destroy it. This was great if you were just tallying numbers on a tote-board, but it can be really devastating to the smaller units sent out as bait. We call it dangling the bait. We were just sort of out there, if you know, just on the edge, the periphery, and waiting for something to happen.

"Combat is a paradoxical experience. On one hand, it was one of the most debilitating things I went through. I had a platoon that averaged say 25 to 28 people. During one period, that was not quite seven weeks, I took 51 casualties, and when No. 51 got his arm blown off, I sat down next to him and cried like a baby. I had had it. And yet on the other hand, it is an immensely rewarding level of experience on a personal level. It is a meaningful experience more than rewarding, put it that way. It has a deep amount of meaning when you see people around you stripped down to their basics as human beings. You know what the saying is, 'When you are up to your neck in alligators, you don't sit there and keep talking about why you came to drain the swamp.'"

Webb continued: "The whole environment in Vietnam was a day-to-day environment. It didn't matter why you were there. You didn't talk about what patrols you had; you talked about whether you were getting mail. You talked about how many days you have left on your tour. Again, perhaps maybe because this was rarely emphasized in Vietnam, because of the filtering process of the draft, there were so many ways to get out of it. You know, there were only 11 percent of the draft-eligible males in this country ever to make it to Vietnam. And at any one time—what was it?—only 10 percent of the Americans in Vietnam were actually in a combat unit. My platoon averaged probably 10th or 11th grade education. They were, on human terms, they were the finest people that I have ever been around in my life. They were a giving people, they were very courageous people, but they were not political people."

"As a platoon leader, there is one thing you never get over, is pointing your finger and telling somebody to go, and then watching them get blown away. You know if you had any degree of sensitivity at all, think that if you are developing a sort of feeling for these people... And as a platoon commander you live with them day in and day out. It's so different from other wars. They become like little brothers, they really do."

"The civilians in many areas were actively against us. We hit a major North Vietnamese unit, a regiment, and in a multi-battalion sweep and block we were sweeping north, and my company was the last company down. And we started to set up around a tank and there was a tree line that came into our village that we were setting in. And there were six guys that were sent out to clear this tree line, because we had enemy moving in. They were approaching through a cemetery and as they got towards it this girl stood up and waved at them. And the team leader, a kid by the name of Ricky, said, 'Wait a minute,' as one of the guys was going to shoot her. 'Wait a minute, it's only a baby san.' So, he stood up and said, 'Hey, baby san, lay down,' just to get her out of the way. And the North Vietnamese opened up on him, and Ricky was shot right in the face, the guy behind him was shot in the chest, and by the time we got there was only one left alive. And you know, it was just typical of a Marine engagement. You get a small unit pinned down, and somebody else would try to help them. And they get pinned down, and you send somebody else to help them and they get pinned down. You know, that is the way things unraveled.

"We were instructed on the rules of engagement, and we were required to read them when we came into the country. And my experience was, with the exception of a few cases where someone would lose control after eight or 10 months under very frustrating circumstances, my experiences were that our people attempted, you know, with great personal loss at that time, to abide by the rules of engagement. There were things like if a person was running from you, and if you went into a village and that person was a civilian and stood perfectly still, they would not be harmed. If somebody then turned and ran, chances were about 95 percent that was a VC or a North Vietnamese. You still had to yell three times for the guy to stop, and if he didn't, then everyone of us knew it.

"And like if you took a civilian detainee you could never make them walk point. I had a friend of mine who had taken a woman detainee and he had a guy walk in front of them, and she walked right over a body trap and started running. And my friend tripped on it and killed his radio officer and you know just blew half his butt off. I would say that, as much could be expected of any human being, basically an emotional animal, we accorded them, you know, the sort of courtesy that our superiors wanted us to.

"You have basically an immature human being. The average age of an American soldier in World War II was 26 years; you had my father's best friend was my age now when he got drafted in World War II. The average age in Vietnam was 19 years old. And you have a collection, you know, of young, immature, very emotional people. And these guys tried like hell," Webb said. "We had a few words we all knew and the civilians knew also. Hand gestures and that sort of thing. In the village, the people's main presentation to us was absolute numbness. You go through and they could just squat there. They learned not to move. That's the main thing. They froze. And if we wanted something from them we would approach them. And some of the things were very basic. You could tell the words that we polluted as the intonations of other language: la dai, 'come here'; dun la, 'stop'; ah dai, 'where.' There were a dozen others we all knew and could communicate with.

"As far as the enemy is concerned, there were good units and bad units. Most of the North Vietnamese units I thought were good units.

And they had a good deal of fire discipline. One of the things that I really admired was the way the North Vietnamese maintained their fire discipline. For a Marine, you are going to hit the first thing you see, mainly because we had so much firepower. But they had the ability to hold fire in an ambush. For instance, when crossing a paddy toward a tree line and you had to prep it (prepare for your advance with covering fire). One company with my regiment moved on line until they were approximately 10 feet away from the tree line, and the North Vietnamese opened up all at once and they killed 18 Marines in about 10 seconds. When they hit you that close, you cannot use supporting arms unless you call them in on your own people, which occasionally happened. That was something that required very good unit discipline to be able to do."

"Another thing, when the communists moved they moved in eight-man groups. When a Marine unit moved we moved as a company, a huge dinosaur floating around, and a sniper could pin down a whole company. And they moved in eight-man cells, even if they have eight hundred people moving, two hundred yards apart. In an ambush, when a Marine gets hit you immediately fall straight down, just fall straight down. If an eight-man enemy unit got hit they would just turn around and run straight back where they came from, they knew the rear was clear. Otherwise, they knew we would come in to blow out everything we saw. Little things like that."

I interviewed Tim O'Brien in his apartment at Cambridge, Massachusetts, soon after the publication of his Vietnam book, "Going After Cacciato," which won the National Book Award for fiction in 1979. O'Brien had earlier won attention for his first novel published in 1973 named "If I Die in a Combat Zone, Box Me Up and Ship Me Home." Another of his best-known books is "The Things They Carried," published in 1990. In our interview, O'Brien said, "I remember a lot of the songs we sang while we were in a military training camp in the state of Washington preparing to go to war. My first book was based on the lyrics of one of them that went, 'If I die in a combat zone, box me up and send me home. If I die on the Russian front, bury me with a Russian cunt.' There was a nice clean one we sang, 'Vietnam Vietnam, every night while you are sleeping, Charlie Cong comes a-creeping all around.' And those are the strains, the music that sort of seeped into your dreams at night. Those songs just seemed to reverberate and resonate in your dreams."

O'Brien's early days experiencing the joys of beach patrol and friendly local Vietnamese at Chu Lai air base ended when his outfit, the U.S. Army's 46th Infantry Regiment, was required to move deeper into the surrounding countryside. He described a typical night patrol: "My platoon was part of an infantry company of about 100 men. And roughly about half of those would group up around midnight and we would set off. We'd sometimes darken our faces and we would throw off our helmets because helmets were useless, they impaired hearing at night, and they were heavy and it was hard to march with them on. We would throw everything aside except our rifles, our ammunition, a canteen of water, a claymore mine and a radio. And begin zig-zagging through this ghost land that we called Vietnam. It was scary. There was almost a mythology about Vietnam among the soldiers, that this land is populated by ghosts. In my platoon, we called them Vietcong ghosts. You know, 'The ghosts are out tonight,' or 'The ghosts will get us tonight.' It was not often 'Charlie' that we called them; it was it was 'ghosts.' And the ghostly feeling was there. It was like a wonderland. It was like an Ichabod Crane driving through Sleepy Hollow at midnight. Trees seemed to be moving, seemed to be actually lifting off the ground, and wavering, shimmering. How much of that is my imagination? Well, part of it probably.

"We called the Vietcong ghosts because we never saw them. You would see a sheet of flame as they would shoot at you, and you might see a shadow, very rarely. They seemed to be capable of incredible things. There was a mythology that they could crawl through barbed wire, that they were immune to barbed wire. I remember an incident when we were operating out in the field where we could see our base in the distance. And one night the whole base lit up with flares and we received a call the next day that our base had been attacked. Our battalion commander, our colonel, who was a very gung-ho black colonel, had been killed. The communist sappers had come into the base through the barbed wire, in that supernatural sort of way, and gone directly to the colonel's hooch and threw satchel charges into his hooch and disappeared. He was the only man killed on the base. This was a protected base. One man was killed and he happened to be the gung-ho commander. These sorts of things bred the mythology, these sorts of deeds, and an image of the enemy began to grow, of an enemy capable of the most incredible sorts of deeds."

O'Brien went on: "I think that there is one important memory I have of my time in Vietnam, it is the memory of ignorance. And I mean utter ignorance. I was a college graduate so I guess I was one of the most attuned people in my platoon, in my company, and I was ignorant. I didn't know the language, I didn't know how to communicate with the Vietnamese except in pidgin English. I knew nothing about the culture of Vietnam. I knew nothing about the village community. I knew nothing about the aims of the people, whether they were for the war or against the war, or didn't care or were indifferent. I knew nothing about the tactics we were pursuing. You search a village and it was like hunting a hummingbird. You would go to one village, nothing there. Another village and nothing there. The enemy — the hummingbird we were after — was just buzzing around. And I had no knowledge of what the enemy was after. No knowledge of what I was after as a soldier. What our purpose was. You secure a village, you search it and you leave. And the village reverts to the enemy.

"It seemed a senseless strategy, and yet I thought perhaps there was some rhyme or reason behind it. I never found out. To this day I haven't found out. I knew nothing of the regime in Saigon and what they were after. I knew nothing about the political leadership of the country. And I knew nothing about warfare. I knew that I was a rural Midwesterner, a kid who graduated from college, so I didn't know what made the guns work. I didn't know what made the shells go off. I didn't know how you aimed an artillery piece so the shells would hit a particular place. So, I was always thinking these guys know more than I do. I sure as hell hope they do. Sometimes they did, and sometimes they didn't. One time they didn't was on a small lagoon we were guarding, when a mortar company blew up a village, by accident. They were firing delta tangos, which were reference points essentially, but they mis-aimed and misfired and killed 30 people in a village which they were supposed to be protecting.

"I mentioned I fought the war ignorant. And the final effect is that of a moron wandering through a foreign land. Or a blind man wandering through a foreign land. It is not quite true that foot soldiers aren't expected to know much about anything other than fighting. In World War II, for example, or Word War I, there was a general understanding that we have to get from point A, that is the beach at Normandy, say, to point B, that is the village of St. Louis. And from St. Lou we have get to the Rhine, and from the Rhine we have to get to Berlin. There is a general sense of progression in that war. In trench warfare, we knew we have to get from our trenches across no man's land to the German trenches. We didn't have that, we didn't have that fundamental sense of understanding of direction. In Vietnam, it was like walking in a maze, and you didn't know where the maze was leading. And you would leave a point and you would walk blindly though some hedgerow, and then take a right turn and then a left and often you would end up sometimes back where you started. No sense of progression.

"And along the way you had mines going off like that (clicking finger)—feet going, legs going, balls going, caused by the most feared mine, the bouncing Betty. It's a one that is conical shaped and has three prongs jutting out of the soil. When your foot hits the prongs, there is a charge that goes off and shoots the mine up in the air, say a yard or two feet high, and it explodes, shooting shrapnel everywhere. It's a mine that obviously goes after the lower legs, the testicles and maybe the lower torso. A terrible mine. Other mines were what they call toe-poppers; they were little bitty things that would blow a heel off or part of a foot or a whole foot. I saw men hobbling after a hitting one like that, with their foot gone.

"And there were huge booby traps with mortar rounds or artillery rounds. I remember a day when we were encamped in a large clearing and an explosion went off maybe 200 yards away, and we had a patrol out. I made the call to the patrol. No answer. And the captain, kind of joking, said, 'That's maybe a stray artillery round.' And half an hour later one of the survivors hobbled back and said, 'It was a mine, a booby trap, and they are all gone.' I said, 'What the hell are gone?' And we check it out, and there were, I guess, two men were still living out of eight or so on the patrol. Ah, it was just a mess. It was like a stew, full of meat and red tissue and white bone. That is what a huge one will do or a huge booby trap mine will do."

O'Brien went on: "And of course, there are variants in all of these kinds. Hand grenades were often turned into mines by placing one into a tin can and pulling the pin out with the tin can stopping what they call the spoon from releasing and setting the grenade off. A string is attached to the grenade and when you walk down a path and you hit the string which pulls the grenade out of the can releasing the spoon, the grenade goes off. It's a clever little device and a very deadly one. And there were things called Chi-Coms which were the Vietnamese-made hand grenades, homemade hand grenades. I remember in my very first fire fight seeing a thing come out of the bushes, a red thing and land beside me. It was a red mackerel can, the sort you saw all over Vietnam. And the thing blew up and killed a friend of mine, and I thought it was mackerel can. I didn't know that it was a grenade and it went off."

I asked Tim O'Brien how he compared Vietnam to other wars. "When it comes down to it, Vietnam, in its essence for the foot soldier, was really identical to every other war I suppose in history. I am talking about things that foot soldiers see. Maiming, death, orphans, widows, loneliness, boredom," he said. "War is boring, basically, not scary. It is basically just monotonous. Sitting around. Opening up C-rations, marching from spot to spot and looking at your watch, marking off the days you have left in Vietnam in a little calendar you have in your helmet. It is monotony punctuated by moments of sheer terror, just horrible stuff. But nonetheless the experience when you are living it is monotonous. And after the war is over, you don't remember the monotony and the mosquitoes and the heat. What you remember are those few moments of real terror. That is what sticks in the memory. That is what is memorable about war.

"In its elements, every war is the same because it boils down to suffering. And the thing about Vietnam which bothers me in retrospect now, in terms of what I read and what I see on television and in the movies, it's that it is a political experience. The sociological experience, the human element of what the soldier goes through and the Vietnamese went through, the human suffering, is not only neglected; it is almost cast aside as superfluous to the political stuff."

I asked Tim O'Brien if a novelist such as himself can correct the imbalance. He replied: "A novelist's obligations aren't to cause—what caused the war, why did we get into it? A novelist's obligation isn't to defining the history of a war, the sociology of the place. Rather the novelist's concern is almost solely with the impact of experience on what it does to the psyche, what a war does to the psyche. That is what Stephen Crane was writing about, Joseph Heller, Hemingway, and that's what I am writing about. What does fear do to a man? What are the reactions of fear? How do we react to ignorance? I was just saying that my feeling about Vietnam was that I was just dumb. I didn't know anything. I compensated for that ignorance in a whole bunch of ways, some evil ways. Blowing things up. Burning huts. That's the frustration of being ignorant.

"My concern as a novelist now in terms of fiction is to try to isolate those key moments of human response to pain, suffering and boredom. And to try to show how the final impact of Vietnam isn't on American foreign policy. The final impact of Vietnam isn't on the posture that America will take vis a vis new Vietnams. Rather that the final impact of Vietnam is in the heads, heads of the men who fought in Vietnam. And if anything, I write just to keep us out of another Vietnam. If anything is to prevent the same mistakes, it has to be the memory of those who fought in that war. And that memory is an experiential memory on the things that I listed—boredom, monotony, anger, bitterness, pain, suffering, and the daily life of the paddy fields, and the night patrols and the ambushes."

14

1967

THE BATTLEFIELDS OF SOUTHEAST ASIA were 10,000 miles away, but from the cabinet room of the White House where he scanned detailed military maps to pick the North Vietnamese bombing "targets of the day" and send out American war planes to hit them, President Lyndon Johnson waged his own personal war against the Vietnamese communists. And in the secure basement Situation Room with its communications links to the war zone, the president would sometimes wait anxiously through the early morning hours to see if the aircraft made it home.

"He thought of every bomber that went out, every flight crew, as his own family or personal property," wrote Vice President Hubert Humphrey. "Some mornings, looking drawn, he would put his arm around my shoulders, almost for support, and say, 'Hubert, I lost four of my boys last night. How am I going to explain to their families why they had to die?'"

Early in 1965, when President Johnson had approved the escalating "Rolling Thunder" air campaign against North Vietnam on the advice of the military's Joint Chiefs of Staff, the enormous firepower being brought to bear by American Navy and Air Force bombers against communist military and industrial targets was presumed to be the most effective method of convincing the communists to stop supplying troops and military equipment to the Vietcong in the South. But two years later, that strategy had failed.

Increasing numbers of American planes were being blown from the skies by sophisticated Soviet-supplied anti-aircraft weaponry surrounding important locations. The notorious "Hanoi Hilton" prison was filing up with captured American flyers. An increasingly concerned President Johnson directly involved himself in target selection. On many nights, he would sit in the cabinet room with a large map of North Vietnam spread before him with several military advisors in attendance.

Vice President Humphrey wrote about a typical session. "The president would ask, 'What are the crucial or strategic targets?' and General Wheeler (Earle Wheeler, the Joint Chiefs chairman) would say that there are 80 or 60 or whatever they thought was important at the moment. Johnson would lament, 'Any damn fool can get a bigger war. What I want is to end the war. What I want is to stop the killing and the shooting and get these people to a conference table so we can settle this thing.' Finally, he and his advisors would select 10 or 12 or 14 targets, with the president feeling he was restraining the military and still proceeding towards his goals."

His military advisors were pressing the president to widen the target area in North Vietnam. He refused. On August 7, 1967, Johnson determined that the bombing of North Vietnam should not be extended beyond the area already approved.

The following day the president met with Secretary of State Dean Rusk, Secretary of Defense Robert McNamara and CIA Chief Richard Helms, and according to a White House transcript, said, "Let's find the least dangerous and most productive targets. I think we should hit every target as quickly as we can. We have some weather now that is my kind of weather." But he added, "There are three areas we are not going to hit. We are not going to bomb Haiphong harbor because we are not going to hit any ships. We are not going to bomb Hanoi because we are not going to hit civilians. And we must be careful about the buffer zone (with China) because of the danger of going over the border." Secretary McNamara said, "We can get the president 20 more targets." Secretary Rusk responded, "It's a question of what you ask a man to die for. Some of these targets aren't worth the men lost."

In his autobiography, Hubert Humphrey reflected on his president's actions. "When you send men into battle, you know that some are going to lose their lives. That is an awful part of political power. I don't suppose it is easy for anyone, but military men are at least trained in war. Most politicians are not. Yet the compassion breeds an irony. Once an early order causes the first person to die, leaders feel required to justify what has been done. Thus, the compassion helps to create an insidious condition that leads, I fear, not to less killing but more."

For Robert McNamara, his growing distaste with the war he enthusiastically helped orchestrate in 1964 became overwhelming. To the president's consternation, McNamara told a Senate hearing mid-year that the intensive Rolling Thunder air campaign had failed to cripple the enemy's war efforts, even though almost as much bomb tonnage had been dropped on the North and it's 17 million people as had been used on Europe in World War II. McNamara also testified that communist forces fighting in the South could exist on just 15 tons of supplies a day but the North was capable of moving 200 tons a day down the Ho Chi Minh trail, despite continued air attacks.

On November 1, 1967, McNamara challenged the policy that the president was following. He wrote in a memo to the president released years later, "I state my opinion that continuing in our present course will not bring us by the end of 1968 enough closer to success, in the eyes of the American public, to prevent the continued erosion of popular support for our involvement in Vietnam." Referring to the planned increase of U.S. combat troops to 525,000 in the coming year, McNamara said, "The additional numbers of combat troops will not produce any significant change in the nature of our military operations. The increase in numbers will likely lead to a proportionate increase in encounters with the enemy and some increase in the number of casualties on both sides, but neither the additional troops now scheduled nor the augmentation of our forces by a greater amount holds great promise of bringing the North Vietnamese and the Vietcong forces visibly closer to collapse within the next 15 months."

McNamara added, "There are no present plans to turn a larger share of the campaign against main enemy forces over to the South Vietnamese. Accordingly, the present U.S. casualty rate will probably increase if the present program is pursued. This would mean between 700 and 1,000 killed in action every month, for a total during the next fifteen months of 10,900 to 15,000 additional American dead and 30,000 to 40,000 additional wounded requiring hospitalization. This would bring our total killed in action in the Vietnam campaign between 24,000 and 30,000, close to the Korean total of 33,000, and 70,000 to 90,000 wounded requiring hospitalization. Continuation of the North Vietnamese attacks across the DMZ and the use of Cambodian and Laotian territory will produce repeated requests for ground operations against these 'sanitary' areas."

President Johnson considered McNamara's advice, but he was increasingly unhappy with what he saw as the negative counsel of his secretary of defense. In an interview with me after the war, a top advisor to Johnson, William Bundy, told me that, "President Johnson had come to the view that this was a too uncertain conduct of the war. The problem is a very real one when one is analyzing problems. One wants to take into account all considerations, plus or minus, wants to fully understand what is going on, what the problem is. One wants to understand the other person's point of view, as well as those people on your side. But once a decision has been made to do something, an effective person must stop analyzing and execute, and I think it was Mr. Johnson's view that Mr. McNamara was still agonizing and re-agonizing at the time when he wanted him to be executing. There was too much of the 'Hamlet' involved."

Later in November, McNamara persuaded an all-too-willing President Johnson to accept his resignation because he felt his efforts in helping launch the war and pursue it were futile and immoral. Johnson's biographer Doris Kearns Goodwin told me in an interview that even though his chief architect of the war was losing faith in it, it did not give the president pause. "Johnson was having even less doubt; he was growing surer of his actions. The way that the president liked to think about it was that McNamara was being wracked by doubt; he wasn't just doubting the policies, he was becoming emotionally disturbed, near the point of cracking up. So, then Johnson would like to tell that magnanimously he'd allowed McNamara to head the World Bank as a way of preserving his sanity." Kearns Goodwin said, "Johnson just did not want a dissenter around, and he didn't want McNamara out there saying he had dissented. It was agreed that McNamara would just sort of slip away into the night but only after a politically healthy interval." McNamara left office on February 29, three months later.

The president favored Clark Clifford as the replacement secretary of defense. In an interview after the war, Secretary of the Navy Paul Nitze said, "Clifford was one of the two leading hawks in Washington. He had not been full time in government, but he was an advisor to President Johnson. He and (U.S. Supreme Court Justice Abe) Fortas were the two outstanding proponents of the toughest possible line both in negotiations and in action vis a vis North Vietnam, and intensifying the war against it. It was my view that President Johnson arranged for Mr. McNamara to become president of the World Bank because he was less than satisfied with Mr. McNamara's conduct or role at work as secretary of defense in the latter part of McNamara's tour of duty. He had more confidence in Mr. Clifford. When Mr. Clifford came in, he did have the view that air attack would bring military effectiveness beyond which I thought effective. He did not think it worthwhile to try to find ways of terminating the war with honor rather than through seeking surrender on the part of the North Vietnamese." While some saw the wavering McNamara as a Prince Hamlet of the war effort, the eager General Westmoreland was seen by President Johnson as a warrior King Henry V, and routinely approved his troop requests and his battlefield strategy.

Westmoreland attended a meeting in the cabinet room of the White House in the summer of 1967 where he made two proposals for possible troop increases. The general told me, "We were discussing additional troops, discussing the results that would accrue if these troops were provided. I had two troop lists. I had what I considered a minimum essential and then I had an optimum. The first proposal involved an increase of 2 1/3 divisions, and five air squadrons, about 80,000 men. The second suggested an increase of 4 2/3 infantry divisions and 10 air squadrons, raising our force level in Vietnam by 200,000 to a total of 680,000 by July 1968. Making the optimum troop list was designed to give us the forces to capitalize on a change in political strategy, or initiative by the enemy, such as the Tet Offensive, where we could follow up and take the war to the enemy. We could cut the Ho Chi Minh trail, we could clean out his sanctuaries in Cambodia, we could block his actions immediately north of the DMZ—and plans were prepared to do all of that."

These proposals envisaged a considerable widening of the war. Westmoreland said, "When I was asked by Mr. McNamara how long it would take with those two increments of troop reinforcements to wind the war down, I said with the minimum essential it will take at least five years, but my estimate is that if we had the optimum we could probably do it in approximately three years. That was under the assumption that all political restraints would be lifted and would allow us to expand the geographical area of the battlefield."

The restraints Westmoreland was concerned about included the use by North Vietnam of neighboring Cambodia and Laos as staging areas for attacking South Vietnam. He complained, "They used Cambodia and Laos frequently, while we were not allowed to move troops into there. Now under the Geneva agreements of 1962, they were not supposed to be there at all. Now they were there, and this was off-limits for us. So that is why I was concentrating American combat forces in those areas. By fighting in the highlands, we wanted to preempt the enemy as soon as we determined his location. The quicker you can hit him when he is getting organized, the easier he is to defeat. If you can beat him on the periphery of Vietnam then you don't have to worry about fighting him among the people in the lowlands and the 44 populated areas. When we fought in populated areas, we had a procedure that before you could fire into an area where you had population, the targets you were going to hit had to be cleared by province chief and the district chief. And this took an awful lot of time."

Westmoreland did succeed in securing strikes along communist supply lines in Laos along the Ho Chi Minh trail using U.S. Air Force B-52 Stratofortress bombers that could carry 35 tons of bombs. But their frequency was disputed by the American ambassador in Laos, William Sullivan. In an interview, he said, "I was restrictive not only on B-52 strikes but also on the strikes of tactical aircraft. These were fast moving airplanes and their navigational controls were not all that precise in those jungle areas. We wanted to be absolutely certain that they were not indiscreetly striking into inhabited areas where villagers were living. So, we made it quite clear, were quite insistent upon having definite proof that they were going into an area that was controlled militarily and that had no civilians in there that might be subject to that sort of bombing. This meant we insisted on photography beforehand, and several times I'm sure that Westmoreland was impatient with the delay that came about from that. On the other hand, I don't think their accuracy or their effectiveness was such that we really needed to obliterate the concern for unarmed civilians in the area merely for the sake of getting a rapid strike."

For all his public prominence in having the prime responsibility for the war effort, General Westmoreland felt his hands were tied in some key areas. He told me he had little contact with President Johnson. He said in April, 1967, "I stayed at the White House and got to know him pretty well. Now the only other contact I had with him previous to that was in February 1966, the first time I had seen him. The conventional knowledge at the time was that I was on the phone with President Johnson every day. Now, I had a very high regard for President Johnson, we had a very warm relationship. He was always very nice to me. And I liked him very much personally. But I never talked with President Johnson one time from Saigon over the telephone. I only recall once when I had a call from the White House, from one of his assistants, Walt Rostow.

"Now my boss was the ambassador who had full authority over me, to include the military decisions I had to make. But of course, he never exercised those prerogatives because I had good relations with the ambassadors; there was confidence between us. My military boss was Admiral Sharp in Honolulu, and he reported to the Joint Chiefs of Staff. And normally my communications came from the chairman of the Joint Chiefs. And indeed, I think that President Johnson talked to him frequently. I did not have responsibility for the air campaign in the north. Authority was vested in Admiral Sharp, commander in chief of the Pacific. I had responsibility for the ground operations in Vietnam, the tactical in support of those ground operations, and operations very close to the geographical area of South Vietnam.

"The responsibility of the war was a divided one. It was divided between the ambassador and myself, and the commander in chief of the Pacific and the Joint Chiefs of Staff. I feel it would have been better if it could have been a unified effort, which would have run contrary to some of the service doctrines but I think would have been accepted by the services."

By mid-1967, the political ground at home was shifting under President Johnson's feet. He was looking to run for a second term in the elections of 1968, but fellow Democrats, unhappy about his administration's Vietnam policies, were looking for alternative candidates. The former ambassador and John F. Kennedy confidant John Kenneth Galbraith told me in an interview in Cambridge, Massachusetts, after the war: "In 1967, I became the head of the Americans for Democratic Action, and we were looking for someone to carry the flag, our message against the Vietnam War. We moved to search for a candidate.

"Robert Kennedy would have been our first choice," Galbraith continued, "and sometime in the late summer of 1967, I had a long talk with Robert Kennedy about this in his office in Washington. And he was reluctant because of his past bad relations with Lyndon Johnson, and this would be interpreted as a personal vendetta and as a personal action. It would be too much of a hurdle to get over. He suggested Gene McCarthy. They were not very close friends, but I thought that he believed the one person thinking along those lines would be Eugene McCarthy. That same day I went down and saw Gene and he told me he was. He came up a few days later to Cambridge here, where we are talking today, and we talked further. By that time, he had come to a decision that he would make the run, to enter the race for the Democratic nomination. I again want to stress that I don't want to exaggerate my role in persuading him. Nobody ever persuaded Gene McCarthy at anything; he was a man with a singular ability to make up his own mind. But I can attest at my delight when he decided to make the run."

By late October the antiwar movement manifested itself in Washington, D.C., in a major demonstration against the Pentagon. Beginning with 100,000 people massing in front of the Lincoln Memorial, many waving the red, blue and gold flag of the Vietcong, they marched to the Pentagon and surrounded and besieged the military nerve center in the early hours of October 23, 1967. By the time it was all over, there were nearly 700 people arrested, including the novelist Norman Mailer. One of the prime organizers of the march was Jerry Rubin, a young American social activist who organized like-minded antiwar activists. In an interview after the war for a documentary I was writing, he said, "My idea was that the antiwar movement had to be daring, had to be bold, had to be confrontational, had really to grab the imagination of the country. And so, we said we were going to close down the Pentagon. No halfway measures. We had to create the image then of a massive outpouring of public reaction against the war aimed at the Pentagon. I believe the Pentagon demonstration was the turning point in the antiwar effort. I believe it was the most important demonstration that took place in the entire decade against the war. I believe it captured the imagination of young people. It gave those middle-class people who were already beginning to be quizzical about the war, gave then something to hold on to. And it really laid down the point that this was a moral issue, it's good versus evil, it's right versus wrong. We believed the United States was wrong in Vietnam. We are committing moral crimes, and it was up to the youth of America that stood up and pointed their finger at the elders and said, 'You are wrong, and we are judging you, and we are saying stop the bombs'."

Rubin said, "I didn't particularly want LBJ to withdraw. That wasn't the goal. The goal was to build the mass movement from below that would just, you know, engulf the entire political-military system. Yes, that was the end result of the demonstration because the demonstration did shock the conscience of the country. It did get people mobilized. It did get businessmen wearing arm bands. We had the idea that we wanted everybody to take some steps against the war from wherever they were at. If they were unemployed and young and hip they could get arrested and go to jail. If they were strategically placed within a corporation they could just wear a black armband. If people say, 'What's your armband?' you'd say, 'I'm against the war in Vietnam.'

"The antiwar slogans all fit the emotion and the state of the antiwar movement at that time. It started out with something simple like, 'Let's discuss the war.' And they progressed every six months. The slogans got more and more aggressive because the antiwar movement got larger and stronger and more aggressive. The first phase was teach-ins, and then it went to resistance, resist the draft. Then finally it climaxed in the late '60s with 'bring the war home' — the only way the war is going to end is if we have war in the streets. And when people see that there's going to be a war on the streets of America then they're going to stop bombing Vietnam 10,000 miles away to stop the war at home. That was the eventual slogan."

Researcher Brian Jenkins of the RAND Corporation, commenting on the growing frustration on the home front, said in an interview, "The American people wanted an end to the war. The people wanted our involvement and our military involvement to cease. The military mistakes however added fuel to the antiwar movement. Had the U.S. armed forces been able to deliver a swift victory in 1966 or 1967 then in my view the antiwar movement would have been remembered only as an obscure sidelight to the history of the way we recall the war.

"But the fact that the American military establishment and our political leaders not only could not deliver that swift military victory but could not even define what that victory was or might appear to be, led many people, a growing proportion of the population, to perceive the war as simply bringing endless destruction both to the South Vietnamese landscape and lives, and destruction to American lives, and at that point it became intolerable to the American public."

15

THE LIGHT AT THE END OF THE TUNNEL

ON NOVEMBER 1, 1967, LYNDON JOHNSON welcomed to the White House a group of elder statesmen informally known as "The Wise Men." They were summoned to consider and hopefully to approve his stewardship of the Vietnam War. It was a critical time for the 36th president of the United States, who would soon be seeking a second term in office even as the war was stalemated and a rising tide of antiwar protest was washing across the home front. Three years earlier, a Wise Men group had met at the White House when Johnson was contemplating sending American combat troops to South Vietnam. Their approval of his policies then had been an important element in his decision to wage war against the communist forces threatening the independence of South Vietnam.

The newly assembled group included General Omar Bradley, Supreme Court Justice Abe Fortas, former Secretary of State Dean Acheson, and Clark Clifford, who was well known as a Washington lawyer and advisor to Democratic presidents. The president greeted them around the cabinet table and told them, according to a declassified official document, "I have a particular confidence in you as patriots and that is why I have picked you." He said he wanted to know if his course in Vietnam was right. If not, how should it be modified? He said he was deeply concerned about the deterioration of public support and the lack of editorial support for his policies. He pointed out that "if a bomb kills two civilians in North Vietnam it makes banner headlines. However, they can lob mortar shells into the palace grounds in Saigon and there are no editorial complaints about it."

But few of the Wise Men were privy to the sometimes raging debate about war policy within the president's innermost circles. The issues: How to unite the American public over Vietnam policies, alternative courses of action including bombing, more troops, negotiating a withdrawal, or all three. All of the group were iconic members of establishment policy-making over the previous 40 years. They sat through generally positive briefings from top cabinet officials and two days of discussions. They determined, not surprisingly, that the president should stay on course in Vietnam and put the best face forward. The Wise Men would be called to another White House meeting four months later, this time to ponder a decision that would change American history.

The policy change that did come out of the White House meeting in November was the inspiration for an all-out propaganda campaign to convince increasing numbers of skeptical Americans to agree with the Wise Men, that the war was on course. Johnson had told the assembled elders that "the main front of the Vietnam War is now in the United States." And Walt Rostow, his special assistant for security affairs and an avowed hawk on policy, told them that while he doubted that the war would ever be a popular one there was progress enough to win support. Rostow said, "There are ways of guiding the press to show that there is light at the end of the tunnel." Within a few days, American officials in Saigon were advised that both General Westmoreland and Ambassador Ellsworth Bunker would be required to report to Washington, D.C., within days to appear on national television, in press conferences and media interviews to promote the official view from the battlefield that the war was being won.

Westmoreland was particularly optimistic in a speech at the National Press Club on November 21, 1967. He insisted that the enemy's ability to carry on the struggle had deteriorated. He estimated that the 40,000 communist troops lost during the summer of 1967 could not be replaced. In a telegram to his deputy commander in Saigon, General Creighton Abrams, two days later, Westmoreland said that in appearances in Washington, "I presented in full or part the following: We are grinding down the enemy in South Vietnam. Our forces are becoming stronger and growing more proficient in the environment. The Vietnamese armed forces are getting stronger and becoming more effective on the battlefield. These trends should continue with the enemy becoming weaker and the GVN becoming stronger to the point where in two years or less the Vietnamese conceivably can shoulder a larger share of the war and thereby permit the U.S. to begin phasing down the level of its commitment. The phase-down will probably be token at first."

Westmoreland added, "The concept is compatible with evolution of the war since our initial commitment, and portrays to the American people 'some light at the end of the tunnel.' This concept justifies the augmentation of troops I have asked for based on the principle of reinforcing success, and also supports an increase in the strength of the Vietnamese force and their modernization."

In the weeks remaining in 1967, pollsters were recording an uptick in public support for the war, or at least in acceptance, an indication of the success of the White House aides' "light at the end of the tunnel" viewpoint that General Westmoreland and Ambassador Bunker were relaying to national audiences. But within the White House for the first time the full authority that General Westmoreland had been given to set battlefield strategy began coming into question. The protagonists were his former close supporters, General Maxwell Taylor and Henry Cabot Lodge, who as ambassadors to South Vietnam in 1964 through early 1967 were technically Westmoreland's superiors but rarely exercised their authority. In a memo to the president on November 10, McGeorge Bundy, who as a former assistant secretary of state attended the Wise Men discussions along with Lodge and Taylor, wrote: "Lodge and Taylor were the two men with most direct experience in Vietnam, and I found it interesting and troubling that both of them raised troubling questions about the military tactics now being followed. Taylor was worried about fixed positions on the DMZ and in the highlands. Ambassador Lodge questioned the wisdom of large scale search-and-destroy operations such as those planned for the Delta. Lodge and I raised questions about whether American casualties must be expected to continue at their present level and even increase. This specific question was related to the general comment of several others that the prospect of endless inconclusive fighting is the single most serious cause of domestic disquiet about the war."

Bundy went on to write, "If battles near the borders are not wise, or if search- and-destroy operations in heavily populated areas are likely to be politically destructive, then the plans of the field commander must be seriously questioned. I see no alternative here but to have a very carefully prepared discussion with General Westmoreland, preferably after a good hard look on the spot by young officers who might be chosen specifically for their acceptability in Saigon. I should emphasize that what I am suggesting has not been done in Saigon so far. For extremely good reasons the top men in Washington have kept their hands off the tactical conduct of the war. I believe the commander-in-chief has the right and duty to go further."

Bundy concluded, "What I am recommending is simply that the commander-in-chief should visibly take command of a contest that is more political in its character than any since the Civil War (where Lincoln interfered much more than you have). I think that the visible exercise of this authority is not only best for the war but also best for public opinion — and also best for the internal confidence of the government. Briefings which cite the latest statistics have lost their power to persuade. So have spectacular summits. These things are not worth one quarter of what would be gained with the gradual emergence of the fact that the president himself — in his capacity as political leader and commander-in-chief — is shaping a campaign which is gradually increasing in its success and gradually decreasing its cost in American lives and money."

In mid-November while Saigon's two top people, Westmoreland and Bunker, were in Washington proclaiming that a corner had been turned in the war, I joined other reporters covering a developing story in the remote Dak To Valley in the Central Highlands. The bland official story was that in three actions from November 3 to November 13, American forces led by the U.S. Army's 173rd Airborne Brigade lost 102 soldiers killed, with 636 North Vietnamese enemy bodies found.

The Pentagon announced that 102 bombing strikes were delivered by B-52 Stratofortress in support. In a meeting of the National Security Council, General Earle Wheeler told the president that the communists were "attempting to achieve a dramatic victory and to draw forces away from the pacification effort along the coast."

When I arrived to join an Associated Press reporting team already assembled there, the full dimensions of the story became evident. The Dak To Valley, winding between heavily jungled mountains along the Laos border, had never seriously been defended because of its remoteness, even though it was a known entry point of communist reinforcements coming in from the Ho Chi Minh trail. The appearance of communist ground forces apparently willing to fight played into Westmoreland's tactics of finding and destroying the enemy using superior force. The U.S. 4th Infantry Division, commanded by Major General William R. Peers and based in the highlands city of Pleiku, was eager to fight. The stage was set for a pivotal battle, the latest in a series that began in November 1965 at the equally remote Ia Drang Valley that pitted the recently arrived U.S. 1st Air Cavalry Division against the North Vietnamese 304th infantry division, equally newly arrived from North Vietnam to fight the Americans. In that action, 250 Americans died; the estimate of enemy dead was 1,000. It was a foretaste of the brutal border wars that followed.

In Dak To, North Vietnamese soldiers had been methodically preparing the hilltops and ridgelines for war, concealing their efforts under the thick cover of triple-canopy jungle. They dug extensive bunkers and trench systems, and tunnels leading to caverns lined with log floors and woven bamboo walls for comfort. Each hilltop bunker system was built to withstand the severest bombing, some 30 feet deep with six feet of earth and log cover on their roofs. The winding entrances were designed to seal the inhabitants against air strikes of flaming napalm projectiles. The evening I arrived I saw the hills around the valley aflame with American and Vietnamese air strikes. But it was becoming clear to the American infantrymen engaged in the battle that the only way to beat the enemy in Dak To was in face-to-face encounters because the bombing and artillery barrages were not dislodging them from their prepared positions.

I joined two new colleagues to cover a paratrooper battalion of the 173rd airborne brigade, the 4th of the 503rd, that was deeply committed in the battle for a place called Hill 875, an uninhabited bump in the valley edge named for its height in meters. A sister paratrooper unit, the 2nd of the 503rd, had been severely mauled over the previous day and evening in a fight with entrenched North Vietnamese troops. They had been ambushed just 300 meters from the summit by a North Vietnamese unit, the 2nd of the 174th regiment, that was using machine guns and B-40 hand-held rockets and recoilless rifle fire. Attempts by the Americans to continue the advance were stalled by communist troops using small arms and grenades from deep trenches and bunkers. U.S. airstrikes were called in along with artillery, but they were of little use because of the dense foliage on the hillside. Resupply and medevac helicopters tried to get in but failed, with six aircraft shot down or severely damaged.

The mission of the 300-paratrooper patrol we had joined was to determine the fate of their sister unit. We moved out on foot mid-morning through tall elephant grass on the approaches to 875, and then pushed past tangled jungle on the steep hillside. By early evening we were being fired upon by snipers concealed in the jungle, and soon an officer called for flares that cast a yellow light through the towering trunks of trees splintered by bombing. By mid-evening we were stumbling over dead bodies, at first thought to be North Vietnamese fighters before we realized they were American soldiers, killed the previous day. By late evening the rescuers reached the remnants of the second paratrooper battalion, a shocking scene, illuminated by flares, of mounds of dead bodies, and of the wounded sheltering behind fallen trees and desperate for water. The defenders who were still able to do so had gathered themselves into a tight circle, pulling the wounded in with them. At dawn the communist mortars began, fired from positions a few hundred or so meters distant.

I scrambled into a bunker where three soldiers were concealed. One said he was Private First Class Angel Flores from New York City. He murmured as though to himself, fingering the plastic rosary around his neck and kissing it.

"Does that do you any good?" one of his buddies asked.

"Well, I'm still alive," the private answered.

"Hell," his buddy said, "The chaplain who gave you that was killed on Sunday." But Flores kept kissing his rosary.

Rockets were whizzing through the trees when I visited Lieutenant Bryan MacDonough at his bunker facing the hill. He said eight of his fellow officers were dead and the eight others wounded; he had started out with 27 men 30 hours earlier and only had nine left.

By mid-evening of November 21, the 173rd paratroopers began evacuating wounded by helicopters from a landing area they had hacked from the trees. An attempt a few hours earlier to drive the communist troops from their emplacements at the summit of Hill 875 failed, leaving it to airstrikes over the next two days to pound them into submission. When paratroopers eventually made it to the summit, they found a dozen or so bodies and a few rifles, but nothing else. The North Vietnamese had abandoned it.

We newsmen were put aboard the final medical evacuation helicopter leaving that evening, the loadmaster shouting out to his buddies, "This is the last one of the day. We moved 140 wounded, 90 dead and three newsmen outta here." I waited at the Dak To airstrip until dawn, and hitched a ride on an Air Force C-130 transport plane to the U.S. Army base at Qui Nhon. At the press office, an obliging desk sergeant called our Saigon bureau and began reading my story to our desk editor, Ed White, as I wrote it: "War painted the living and the dead the same gray pallor on Hill 875. The only way to tell who was alive and who was dead amongst the exhausted men was to watch when the enemy mortars came crashing in. The living rushed unashamedly to the tiny bunkers dug into the red clay of the hilltop. The wounded squirmed to the shelter of the tress that had been blasted to the ground. Only the dead didn't move, propped up in the bunkers where they had died in direct mortar hits."

I heard the sergeant gasp as he began reading my account, but he persevered through the 11 typewritten pages. I hitched a ride back to Saigon with my film on the only flight available, a transport plane loaded with black rubber body bags holding the remains of 100 American soldiers killed at Dak To. I was sitting in the cargo cabin and I saw that the body bags were leaking on the deck. As we began our steep descent the viscid liquids surged over my ankles before the plane leveled off and landed at Tan Son Nhut airport.

Just as in the fierce battles that preceded it, General Westmoreland claimed the Dak To engagement a victory for the American side. "We had soundly defeated the enemy without unduly sacrificing operations in other areas. The enemy's return was nil." The announced American casualties during the Dak To battle were 361 killed and 15 missing with 1,441 wounded. The claimed enemy dead, by unreliable body counts, ranged from 1,000 to 1,600. But even if the statistics were accurate, the friendly-to-enemy loss ratio was of concern to officials aware of the rapidly-growing casualty toll of American soldiers in Vietnam, now reaching 15,000 dead in the 30 months of the war. U.S. Marine Corps General John Chiasson was quoted as questioning Westmoreland's tactics: "Is it a victory when you lose 362 friendlies in three weeks when, by your own spurious body count, you get only 1,200?"

There were broader strategic implications arising from the battle at Dak To. A brutal action around the U.S. Marine base at Con Thin near the demilitarized zone a few months earlier, and the portending confrontation at another Marine border base at Khe Sanh, were pulling America's combat units away from the cities and the populated lowlands, drawing them towards the borders of South Vietnam.

In the fall of 1967 I wrote an account about the battlefield stalemate in Vietnam in a news analysis for the AP. "Thirty months of hard incisive fighting in Vietnam," my report said, "has forced American military commanders to acknowledge a crucial fact: Unless the dispirited Vietnamese army can be revitalized into a fighting army, U.S. troops will be tied down for at least a decade just holding the lid on the communists all over the country. Westmoreland has tried to go it alone, pulling the Vietnamese Army along by the bootstraps as the enemy was crushed by U.S. infantry and Marines. But such tactics have been thwarted by the resilience of the communists. Hopes of quick success have died with the lives of the 13,000 Americans already killed."

In my end-of-1967 war assessment, I felt no need to change any of my earlier analysis. In fact, I was seeing a graver picture. I looked back at the battles I had covered and my conversations with knowledgeable

American military and civilian sources and concluded that 1967 was a curtain-raiser for a military showdown in Vietnam in 1968. I predicted for the New Year, "the biggest and bloodiest battles are still to be fought despite a long year of mauling, brawling actions from one end of the country to the other."

I wrote that "both sides were optimistic, which from their viewpoint made sense, because American commanders still analyze Vietnam in terms of World War II, and the communists analyze the war on terms of their fight to oust the French in the 1950s." My analysis was well used by AP member newspapers. I was aware that other reporters were reflecting in their stories the rosier confidence of the American high command.

I asked Westmoreland after the war about the criticism of his tactical abilities. He repeated that the responsibility for the war was "a divided one," with the U.S. ambassador and himself running the ground war and the commander-in-chief of Pacific forces running the air war. "I was somewhat critical of this in my book ("A Soldier Reports") because I feel it would have been better if it could have been a united effort . . . A commander has to exercise initiative, he has to be audacious and to take chances to be successful on the battlefield. But on the other hand, he has to be prudent to avoid casualties. He must take every step to minimize casualties. In going into traditional enemy strongholds, we had to plan our operations carefully. We had to commit the forces necessary to avoid that. And when we went into war in war zones C and D and into the Ashau Valley, we went in with the necessary force to do the job and which didn't jeopardize any particular unit. If I had tried to accomplish these tasks with minimum force, we would have had our people mangled."

In a top-secret letter in December 1967, Westmoreland was advised by the chairman of the Joint Chiefs of Staff, General Earle Wheeler, that they planned to move him from Vietnam in the summer of 1968. Westmoreland told me after the war that his removal had nothing to do with his work performance. "The personnel planning was that I had been there so long — four years — that they were, as a matter of routine, giving me another assignment." But before his tour of duty was over, Westmoreland's four-year record as commander-in-chief of all

American ground forces in Vietnam would be permanently tarnished by the unforeseen resurgence of the communist enemy that for months he'd been suggesting was being beaten.

Before all that happened, I attended a New Year's Eve celebration in Saigon. Some young Americans from the embassy and other official agencies, calling themselves "the flower people of Saigon," held a "light at the end of the tunnel" party at a comfortable villa on the Saigon side of the Bien Hoa bridge. The organizers were making sly fun of official optimism about the war, but the senior people in attendance didn't seem to mind. I joined a crowd of news colleagues, familiar faces from the press center, diplomats, a few Vietnamese officials and some embassy and military people, listening to a Vietnamese band from one of the downtown bars playing foxtrots, and dancing and drinking the night away. It was a pleasing respite from the war, a short respite.

16

CALM BEFORE THE STORM

THE APPROACHING TET FESTIVAL IN SAIGON in January 1968 celebrated the "Year of the Monkey" in the Chinese Lunar New Year calendar, with its zodiac sign symbolizing craftiness and opportunism. For the super-stitious Vietnamese, this promised a good year, a view buoyed by an improving economy and seeming political and military improvements, not the least being a seven-day truce in the interminable war offered by the Vietcong enemy. Preparations were underway for the celebration of the most jubilant Tet in years. For President Lyndon Johnson and his White House advisors in distant Washington, D.C., well aware that January 1968 was the first month of a presidential election year, there was satisfaction that the "Vietnam problem" was controllable after nearly four years of ever-increasing military effort and rising domestic concern.

The president's influential special assistant for national security affairs, Walt Rostow, noted in a January 4 memo: "For at least a year we have known that the object of their [Vietcong] military operations was not victory in the field in Vietnam but political victory in the United States. We have generally believed that they are holding on until November 1968, on the hope that American political life will produce a Mendes France who would accept defeat as the French had on 1954. But they may have decided that a pre-election Johnson will give them a better deal than a post-election Johnson or a Nixon/Rockefeller reign with four years to go."

President Johnson was hearing from some of his advisors that it was time to level off the U.S. effort in Vietnam and turn more of the burden over to the South Vietnamese. The idea to place limits on the expansion of the American effort in Vietnam was first advanced by Secretary of Defense Robert McNamara in a memo to the president on November 1, 1967, and supported by Secretary of State Dean Rusk several days later. They rejected further military escalation, believing this approach would help maintain public support for the war and reconcile the public to a prolonged struggle. The administration was opposed to any formal announcement of the leveling off, an approach that turned on the assumption of a reasonably stable situation—slowly improving, at best, and at worst, a military stalemate. The decision represented that the troop level of 525,000 was the maximum that could be sent without a divisive reserve mobilization.

President Johnson's hopes of shifting more of the war effort to the Vietnamese were dependent on an effectively functioning Saigon government, but unlike the optimism emanating from American officials over the military situation, there were continued frustrations over dealing with the newly elected President Nguyen Van Thieu. A visiting National Security Council officer, Major General William DePuy, reported in a memo of record on January 17 that some U.S. officials, including Robert Komer, who headed an anti-Vietcong pacification effort, the Civil Operations and Revolutionary Development Support Program, and others in Saigon, "were extremely disquieted by the situation in Vietnam at this time. The basis for their unhappiness goes something like this. The government of South Vietnam is simply not functioning at this time, the various ministries have not launched the new programs mentioned by Thieu in his inaugural statement, and the reorganization of the military which was worked out with the U.S. command which would reduce the power of the corps commanders and division commanders has been frustrated by a series of crippling stipulations."

In the memo, sent to the Joint Chiefs chairman, General Earle Wheeler, DePuy wrote that "corrupt province chiefs have not been removed and the junior officers of the army are increasingly restive in that nothing has been done about corruption in the armed forces. The government ministers and ministries feel they have no authority to move out on new programs nor are they getting any support from Thieu. It may be necessary for the U.S. high command in Saigon not only to make certain demands on the Vietnamese government for specific actions, such as reorganization, but also to involve itself in whatever scenarios may be necessary to remove the power of the corps commanders. Of all the things regarding SVN that should be worrying Washington now, it is my opinion that this subject should be number one."

The White House was aware of the continuing potential for battlefield violence. The North Vietnamese leadership had openly signaled its intention to launch a "winter-spring offensive" across the country, with the opening shots already fired in the biggest battle of the war to date, at the remote Dak To Valley in November 1967. American intelligence agencies were anticipating an upsurge in enemy activity either before or after the upcoming Tet holiday.

Washington was also aware of a growing buildup of enemy forces near the Khe Sanh Combat Base at the northwestern corner of the U.S. Marine defense line along the demilitarized zone with North Vietnam. President Johnson was giving it his personal attention, particularly after General Wheeler informed McNamara on January 13 that it "has come to my attention" that one view of Khe Sanh was that a complete withdrawal from the base might be necessary "because the enemy is building toward a Dien Bien Phu." Wheeler was referring to the climactic battle of the French Indochina War in 1954.

In a message in response, Westmoreland said withdrawal from Khe Sanh "would be a big step backwards. Its abandonment would result in a major propaganda victory for the VC." The White House and the Defense Department accepted Westmoreland's view that the major thrust of the communist winter/spring offensive would come against Khe Sanh and not the cities, as some CIA intelligence reports had suggested.

On January 22, the communists did launch a preliminary attack on Khe Sanh, with a massive artillery bombardment that leveled the above-ground buildings on the base and destroyed 90 percent of stored ammunition. Twenty Marines were killed and 109 wounded in the first minutes of the attack. But Westmoreland remained confident Khe Sanh would hold. In a January 22 message to the Joint Chiefs of Staff he wrote, "The bulk of our evidence suggests that the enemy is conducting a short-term surge effort, possibly designed to improve his chances of achieving his ends through political means, perhaps to negotiations leading to some form of coalition government."

On January 24, one week before the annual Tet celebrations began in Vietnam, President Johnson, long a bitter critic of press coverage of the war, informed a meeting of the National Security Council in the White House cabinet room that efforts to rein in press criticism were having an effect. He said, "We have been getting unusually good press from South Vietnam recently, and I think that McNamara and General Wheeler should pass that along to the people who are handling our press relations out there." Walt Rostow commented that the new press officer, Major General Winant Sidle, "Is an excellent man who is moving the Vietnamese military out in front of the press." General Wheeler said, "Sidle has a good program and is also making Westy more prominent in the news."

From Saigon, American Ambassador Ellsworth Bunker took the opportunity to message a response, giving voice to his deep frustrations with news coverage that challenged the official view of the war. "Our defects in the field of public affairs both here as well as in Washington have required imagination and energy. We have sought to present the true dimensions of the conflict in Vietnam to American and world public opinion as objectively and fairly as we can. But we have had to do this through a press which it seems to me has been unusually skeptical and cynical. One experienced journalist gave an explanation for this which may have validity, i.e., that there is a generation gap here in that many of the young reporters have never seen or experienced war before and consequently suffer from an emotional trauma which results in subjective reporting. However, that may be, the result of all this is that there tend to be two separate and only partially connected realities: the view of Vietnam as we see it here in Vietnam and the view that is being presented to American and world public opinion. This problem has engaged major attention during the past year and will continue to have our attention in the future. I think we made have made some, though limited, progress in dealing with it."

Ambassador Bunker's mention of the "two separate and partially connected realities" was better known to the public as "the credibility gap" that had emerged early in the war when both President Kennedy and President Johnson had concealed significant policy decisions on Vietnam behind a wall of secrecy.

The president's perceived honeymoon with the Saigon press corps would last just seven days, dramatically ended by the extensive news coverage of the upending of American policy by the violent and spectacular communist onslaught during the annual Tet Lunar New Year celebrations of the Year of the Monkey. Also arguable were Ambassador Bunker's confident assertions that "cynical" and "emotional" younger journalists had been misreading the situation in Vietnam from the beginning by ignoring the official view from the American embassy, Saigon military headquarters and the White House.

17

SMOKE AND MIRRORS

A S THE 1968 YEAR OF THE MONKEY approached, the communist Vietnamese authorities saw the upcoming Tet holidays as an opportunity for military action rather than a time of peaceful festivity. Few American and Saigon government officials believed that the communists would attack during Tet. Nor did the Vietnamese public. It is the most important holiday in Vietnam, observed by all members of every family including Buddhists, Christians and communists, and such an action would generate antagonism. For not the first time, the communists chose deception not celebration in an effort to achieve their military and political goals.

As President Johnson and his foreign policy advisors struggled to find acceptable solutions to the Vietnam quagmire in 1967, so too did the communists seek a way forward from the battlefield stalemate. From April to June the senior North Vietnamese political leadership, along with the senior members of the military general staff, met secretly in Hanoi. They agreed that communist forces would attempt a "decisive victory" while the U.S. was preparing for the upcoming presidential election and a possible shift in its military strategy. Secrecy had always been one of the guiding principles of those at the highest decision-making level in Communist Party headquarters in Hanoi, and all the way down to those responsible for implementing those decisions in the battlefields in the South. So effective was this policy that it was only near the end of the Vietnam War that American intelligence began realizing that the three

North Vietnamese leaders seen as the proponents of the war, President Ho Chi Minh, General Vo Nguyen Giap and Prime Minister Pham Van Dong, had long been sidelined in critical military decision-making by a much lesser known senior official. In fact, the architect of Vietnam's war effort, the main strategist and the commander in chief was the General Secretary of the Central Committee of the Communist Party of Vietnam, Le Duan.

He was one of the original Vietnamese revolutionaries, a southerner and a founding member of the party in 1930. In the 1950s, he was an aggressive voice in the communist hierarchy for reunification of the two Vietnams through war. While Western military strategists and journalists studied the writings of General Vo Nguyen Giap and China's Mao Zedong to better understand the nature of the fighting waged by the communists in South Vietnam, Le Duan's strategy of constant attack as the key to victory prevailed. The historian Lien-Hang T. Nguyen, in her authoritative 2012 book, "Hanoi's War," wrote: "Le Duan drew from his military experiences in the Mekong Delta, where he learned that in order to wage a successful revolution one must always be on the offensive. Although the majority of the military leadership led by General Giap did not believe anti-revolutionary forces were ready to launch those attacks against the cities and towns, Le Duan was ready to take the chance in 1968."

The nature of that victory would be the "General Offensive, General Uprising," a campaign that sprung from Le Duan's conviction that, contrary to the conservative guerrilla war teachings of Giap and Mao, South Vietnam's cities could be overwhelmed and a decisive victory achieved by direct action. Le Duan had tried it before, in 1964 and 1965, when Vietcong fighters rose up from the countryside in the chaos that followed the assassination of President Ngo Dinh Diem and began overwhelming South Vietnamese military forces. Only the introduction of United States combat forces in 1965 prevented their victory. Now, Le Duan would try it again, emboldened, according to historian Lien-Hang T. Nguyen, "by the Cuban model, where Castro attacked the cities three times before achieving power."

The formal authorization of the offensive came on October 25, 1967, when the Vietnamese party central committee issued Resolution 14, later detailed by the senior communist commander in South Vietnam, General Tran Van Tra, as instructing: "The upcoming general offensive/ general uprising will be a period, a process, of intensive and complicated strategic offensives by military, political and diplomatic means... The general offensive/general uprising is a process by which we will attack and advance on the enemy continuously both militarily and politically."

The Tet greeting of chairman Ho Chi Minh was designated the combat order for the communist army and the population, and it would be broadcast across the country in the form of his celebration poem, that read: "This spring far outshines the previous spring. Of victories throughout the land come happy tidings. Let north and south educate each other fighting the U.S. aggressors. Forward. Total victory will be ours."

The ability to place well-trained covert agents inside the governing institutions and within the social landscape of South Vietnam's major cities was a key advantage the communist side enjoyed as it made elaborate preparations. I was regularly in contact with one of Le Duan's key espionage agents in Saigon, as were my journalist colleagues. None of us had a clue as to his real mission. He seemed always in plain sight.

One of my indulgences in Saigon while taking a few days' break from war reporting was to stroll along the street from the Associated Press bureau to Givrals Café for coffee and croissants. If it was late morning or early evening, more often than not I would see the Vietnamese journalist, Pham Xuan An, at a table there, chatting with his companions with an eye on the plate glass window that looked out on Lam Son square while patting his dog sprawled at his feet, a surly German shepherd named Berger.

Givrals Café, founded a decade earlier by French master baker Alain Pottier, was a favored coffee shop in the Saigon of the 1960s. It was tucked in a street-side corner of the big Eden building across from the Hotel Continental where a patron saint of the Western press corps, journalist and author Graham Greene, had lived during the French war while he was writing his iconic novel "The Quiet American." From his table in Givrals, Pham Xuan An could look across the square to the ornate former French opera house, then the seat of the National Assembly, and the neighboring Caravelle Hotel, home to the Saigon bureaus of several mainstream American television and print organizations, and where many visiting Western reporters stayed.

By 1968, at 40 years old, his affable manner and casual style honed during a long sojourn in southern California a decade earlier, Pham Xuan An was becoming an indispensable authority to some influential Western journalists endeavoring to untangle the chaos of the Saigon political scene. And as his early association with Vietnamese intelligence agencies and the security services became better known, his value to competing news organizations grew with the increasing complexity of the war, particularly to Time Magazine, one of the leading news organizations of that era. Time hired Pham Xuan An as a staffer, and often when he slipped away from his affluent new surroundings, he would be seen at Givrals Café with his cronies, visits so frequent that he sometimes joked about being "General Givrals." We learned much, much later that Pham Xuan An had a legitimate military rank at that time, as an officer in the communist Vietnamese People's Army, with his chest already full of medals for his exploits as a senior espionage agent in the Saigon area.

With General Westmoreland obsessed with Khe Sanh in the northwestern corner of the country, the communists moved 15 Vietcong battalions, an estimated 6,000 southern guerrillas, in and around Saigon in January. The primary intended targets would be the symbols of moral and political and administrative strength on the South Vietnamese side. Singled out for denigration and destruction were primarily the American embassy, the presidential palace and the South Vietnamese Joint General Staff headquarters. Elsewhere in the country tens of thousands more Vietcong troops were moving into position, intending to attack most provincial headquarters and police stations with great force. Churches, temples and pagodas would be occupied, and leaders among people sought out for quick murder or kidnapping.

The majority of the communist forces were young recruits from the countryside, familiar with the language and the culture but not with the highways and byways of Saigon or the many other cities and towns they would attack. It was here where Le Duan's master plan included his master stroke of ordering his clandestine network of dedicated spies and agents into action to enable the final phase of the offensive. They would ensure that most of the communist combat forces would evade government security cordons and be in place inside the cities, with their weapons and ammunition on hand, when the order to attack was given. It was a role that the covert spy Pham Xuan An pulled off with aplomb, as he explained in interviews with Western and Vietnamese writers and reporters in Vietnam after the war. By then, he had been promoted to the rank of general officer, with an additional medal for his efforts for the communists in the Tet Offensive.

Pham Xuan An's controller officer was Colonel Nguyen Van Tau who used the alias Tu Cang and was based in the tunnel areas near Cu Chi for most of the 1960s as head of the H.63 intelligence network. The journalist spy said that over the years he would drive to the Ho Bo woods 20 miles northeast of Saigon to see Tu Cang when he had important information or when summoned to receive instructions. A few weeks before the Tet Offensive, Tu Cang came to Saigon with a critically important mission from the communist high command, and that was to make sure that communist combat forces intended for action in the inner Saigon zone be in position beforehand. Tu Cang knew little of the layout of Saigon and didn't know the best access points to the city or the most suitable routes. An, with his Western press credentials in his pocket, obliged his superior by driving him around the city in his old blue Renault car and introducing him, to those who inquired, as a distant relative. Over the next weeks, they cross crossed Saigon on scouting missions, determining the best areas where caches of weapons could be stored, and the homes of sympathetic locals where troops could be concealed. And they surveyed weak points in the defenses of the intended main targets, the U.S. embassy, the presidential palace and the South Vietnamese military headquarters; all were locations where Pham Xuan An was a familiar figure in his other role, that of a trusted journalist working with an influential American news organization. The same pattern was repeated in the other major Vietnamese cities such as Hue and Danang as agents-in-place prepared the ground for the coming communist attacks.

As the Tet holidays neared, a sense of elation spread across the populations of South Vietnam's cities who were lulled, by the relatively calm battlefields and official American optimism, into believing the worst of the war was over. The cities had prospered from the war and were readying to celebrate. Prime Minister Nguyen Van Loc even lifted restraints on the use of fireworks, and soon traditional five-yard long strings of firecrackers could be seen hanging on the gates of Saigon's finer homes, ready to be exploded when the Year of the Monkey arrived.

"The people had forgotten about the dying war. They wanted to celebrate Tet with as much fervor as in the old days," wrote the official historian of the Vietnamese Joint General Staff, Colonel Pham Van Son, in an account of the offensive. "For the city dwellers, the war seemed to be as remote as the moon. They were sometimes reminded of its reality by the sight of long ammunition convoys and the sound of far-off gunfire and bomb explosions. On the whole, the terrible war had no dramatic impact on them beyond the effects of an inflationary spiral that only hit wage earners. The greater availability of money created a semblance of affluence unparalleled in the modern history of South Vietnam."

Colonel Son wrote, "Tet was to give this apparently affluent society a golden opportunity to spend their money surplus. Two weeks before the traditional celebration time, hundreds of parties were given each night in Saigon without regard for their high cost. The celebrations were not just limited to the rich and very rich. Employees of U.S. agencies and the great majority of the working classes who had been enjoying incomparable pay conditions thanks to the shortage of labor, also had plenty of money to buy whatever they pleased. Prostitutes and their great purchasing power also contributed to the creation of an atmosphere of unparalleled prosperity. Even servicemen and civil servants, the poorest of them all in the new social structure, did their best to join in the buying spree, unwilling to give their loved ones the impression that they had gone down the last step in the social scale. There were many cases of wage-earners pawning their most precious possessions in order to give their children a decent Tet. To share in the amount of luck of the New Year, even the poorest of the poor joined in the fun."

For the 4 million people of Saigon on the evening of January 30, 1968, who were spilling onto the vehicle-clogged streets amid the deafening crackle of firecrackers and blasts of car horns to celebrate the first day of

Tet, the lifting of the nighttime curfew was an unaccustomed freedom to gather together as the midnight hour approached. The crescendo of noise peaked as this first day of the Year of the Monkey ended and homes across the city blasted off their remaining stocks of fireworks.

Some exhausted revelers bedding down for the night may have noticed in the early hours the distinctive crack of heavy weapons fire that competed with the lingering echoes of firecrackers. The morning for Saigon's population would bring not pleasant recollections of an important holiday well observed, but blood-chilling fear for their lives and the lives of their families. The war of the countryside that for many had been the responsibility of others had now arrived at their own doorsteps.

18

DEFINING VICTORY

BEFORE DAWN, IN THE OPENING HOURS of the Lunar New Year in 1968, communist assault forces began sweeping through the sleeping cities of South Vietnam intent on overthrowing the government. In the midst of a seven-day ceasefire they'd declared a month earlier, the Vietcong used surprise and deceit to launch their attacks, like the Greek soldiers of legend who had hidden inside a wooden horse to infiltrate Troy and overthrow the defenders. The black-clad communist guerrillas emerged from safe houses they'd sneaked into days earlier from their bases in the countryside, picked up weapons from hidden caches in graveyards and rubbish dumps, and assaulted the centers of government power in the capital, the six largest cities, and 34 of 44 provincial capitals. By morning, heavy fighting was erupting throughout Saigon, particularly on the grounds of the American embassy and the presidential palace and at Tan Son Nhut Airport and the Vietnamese Joint General Staff headquarters. The streets of the cities of Hue and Danang and important provincial capitals were running red with blood as surprised security units struggled to regain control.

Vietnamese military historian Colonel Pham Van Son later wrote, "With the nationwide Vietcong offensive on, and gaining momentum in the first hours of the campaign, it was feared that Hanoi was about to realize its final objective of conquering South Vietnam."

In a message announced too late to adequately inform the military, the official Radio Saigon denounced the unfolding attacks, abrogated the government truce order and required the return to barracks of the half of the armed forces given leave to celebrate the Tet holidays. Many didn't hear the broadcasts. Too late, too, for the commanding American general in Vietnam, William Westmoreland, to inform the Vietnamese government and his own supreme commander in the White House, President Lyndon Johnson, of updated intelligence assessments that a large-scale offensive against the cities was imminent. At his headquarters in Bien Hoa, John Paul Vann, deputy director of civil operations in the region around Saigon and a veteran of six years in Vietnam as soldier and civilian advisor, told me later in the day, "Christ, we knew the VC were up to something, but nothing this extensive, nothing." And he mopped his face and shook his head in wonder. The Tet Offensive had confirmed his warnings. Vann had always argued that the fate of South Vietnam rested on improving the motivation and ability of its own armed forces. But the Vietcong had exposed the perennial weaknesses of the South Vietnamese military and police, particularly the hopelessly inadequate security cordons around Saigon and the 43 provincial capitals under attack.

Other than at the remote Khe Sanh combat base in the northwestern border with Laos and North Vietnam, whose U.S. Marine defenders were under increasingly violent attack, the bases of America's half million troops in Vietnam were initially ignored by the enemy. General Westmoreland had gambled that the predicted communist winter-spring offensive would center on the overthrow of the Khe Sanh base, and he was shifting the full emphasis of the American military effort to the northwest. Even as the general became aware of emerging threats to the cities, he discounted them as primarily diversionary. He was asleep at his residence in downtown Saigon when the first shots were fired at the American embassy.

The initial communist assault on Saigon's centers of power was by commandos and sapper units specially trained for the task. They were the spearhead of a 10,000-man communist military force already secretly inside the environs of the Vietnamese capital and poised to take advantage of any successful assault missions. If communist soldiers succeeded in occupying important locations such as the presidential palace and the American embassy, retaking those places would require punishing, destructive assaults. In Hue, the historically important walled Citadel and the imperial palace were quickly captured by attacking Vietcong and became the scene of desperate, highly publicized battles pitting U.S. Marines and South Vietnamese soldiers against the enemy. Much of the historic district of the city was destroyed.

It was a close-run thing in Saigon. The margin between initial success and failure was razor thin. The leader of the communist assault team that attacked the American embassy was killed within the first few minutes of blowing an entrance hole in the protective wall, disrupting plans to smash open the heavy embassy door with satchels filled with explosives. The attack on Tan Son Nhut airport was foiled by the unexpected presence of a battle-hardened South Vietnamese paratrooper battalion accidentally delayed in an overnight flight to support the military buildup in the northern provinces. The guerrilla assault team that arrived at the gates of the Vietnamese Joint General Staff headquarters were dissuaded from attacking by the unexpected presence of an America military security team guarding the gates. A guerrilla force that arrived in taxis to attack the main gate of the presidential palace were surprised by an alert guard patrolling the grounds, and lost a dozen men killed before fleeing to an adjacent empty building.

With the significant contribution of American combat forces quickly assembled from their regional operational areas in the Saigon region, the initial communist attacks against primary targets were beaten off. By the end of the day there were 14 American infantry battalions fighting inside Saigon. The communist hopes of a general uprising by the public against the national government were not realized. President Johnson, caught unawares as were his senior advisors by the Tet attacks, anxiously watched the evening news programs. He was buoyed by Westmoreland's confident assertions of victory, delivered to network television cameras from the bloodied, body-strewn wreckage of the American embassy grounds. The general confidently described the actions of the day as "a massive military defeat" for the enemy. The president ordered that

Westmoreland give two press conferences a day, rather than just the one he had planned, and stay on message.

In an early morning telephone call on January 31 Washington time, President Johnson asked Robert McNamara his assessment of the communist attacks, and he defense secretary responded: "Well, I think it shows two things, Mr. President. First that they have more power than some credit them with. I don't think that it is a last gasp action. I do think that it represents a maximum action in the sense that they've poured out all their assets, and my guess is that we will inflict very heavy losses on them both in terms of personal and materiel. This will set them back some, but after they absorb the losses, they will remain a substantial force. I don't anticipate that we will hit them so hard that they will be knocked out for an extended period or forced to drop back in the level of effort against us."

McNamara continued: "I do think that this is such a well-coordinated, such an obviously advance-planned operation that it probably relates to negotiations in some way. I expect that, were they successful here, they would then move forwards more forcefully on the negotiation front, thinking they have a stronger position on which to bargain. I don't believe they are going to be successful. I think that in the case we're going to have a real military engagement, I believe we'll deal them a heavy defeat. I think in the other areas it's largely a propaganda effort and publicity effort. I think they'll gain that way. I imagine our people across our country this morning will feel that they're (the enemy) much stronger than they had previously anticipated they were, and in this sense, I think they gain."

The slaughter that was enveloping Vietnam plucked at every layer of Vietnamese and American life. A wealthy Chinese importer gunned his late model French car through a Saigon intersection instead of heeding the stop whistle of an American military policeman. He was shot dead by the nervous sentry. Two American employees of Pacific Architects and Engineers, Doyle V. Clark and Billy C. Stein, both from California, leaped into their jeep when fighting erupted near their home beside the Saigon golf course. They attempted to drive down a bullet-flecked road to the city center and both were killed 20 yards from their gate. Their neighbor, Mike Mealy, a young Californian, elected to stay under his bed for 29 hours. He survived. Trained Vietcong murder squads prowled the environs of Saigon and Hue in particular, seeking known government, police and military officials and killing them, a practice perfected in the years of the clandestine wars in the villages of the countryside.

The communists sometimes picked their victims at random. In the Central Highlands city of Ban Me Thuot, they occupied the home of an American education specialist, Dr. Jane Ford, and let her live even though they harassed her during the time they used her home as a command post. But in the same city, they overran the Christian and Missionary Alliance compound and slew six American missionaries based there, capturing two others, nurse Betty Olsen and translator Hank Blood. Along with American civilian aid specialist Mike Benge, an expert on the indigenous Montagnards who was based in Ban Me Thuot, they disappeared into Vietcong captivity. Only Benge survived, released three years later to report that both his companions had died under the brutal conditions of their captivity.

In the Mekong Delta city of Chau Doc, the Vietcong pushed half a dozen American nurses into the bathroom of their medical clinic, locking them in for the 30 hours they held the building before they were released by rescuing soldiers. But in the nearby province of Vinh Long, New Life hamlet specialist Hugh Lobit, a big, rangy Texan in his mid-30s, was gunned down in his favorite pacified village when he was showing a newsman around. Other foreigners disappeared for months, like Keith Hyland, a reputed Australian millionaire who made his money in duck feathers. A trim debonair 54-year-old when captured by the Vietcong while visiting his factory in the Saigon suburb of Cholon, he was held until late November, bound and blindfolded and marched through the jungle, sometimes confined to a cage or a pit, and interrogated constantly. When released, he was gaunt and suffering from dysentery.

Some fought back, including Ron Fleming, a 20-year-old American psywar operative who I saw crouching outside his home, like a pioneer in the West defending his log cabin from attack. He had a pistol strapped to his leg and a high-powered rifle in his hands. His clothes were dirty and he hadn't shaved for several days. The young Harvard graduate crept along the high concrete wall of his Saigon compound as I approached, and put his fingers to his lips for silence. At the corner he raised his M-14 rifle to his shoulder and fired. The crack of the rifle echoed around the small cluster of homes in the compound. "He's not there now," he said. "Maybe I got him. That might be the end of the friendly neighborhood sniper." A few minutes later, though, bullets cracked in the air. The sniper was still there.

Fleming began stalking him again, just as he had been doing for the previous 36 hours. Living in other homes in Fleming's compound were nine other Americans, including three women and two children. The streets outside the compound were deserted. Some of the heaviest fighting of the offensive had erupted around their suburban area, and Fleming worried that the sniper might be an advance man. "We sort of look upon ourselves as a frontier community. It has brought out the frontier spirit in all of us. Two hardened U.S. embassy people who hadn't spoken to each other in months because of the conflicting nature of their work, are good buddies now. This siege has brought them together. But I found out one thing: The compound's self-described killer, a veteran of the U.S. Army who toted a gleaming Swedish K machine gun and kept bragging about how many Vietcong he would kill if he got the chance, bugged out the moment the going got tough."

Fleming enlisted Don Wilson, a neighbor who was an American diplomat and had been in Vietnam nine months, as long as he had, to assist in the defense. The following day they saw a black clad Vietcong soldier wedging himself on the roof of a nearby building. Fleming fired at him and he disappeared from view. "I don't know whether I hit anyone or not," Fleming told me. "I'm a dreadful shot."

While American and South Vietnamese forces were heavily engaged with communist troops threatening government centers, Vietcong soldiers and cadres began appearing openly in some heavily populated areas of Saigon and Cholon. They were knocking on doors and telling house occupants and passersby that, "We are from the National Liberation Front (the communist southern political organization). We have come to liberate Saigon." Their activities seemed part the overall communist strategy to get the best possible mileage out of the offensive. AP photographer Le Cong Cung was given a similar message by a Vietnamese male dressed in green shirt and blue trousers near the An Quang Pagoda. The man was carrying a carbine rifle. The photographer saw a score of men similarly clad and carrying weapons. He was told not to take pictures, and informed, "There are more than a hundred of us."

Combat casualties were rapidly rising. In the first day, 189 American soldiers were killed, along with 229 South Vietnamese troops. General Westmoreland announced that 4,320 Vietcong had been killed. The ratio of allied killed to enemy, roughly 10-to-1, would push enemy dead into the tens of thousands by month's end. There were the revenge killings, most notably by the National Police Chief, General Nguyen Ngoc Loan, who fired his pistol into the head of an alleged Vietcong death squad leader, Nguyen Van Lem, also known as Bay Loc. A photograph of the incident taken by the Associated Press's Eddie Adams on the second morning of the offensive became symbolic of Vietnam's descent into chaos. And the AP reported on an incident in the Gia Dinh area where a staff photographer had watched angry South Vietnamese troops kill alleged Vietcong wounded, who were lying at the side of a road.

But almost as injurious as the communist attacks were the severe military measures taken to repel them. We watched whole city blocks in the Cholon district of Saigon become free-fire zones for American gunships and tanks, permitting unrestricted attacks on enemy soldiers using as hiding places the rice warehouses, businesses and homes of the primarily Chinese residents. From a helicopter overhead, the patches of rubble and ash scouring the city looked as though some giant wearing hobnailed boots had visited. Ugly bomb holes gaped from the city floor where there had once been clusters of homes, shops and offices. The heaviest fighting was in the rabbit warrens of lanes and homes where Cholon merged with Saigon. The American forces brought in to defeat the Vietcong used tactics perfected in the countryside war. U.S. Army helicopters sought out the Vietcong, roaring low over the city with machine guns, spitting bullets and rockets into the crowded communities below. Vietnamese Air Force Skyraider bombers flattened the tar paper shacks of the poorest residents along canals. Tanks and armored troop carriers and their wide-eyed American crews just in from the paddy fields and jungles were facing an unfamiliar battleground.

Less than two weeks into the offensive, the anonymous dead were laid to rest in three huge mass graves dug at the western edge of the city, with only a few street waifs, some wearing toy gas masks against the stench, and a few Western journalists looking on. One 500-foot grave, carved out of a previous burial ground covered with weeds, was filled with 600 bodies before being covered with dirt. A second mass grave contained 200, and a third held 250 remains of men, women and children. Cemetery officials said the majority of the bodies were those of Vietcong soldiers cleared off the streets of Cholon. Others being buried included around 200 civilians, murdered by Vietcong death squads or accidental casualties in the fighting.

I saw a woman sobbing beside a headstone as she waited for trash trucks to drive up with more remains. She said she was looking for the body of her young son. A man discovered the body of his wife in the top row of one mass grave, and called to cemetery officials to assist him in removing it. But for the majority of those in the mass graves of Saigon, they were buried as anonymously as they had died.

The Tet Offensive stretched beyond Saigon across the whole country. Communist insurgents had emerged from the countryside and streamed past government security forces and into the population centers. Just a few days earlier, the U.S. mission's pacification chief, Robert Komer, had bragged to reporters that the primary highway, Route 1, was open from Saigon all the way to the demilitarized zone border with North Vietnam. When I saw John Paul Vann in Bien Hoa the day after the attacks began he made a joke of it: "The highway might be open, but watch out for the cities and towns en route. They're dangerous."

The reports coming in from the countryside told of unprecedented destruction to towns and villages occupied by the Vietcong who were then driven out by American firepower. AP's Eddie Adams visited the cities of My Tho and Vinh Long and returned with photographs of the battle scenes. He told me, "The damage was devastating, man. The ruins were still smoldering, the population was silent and were looking angrily at us. They don't like us down there because of the bombing and the gunships."

I wanted to see it for myself. I joined a press trip on February 7 to the city of Ben Tre, a small Mekong Delta provincial capital I had visited in early January on a reporting trip. Jeeps were waiting at the airport to take us into the city, but I let my colleagues go ahead and walked over to the wooden control tower where I had seen the familiar face of Major Chester L. Brown, an American Air Force officer who had flown me around in his L-19 spotter plane on my earlier visit. He warned me that I would be shocked at what I saw, that much of Ben Tre was in ruins and many people had died. Major Brown explained, "It is always a pity about the civilians. In the mass confusion of this sort of thing, the people don't know where the lines are, they don't know where to hide, and some of the weapons we were using were area weapons instead of against specific targets, and that way people get hurt."

I drove with Major Brown into Ben Tre and saw rows of blackened palm trees with their tops burned off and the wreckage of roadside homes and small shops. In town, we passed the giant shells of two- and three-story office buildings. The once handsome Kien Hoa market where I had purchased durian and star fruit three weeks earlier was a crumpled ruin. We arrived at the administrative center of the city along the riverside where the U.S. Army Advisory Team 93 was buried in protective sandbags. The province chief's home and the Vietnamese tactical center were similarly shielded across the grassy compound. From a wooden landing, I looked across the river to the opposite bank where a two-mile stretch of thatch-roofed homes had been reduced to ashes. The squatter district and lower-class housing on the western and northern sides of the city were similarly leveled, just piles of junk.

I asked the army advisory team commander how many civilians had died, and he estimated 500 to 1,000, "but we will never know for sure because many families are permanently buried under the rubble." We had met before and I liked him. I asked how it could have happened that so many could have died in a town of only 35,000 people. He looked at my notebook, shook his head and said, "None of us can talk about that. We know we can't go on record criticizing our Vietnamese counterparts, not at a time like this." There was a murmur of ascent from the group of American officers around him. I put away my notebook and tucked my pen into my belt. I said, "Now, you know me. I've been down here before. Talk to me, trust me, and I won't quote you on anything that'll hurt you. I never do that."

A picture emerged of chaos and ineptitude in the defense of the city. The Vietcong had sneaked in during the night of February 1, the day after the attack on Saigon. The attacks were launched against an unprepared defense force, half depleted by holiday passes. Ben Tre's commercial center and residential areas were under insurgent control by dawn, and the guerrillas were threatening the administrative center and the Vietnamese barracks whose troops were unwilling to launch counter attacks. One of the officers, a major, who had helped defend the compound, told me that the decision to use the heaviest of firepower against the enemy was not taken lightly. "They are our friends out there. We waited until we had no choice." He said, "The Vietnamese chief of staff had to bring in an airstrike on the house of his neighbor because the communists had occupied it. Our own positions were being threatened, the government center nearly overrun. It became necessary to destroy the town in order to save it." The stratagem to use fighter-bombers dropping napalm and heavy projectiles, along with armed helicopters and artillery barrages, was approved by the corps headquarters at Can Tho.

When we drove back to the airstrip, Major Brown said, "It wasn't all bad. There could have been many more killed. I think I saved hundreds of civilians." He told me how in the midmorning hours of the battle he was ordered to guide airstrikes in on what he was told were a thousand Vietcong retreating north from the city. He buzzed down low in his spotter plane and saw scores of mostly women and children carrying bed rolls and household goods, clearly fleeing from their destroyed homes. "Some Vietcong may have been amongst those people but most of them were refugees, and I wasn't about to bring napalm on them, so I called off the planned airstrike," Major Brown said.

On the return flight to Saigon I thought about what I'd seen and heard in Ben Tre. The phrase I had surreptitiously written in my notebook, "It became necessary to destroy the town in order to save it," leaped out as a comment on the essential dilemma of the Tet Offensive: The authorities had not only to defeat the enemy, but to protect the civilians in embattled cities. At the AP office, I sat at my typewriter long into the night. Eventually I began my story, "At what point do you turn your heavy guns and jet fighters on the streets of your own city? Where does the infliction of civilian casualties become irrelevant as long as the enemy is destroyed? The answers to both these questions came in the first hours of the battle for Ben Tre, a once placid river city of 35,000 people. 'It became necessary to destroy the town to save it,' a U.S. major says. The destruction of this provincial capital was drawn out over 50 hours."

I wrote eight pages of copy and at 3 a.m. passed them over to the teleprinter operator who punched the material directly through to our New York foreign desk. I lay down on a cot in the bureau chief Bob Tuckman's office and slept until he came in early to start the news day. Late that evening Tuckman had a call; from a staffer at the U.S. military information office asking me to identify the major who had made the comment I had highlighted in my story. I rejected the request out of hand because we routinely gave anonymity to our many nervous sources who requested it. This was the first inkling of how controversial the story was becoming. The next day, the AP foreign desk advised that the quote had echoed from Fleet Street in London to Seoul, South Korea, and was subject of editorial comment in the United States. A secretary in the office of Barry Zorthian, chief of information in the Saigon mission, said the message traffic indicated that President Johnson himself was demanding to know the name of the major, and a few days later, Peter Kann, of the Wall Street Journal, told me that a helicopter full of senior American officers had descended into Ben Tre while he was visiting, demanding to know the name of the culprit.

Washington's concern — and impatience — with events in Vietnam became apparent in a message from Secretary of State Dean Rusk to the American embassy on February 4. "President Thieu and the GVN (Government of South Vietnam) have been dealt a significant blow and Thieu must move more energetically if GVN is to recover from it. A useful byproduct of recent developments might be a modification in Thieu's sense of timing and priorities. As a result of the crisis he might shift from his cautious, methodical approach to problems and programs to a more dramatic energetic one — or at least give freer rein to those who normally take a more activist posture. We might come hopefully to find him more receptive to our advice in future."

That same day Ambassador Bunker, who had heaped praise on the response of the South Vietnamese and American military to the Tet attacks, modified some of his earlier self-assurance, admitting to some failings. "It was evident that the initial success of the attacks was due in part to the element of surprise and the fact that they were made in flagrant violation of the Tet period, which Hanoi as well as the GVN had proclaimed. I think it is fair to say also that there was some failure of intelligence on our side, for a sizable number of GVN troops and many GVN officials were on leave."

President Johnson was also hearing direct criticism about his Vietnam policies. At a breakfast for congressional leadership he hosted on February 6, a White House note-taker wrote: "Senator Robert Byrd of West Virginia said of the situation: Poor intelligence, poor preparation for these recent attacks, underestimated Vietcong morale and vitality, underestimated support of South Vietnamese people and army. LBJ said he was alarmed at this, and the attitude expressed by Senator Byrd seemed to be reflected by much of the comment heard in Washington not only by politicians but also the press. LBJ also said, this is all part of a political offensive. They said we had the people believing we were doing very well in Vietnam when we actually were not."

The following day, General Earle Wheeler, the Joint Chiefs chairman, put a damper on hopes that the earlier successes against the communist attacks would quickly end the offensive. He told a cabinet meeting, "There is continued fighting in the Cholon sector of Saigon. We have intelligence that there are two divisions of NVA/VC in the Saigon area. At Hue and Danang the situation is most serious. The enemy remains in Hue and the strength of the ARVN battalions is down. Early reports say the AVRN units are running out of gas." Wheeler also reported on a heavy attack on the Special Forces camp at Lang Vei four miles from Khe Sanh, and that for first time an attack was supported by Soviet-supplied tanks, nine of them. The camp held out to daylight, he reported, and then was evacuated. Seventeen Americans were killed along with 100 enemy in that action, bringing the total

U.S. casualties at the end of the first week of the offensive to 670 dead and 3,565 wounded.

Two days later, as the battles in Hue and Khe Sanh gathered ferocity, General Westmoreland indicated to the head of the Joint Chiefs of Staff that he might require reinforcements, and mentioned 15 more infantry battalions. General Wheeler told a cabinet meeting on February 9, "Since December, the NVA infantry has increased from 78 battalions to 105. That is approximately 15,000."

At the same cabinet meeting, President Johnson began what became the first of a series of sometimes acrimonious debates about additional American troop levels in Vietnam. Tape transcripts reflect the strong words.

President Johnson to General Wheeler: "What you are saying is that since last week we have information that we did not know about earlier, and this is the addition of 15,000 NVA in the northern part of the country. Because of that we need 15 battalions? Because of the increase of 15,000 we need 45,000?"

Wheeler: "Westy needs reinforcements for several reasons. The reinforcement he has in mind are the 82nd Airborne Division and two-thirds of a Marine division, a total of 15 battalions."

Johnson: "All last week I asked two questions. The first was: Did Westmoreland have all that he needed? You answered yes. The second question was: Can Westmorland take care of the situation with what he has there now? The answer was yes. Tell me what has happened to change the situation between then and now?"

Secretary of Defense designate Clark Clifford, in the first of a series of critical observations over the next few weeks, said: "There is a very strange contradiction in what we are saying and doing. On one hand, we say we have known of this buildup. We know that the NVA and the Vietcong launched this type of effort in the cities. We have publicly told the American people that communist efforts did not produce a victory, produced no uprising amongst the Vietnamese people, in support of the enemy, and that they have lost 20,000 to 25,000 troops. Our reaction to all this is to say that the situation is more dangerous today than it was before all this. We are saying that we need more troops, that we need more ammunition and that we need to call up the reserves. I think we should give some serious thought to how we explain saying on one hand that the enemy did not win a victory and yet we are in need of many more troops and possibly an emergency call-up."

Johnson: "The only explanation I can see is that the enemy has changed its tactics. They are putting all their chips in. We have to be prepared for all we might face."

Two days later at a meeting on February 11, President Johnson asked Wheeler, "I want to be completely clear in my mind. Is it true that Westmorland is not requesting or recommending or requesting additional troops now?"

Wheeler: "That is true."

Johnson to Defense Secretary McNamara: "If Westmoreland asks for the 82nd Airborne would you give it to him?"

McNamara, who continued to attend White House meetings until his retirement at the end of the month: "No, I would not. I read this as a permanent augmentation of forces. We are carrying too much of the war there now. All this would do is shift more of the burden on to us."

On February 12, Westmoreland sent a message to the Joint Chiefs of Staff confirming his demand: "I am expressing a firm request for additional troops not because I fear defeat if I am not reinforcing but because I do not feel I can fully grab the initiative from the recently reinforced enemy without them. On the other hand, a setback is fully possible if I am not reinforced, and it is likely we will lose ground in other areas if I am required to make substantial reinforcement of I Corps."

In an 8:29 a.m. phone call the same day Washington time, McNamara told President Johnson, "We've just had a message from Westmoreland. He states categorically he wants six battalions immediately."

Johnson: "I don't have a position of deserting my commander in time of war. I don't have a position of deserting my home folks and acting imprudently and getting involved where I can't pull out."

On February 27, an influential member of the Saigon embassy's mission council, General Edward Lansdale, questioned official assessments of the Tet Offensive in a confidential memo to President Johnson's special assistant for national security affairs, Walt Rostow. "The high cost to the enemy was not vital to him. It could be made vital if there were retributions from an aroused Vietnamese population who were led with more spark and spunk than the present Neville Chamberlain-style of Vietnamese leadership. As it is, one month after Tet the enemy has the initiative in the war. Today, many Vietnamese civilians and soldiers have a sinking feeling in their gut that the enemy is going to outwit us with this initiative. It will take some tough policies and psychological judo on top of military muscle to throw down the enemy.

"Destruction resulting from United States and Vietnamese bombing and artillery firepower has created some deep resentments against Americans and the government particularly in the refugee camps where Vietcong agitators are at work. Vietcong atrocities have created mostly fear but not widespread antagonism except in families that suffered personal losses. Vietcong propaganda still seems to have more credibility with the people at this point than does the information campaign on our side. This can be reversed but time is running out."

"The enemy's Tet offensive demonstrated once again the ability of communist leaders to make a hard strategic decision, marshalling their resources in an extremely disciplined way, and dealt us a hard blow. At present our strategy is less clear and our resources are not being used in a concerted and disciplined fashion as the enemy's (are), at least not in the political sphere. In case of another enemy attack, individuals will feel highly vulnerable, their main recourse to safety being only within their immediate family.

"Much of this has been caused by the attitude and behavior of the police. Even as the security of Saigon/Cholon owes a debt to the energy and resourcefulness of General Loan, he also portrayed the image of an emotionally unstable, suspicious, vindictive and willful person. This image has rubbed off on the force he commands, further tarnishing their reputation for corrupt venality and saving their own hides in times of trouble. Unless their image is changed, unless some bond is created between police and the people, we will be leaving a grievous chink in our armor for the enemy to exploit."

General Westmoreland's request for additional forces earlier in February was eventually granted by the White House, bringing the total strength of American forces fighting in Vietnam up to more than 500,000 by month's end. Westmoreland would soon ask for many more troops, a request that would have unforeseen political consequences and would change the course of America's history in Vietnam.

GALLERY
THE KEY PLAYERS

President John F. Kennedy's decision to send military advisors to South Vietnam after taking office strengthened America's commitment to defend the country against communist attacks. But his approval of a coup d'état against President Ngo Dinh Diem two years later seriously weakened the U.S. effort.

National Security Advisor McGeorge Bundy worked closely with President Kennedy on the Cuban Missile Crisis, and was a strong proponent of the sustained bombing of North Vietnam in 1965, along with the commitment of hundreds of thousands of US troops to the war effort to prevent a communist takeover of South Vietnam.

Secretary of Defense Robert McNamara played a major role in the escalation of the war, believing that the fall of South Vietnam would lead to the fall of neighboring countries to communism. But the failure of his defense strategy of limited war led to his own disillusionment and departure from office.

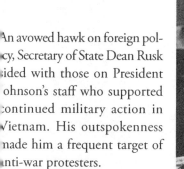

An avowed hawk on foreign policy, Secretary of State Dean Rusk sided with those on President Johnson's staff who supported continued military action in Vietnam. His outspokenness made him a frequent target of anti-war protesters.

An important Republican political figure and a member of the well-known Lodge family, Henry Cabot Lodge was assigned as Ambassador to South Vietnam in July, 1963, under instructions from President Kennedy to persuade President Ngo Dinh Diem to be supportive of America's Vietnam policies. Unable to achieve his goals, Lodge became an important enabler for the Vietnamese military officers who overthrew the Diem in a coup d'état.

A distinguished officer in World War II, a chairman of the joint chiefs of staff and a confidant of President Kennedy, General Maxwell Taylor was an early proponent of American advisory assistance to Vietnam, but as ambassador to Saigon early in the Johnson Administration cautioned against committing American ground troops to the war, and doubted that the bombing of North Vietnam would be effective.

Assigned to South Vietnam in 1964 as Commander of U.S. Forces, General William Westmoreland adopted a strategy of attrition against the Vietcong and communist North Vietnamese troops. His relentless use of air power and artillery resulted in scores of thousands of casualties but did not break the enemy's will. His claim that there was "light at the end of the tunnel" late in 1967 was followed two months later by the communist Tet Offensive that lost him the support of President Johnson.

As Assistant Secretary of State for East Asian and Pacific Affairs, William Bundy had key roles in planning the Vietnam war under Presidents Kennedy and Johnson. He was seen as more dovish that his brother McGeorge Bundy.

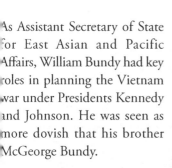

General Earle Wheeler with Robert McNamara (left) often urged President Johnson to strike North Vietnam harder with increased air strikes. As the Chief of the Joint Chiefs of Staff, he fully supported General Westmoreland, backing the field commander's requests for more troops and more authority.

A prominent Washington law-yer and important political advisor to Presidents Truman, Kennedy and Johnson, Secre-tary of Defense Clark Gifford challenged the administration's war policies when he took over the Defense Department from McNamara during the Tet Offensive. He was primarily responsible for persuading President Johnson to make his radical changes.

President Lyndon B. Johnson's decision after taking office to begin bombing North Vietnam mid-1964 and to begin sending combat troops to South Vietnam in March 1965 cemented America's involvement in the war. Mounting US casualties in a stale-mated war and rising anti-war resistance at home after an unexpected communist Tet Offensive compelled him in March 1968 to end most of the bombing in the north, limit the troop deployments to the war zone, and announce that he would not run for re-election.

Chairman of the Senate Foreign relations committee and senator from Arkansas, William Fulbright was the most critical senatorial opponent of the Vietnam War policies of the Johnson Administration, particularly of the view that the Vietnam intervention became necessary because of the Cold War. He held several combative series of hearings on Vietnam, some of them televised nationally.

Elected as the first President of the American-backed Republic of South Vietnam in 1955, Ngo Dinh Diem lost the confidence of President Kennedy by his mishandling of an uprising by Buddhist leaders in 1963, and was overthrown in a coup d'état on November 1, 1963, and murdered along with his younger brother and advisor, Ngo Dinh Nhu.

Chief of State Nguyen Van Thieu was one of several South Vietnamese generals who overthrew President Ngo Dinh Diem in 1963. In 1965 he led a military government until his election as President in 1967. He was forced to flee the country when North Vietnamese forces were advancing on Saigon in April, 1975.

Little known to American intelligence during the Vietnam War, and as President Ho Chi Minh's health was failing, General Secretary of the Central Committee of the Communist Party Le Duan became the top decision-maker in Vietnam, advocating an aggressive military strategy of attack as the best path to victory. It was his secret planning that produced the explosive Tet Offensive in early 1968 that failed to achieve its military goals, but resulted in a political and psychological victory.

19

THE BATTLE FOR HUE

IT WAS BRUTAL AND UNEXPECTED, the Tet Offensive battle that smashed for nearly a month across the old imperial city of Hue, long known as the cultural and religious center of South Vietnam. It echoed the attacks of French colonial troops ravaging its riches in the 19th century, and the Japanese Army's violent suppression of resistance near the end of World War II. But this time it was much worse than the historical record of the past, with high casualties and appalling destruction not seen before.

An American Marine captain, Myron C. Harrington, recalled his first glimpse of the battered city, several days into the battle that began in the early hours of January 31, 1968, with an unexpected communist attack on the city. In an interview after the war for a documentary I was writing, Harrington said, "We entered Hue on a convoy and were let off at the south side of the city, and we were very nervous. I think the first impression that I got was the desolation, the smell of death that was hanging over the city along with the smoke. It looked just like a movie set that we were walking into except the props were eerie and real-looking. I mean the burned-out tanks and trucks, the automobiles that were turned over. The main bridge across the Perfume River had been blown. Most of the houses and small wooden huts the Vietnamese lived in were completely blown away. The concrete and stone structures had been partially destroyed. Roofs were caved in, and in the business district all the windows were blown out in the tall buildings and rubble was all over the place. It was very much devastated. In many cases the bodies were still lying around, and it was very nerve-wracking and a little bit frightening when you walked in and saw this kind of desolation, and you knew right away you were not going on a picnic and it was going to be difficult."

No picnic, indeed. Looking north across the slow-moving Perfume River, Harrington's Marines could see the emblem of the communist Vietcong, the gold-starred, blue-and-red National Liberation Front banner, flying from atop the 120-foot tall flagpole over the front tower of the massive stone fortifications of the Citadel, built by Emperor Gia Long in 1804. An overwhelming force of North Vietnamese and Vietcong combat troops spearheaded by the enemy's 6th Infantry Regiment had swept into Hue from the countryside in an unforeseen onslaught in the early hours of January 31. The surprise tactics were used across the country against cities and towns. Unlike in Saigon and Danang, where defenders strongly resisted, Hue's defenders were caught off-guard; the headquarters of the South Vietnamese 9th Infantry Division was left clinging to the northeast corner of the Citadel and its neighboring airstrip, while the attacking force routed most of Hue's defenders. Ultimately, 10 communist infantry battalions were committed to the battle. They quickly set about building gun positions in the nearly four square miles of the Citadel and in the imperial palace in the center of it. And by dawn of that first day the communists had pulled down the flag of South Vietnam from the battlements and raised their own. The mission of Captain Harrington's company and nearly 2,000 fellow Marine riflemen eventually committed to the battle was to help an overwhelmed South Vietnamese force to tear down that flag and drive the communists from the city.

As the ancient imperial capital, Hue was the symbol of a unified state to all Vietnamese. Its capture by the communists would have a profound psychological impact on people in the North and the South. The majority of the population had remained aloof from the war and some were actively involved in political groups that opposed the central government. That outlook played into the hands of the communists.

The American military commander, General Westmoreland, wrote in his autobiography, "Of all the Communist targets in the Tet Offensive,

Hue, population 140,000, Vietnam's third city, may have been the least prepared for what lay in store. Although I had reported to Washington on January 22 that a multi-battalion attack might be expected at Hue, for some reason, I learned later, that information failed to reach a small American advisory group in a little walled compound within the city. Except for some civilians and advisors with the South Vietnamese 9th Infantry Division headquarters, they were the only American presence in Hue."

Brigadier General Ngo Quang Truong, commander of the South Vietnamese 9th Infantry Division, had placed his troops on full alert when he was advised of attacks the previous day against Nha Trang and Qui Nhon, and he remained at his post throughout the night. He was attempting to bring his troops back from their holiday festivities when the attack began.

The surprise of the communist attack on Hue was complete. The official historian of the South Vietnamese Armed Forces Joint General Staff, Lieutenant Colonel Pham Van Son, wrote in an after-action report: "Hue was very much alive on the eve of the New Year. The Dong Ba market was crowded with people. Many strangers were noticed strolling among the crowds. No one apparently paid much attention to them or thought anything unusual might happen in their peaceful city. Throughout Tet eve and New Year's Day firecrackers exploded endlessly and people went about their customary visits to relatives as if nothing were to happen.

"After the swift communist attacks had taken over most of the city, the local residents were shocked at seeing that from the second through the fourth day of Tet the Vietcong moved freely in the streets of Hue. There were no reactions from friendly forces at this time. During this period, the enemy had a field day making political propaganda for what it called The People's Alliance for Democracy and Freedom. On the local front, this organization was led by the former Hue University teacher Le Vim Hao who had sneaked out of town three days earlier to join the Vietcong. A number of college students and civilians who had participated in the abortive Buddhist-led antigovernment campaigns in previous years supported the alliance and played a fairly active part in the Hue chapter."

Soon after the attacks began, senior Vietnamese military officials and the American 3rd Marine Amphibious Force in the regional capital of Danang established broad policy guidelines regarding clearing up operations inside and outside of Hue. The Vietnamese would take care of subduing the Citadel and the populated communities to the east; the Americans would handle the south side of Hue, with the Perfume River the boundary. On the third, fourth and fifth days of the Tet Offensive, American forces began arriving in Hue. The advance group included three Marine infantry companies and one armor battalion from the 1st Marine Division, called Task Force X-Ray and commanded by Brigadier General Foster LaHue.

Captain George R. Christmas was one of the first Marine reinforcements to arrive. "I was commanding officer of company H or hotel as we call it, of the 2nd Battalion, 5th Marines. And we had fought throughout the northern part of Vietnam from west of Danang and finally into the battle of Hue city. There were no U.S. combat forces inside the city of Hue by prior agreement; it was strictly run by the Vietnamese government and South Vietnamese armed forces. So, we had assumed no tactical responsibility there at all."

Christmas's unit had convoyed up Route One to Hue from the Marine base at Phu Bai on February 3 expecting ambushes and passed a lot of devastation but nothing of the enemy. They got into the city and still nothing. Christmas remembered, "We were about two blocks away from the American advisory compound and then, 'boom,' a major ambush hit us. Fortunately, we were well prepared. We parked the trucks very quickly and attacked the ambush position, and were able to drive them off. We moved all but one destroyed truck to the compound. We were welcomed by the American advisors, and it was pretty obvious they had gone through some difficult evenings. I can remember one of my young troopers in the back of a truck saying, 'Look, they're all smiling at us,' and I felt it was a smile of relief. We had brought ammunition, food and water to replenish their supplies."

Gulf company from 2nd Battalion, 5th Marines, and Alfa and Bravo companies from the 1st Battalion, 1st Marines had been the first ones into the city. They had been able to get all the way up into the southern part of Hue and they raised the siege on the American military advisory compound. But they would soon become the first American casualties of the battle for Hue.

Captain Christmas said, "They did not really know what we had against us. Things seemed pretty quiet and normal, and they sent Gulf and Alpha companies across the main bridge over the Perfume River toward the north side, not realizing at that time how heavily defended by the communists the Citadel had become. Gulf Company got three-quarters of the way across the bridge when there was just deafening fire. They were able to fight the North Vietnamese to 200 yards on the other side of the bridge, but they had lost half the company, and quite frankly had to be brought back that night to the south side. There was the recognition at that time that there's more here than we realize. The very next day Fox company from 2nd Battalion, 5th Marines, was flown in by helicopters to reinforce and were fired upon but landed their loads."

Christmas was blunt in his criticism of the early period of the battle. "How did the communists get in? Well, I think to be quite frank, I think we just totally let down. I think that no one recognized that the North Vietnamese forces would go after such a large objective. I think that, first if all, the basic reason we were moving units around toward the border areas at that time was because we didn't expect an offensive here at that time. We were moving the entire 3rd Marine Division north. Now this a company commander's viewpoint, looking at it from my level at that time. And obviously the South Vietnamese forces did not think so either. I heard that 50 percent of their forces were on holiday because of Tet and the ceasefire."

Captain Christmas also criticized the early tactics of both sides. "If you look at tactics about how to take a built-up area like a city, one of the first keys is that you must isolate the area. And I think both we and the North Vietnamese failed on this area. The North Vietnamese attempted to isolate us by placing fairly large ambushes on Route One, coming both from the north, where the South Vietnamese tried to reinforce, and from the south where we came to reinforce. However, they were never strong enough to hold those positions and keep us out.

"On our side," he continued, "we also failed to ever really isolate the city of Hue, and this was to cause a great deal of pain for us and that is why the battle in many ways lasted much longer than it should have. I don't think we realized the size of the force that had taken the city, and it was not until the third or fourth day that we realized we had more on our hands than we first thought. Once we realized this, we should have isolated Hue from the western approaches because that is where the North Vietnamese forces came from. We never quite successfully did this, and in fact throughout the entire battle there was a corridor that ran along the Perfume River that the North Vietnamese forces were able to reinforce and move to-and-fro on."

Christmas's company was assigned to help clear the south side of Hue before moving to the north side and the battle for the Citadel. They started out towards the Hue University building at the corner of Le Loi street and Route One where it crossed the Perfume River bridge. Christmas said, "The North Vietnamese used each building as a strongpoint, and a strongpoint normally would take a three-story building generally surrounded by a courtyard and the normal type of stone fence used in the city of Hue. Basically, what they would do is surround the courtyard with spider holes, similar to the old World War II foxhole except you can pull a top over it. A North Vietnamese soldier would be in each, with an AK-47 rifle and a B2 rocket launcher, Within the building itself it was fortified, the upper floors would have snipers, there'd be automatic weapons in the building. Down the exposed flank or street there would be grazing fire that would cover the streets. So, it was a very substantial strongpoint, and we would soon find out where they were.

"We started to fight standard, block-by-block, room-by-room combat, done strictly as one would do by the textbook. By seizing a building, it can provide flanking fire into the next building so another unit can move in. When we went at the enemy, house-by-house, room-by-room, I think it really messed up their game plan. It is not the way the South Vietnamese soldiers fight. The enemy didn't expect it, and when we did that I think that's where we gained the advantage. The aggressiveness, the marinization of the young American Marines did in fact gain the advantage on the regular North Vietnamese soldier.

Even though they were well-defended positions, I think that's why we were victorious. But it wasn't done overnight, it was done through a pretty substantial effort."

Christmas and his Marines found that "a good many" professors and their wives had remained in their university quarters during the communist takeover of the city, and that a North Vietnamese army battalion made its headquarters in one of the apartments. Some Vietnamese professors at the Hue University living compound told Christmas that a number of Vietcong forces that came into the southern portion of the city had formed goon squads. They went into the records of the Thua Thien provincial headquarters and determined where various government officials lived, and took captured Vietnamese military trucks "and literally ran up and down the streets, and as you talked to civilians who could converse in English or French, they would tell you this.

"The Vietcong would literally stop at a house that they had an address and pound on the door and break it down if necessary and search to find anyone in there who worked for the government, leading them aboard the trucks — and off they would go, never to be seen again," Christmas said. "I think this is where many of the graves we later found came from, in that time frame. I was told by professors and their wives in the Hue University compound that the NVA battalion commander put a stop to it when he eventually found out about it, and that's something that should be said. The North Vietnamese soldiers were crack soldiers while the Vietcong was something else."

Christmas's company also joined with two sister Marine companies to seize the sizable Hue Hospital complex. "When we entered the complex fortunately we had been told by some refugees that there that there were some Vietcong who were posing as patients in beds, that in fact they had thrown the patients out," he said. "When our troops entered the hospital complex we were aware of this, and it did save several Marine lives. The most poignant story I think was there is a young Marine going down this corridor of the hospital and towards him comes a Vietnamese in a black habit, and the rifleman looks, and naturally thinks this is a Catholic nun. All of a sudden, the habit comes up, and there is an AK-47." But the weapon jammed, and the Marine was able to kill the supposed nun, who turned out to be a disguised Vietcong, Christmas said. "We had several other incidents like that."

Once the hospital was taken and the battle started to quiet down, Christmas's company held up for a night. He'd been given a platoon from another company for support, and next day they moved along the contested Le Loi street next to the Perfume River. They approached an area where they knew there was a heavy concentration of North Vietnamese soldiers, near the Hue City Yacht Club. Christmas said, "My first platoon commander called in about 17:00 in the evening and said, 'Skipper I've got about five civilians across the street here and they want to come over.' (The civilians were hiding in a building between the lines.) I said, 'All right, send a fire team over and get them out.' Very excitedly a few minutes later he called back and said, 'Well, skipper, I think there's about 25 here.' A few minutes later he called and said now there's close to 50. Well, several hundred civilians later...."

"The problem was that with the first five we had started to receive fire as soon as the concentration of North Vietnamese saw what was coming out of the building. With the other platoons, we were able to reduce that fire and finally quell it. We couldn't take the civilians back up the street because it was still contested by long range snipers and the like. So, we had to take them back through every hole in every courtyard we had blown through, all the way back to the MACV compound. It created a great problem for us, manpower, moving several hundred civilians up a contested area; but it did benefit us, however, because we did find a few Americans hidden in that group that were hiding in a basement. We found some English-speaking Vietnamese and several French speakers. So, we were able to garner some very immediate intelligence, which was very beneficial."

By now, Christmas was learning something about his men. "When we were out fighting in the paddy fields earlier in our tour, the old country boy, as we used to call them, the cow cocky, the farm boy, knew his way around. As soon as we got into the city where the ambushes were well concealed and frequent, and the streets narrow, well, the lads we recruited from Watts and from Harlem and from South Philadelphia and other inner cities became very popular because maybe they had been through a few street fights in their day and they knew exactly where the ambush might be. They got to be very popular with each one of the units and looked upon with a great deal of esteem in their ability to pick out where a good ambush might be."

For the five days as Christmas's men fought towards the Thua Thien province capital building, they were looking at a very large Vietcong flag that flew from the big flagpole in the courtyard. The building was defended by the communists as a major strongpoint. It was about 3 in the afternoon when Christmas's company made the attack, using powerful riot control gas to help clear the way.

"There was still a whiff of tear gas floating around when we entered the courtyard that was surrounded by spider holes," he said. "My men were pulling enemy soldiers out of these holes when my company gunny sergeant and two young Marines came to the flagpole, tore down the Vietcong flag and ran up the Stars and Stripes. Well, first of all, the old gunny looked up and just literally burst into tears. But here I think the greater phenomenon is, here bullets are still cracking around, and all sorts of things are going on. And out of the windows of the capital building where Marines are still clearing rooms, there is this tremendous cheer, you know, that you could hear over the sounds of battle and everything else."

But there was a complication. "I had told my superior officers about our flag," Christmas said, "and was told it was their understanding that we were not supposed to raise American flags over Vietnamese buildings. I was told to 'do it quickly.' Well, we did it and later that evening a young officer arrived with instructions that the flag should come down.

"My position at that time, and I guess I was being a bit ornery, was the fact that the flag would fly until we went into the attack the next day. And then and only then, when the last Marine left the compound, that the flag would come down. Well, I remember the young officer saying something about my bucking authority. I offered him this: He had the right to go out and take the flag down, but I didn't guarantee his safety from the 350 Marines that were in the complex. Well, I guess discretion was the better part of valor. He decided to leave us. We did take the flag down the next morning and of course continued the attack."

Wounded Marines were desperately dragged to safety across the rubble of destroyed buildings, the black body bags of their dead buddies thrown on any vehicle moving to the rear. These were unique scenes in a war already lasting years. In talking about the heavy Marine casualties in the Hue fighting, Christmas said, "There were many casualties, but I think you have to put that in perspective. Combat in a built-up area is a great casualty producer to begin with. Our casualties as far as wounded were concerned were extremely high. When a mortar round or recoilless rifle round strikes a building you not only have the shrapnel effect but also have a tremendous debris effect and many of our Marines were killed or wounded very strictly by debris. The number of killed in action interestingly enough were not that high considering the size of the force that we were against. There were a tremendous amount of wounded, and I know you've seen all the pictures of it, of Marines being evacuated. I think the thing to remember about that and put it into proper perspective, is that, what we did, we used a lot of makeshift ways of getting our wounded back to the medical people. I know that Life magazine had a very poignant picture of a tank loaded with wounded Marines going back to the battalion aid station. And I knew it looked very dramatic and horrible, but that was a very quick way of moving these casualties back. The battalion aid station was never more than two bocks behind you, at least on the southern part of the city."

Christmas and his men were not briefed on what was going on in the Citadel in the northern part of the city. It was strictly a South Vietnamese show. It was his understanding that there had been good fighting on the Vietnamese 9th Infantry Division's part, and they were able to drive the enemy about three-quarters of the way out of the Citadel a few days earlier until they were driven back again. Christmas's company had helped clear the south side, and by now the Vietnamese decided they needed assistance in the Citadel. Task Force X-ray started bringing up the first companies of the 5th Marines to fight in the Citadel, and his company was one of them.

Christmas said, "On the night of February 11, I was given the mission of crossing and holding the only bridge left of the several that crossed the Yang Foo canal to the southeast wall of the Citadel. It was the Dong

Ba bridge. We had an awful lot of trouble in getting and holding the bridge. What was left of a North Vietnamese regiment was on the other side. We used white phosphorus mortar rounds followed by eight to 12 high-explosive shells, and the enemy quickly put his head down. We literally ran an entire company across the bridge in double time, and got to the other side and took positions quickly. We drove the enemy off a square block area and then held it for an entire evening. Quite frankly, that was one of the worst evenings I ever spent in the city because I was very scared and I don't think there was any else with us who wasn't."

On Friday the 13th of February, Christmas's unit struck out again across the canal bridge. "I figured Friday might be unlucky," he acknowledged. They were attacking on the flank of the Hue Railway Station and going through the rail yards. "We didn't realize we were overrunning a Vietcong base camp, and as other of our units were pushing up along the canal invariably we ended up in the middle of it. I moved forward through a graveyard and I looked over as a Vietcong soldier jumped up maybe 75 meters away from behind a gravestone and let fly with a B-40 rocket that landed behind me."

His leg was shattered, he said, "and I rolled over into a foxhole to find myself in company with a dead North Vietnamese soldier. My troops picked me up and moved me to the side of a building where they lay me down. But then—this is something I'll take with me my whole life—as mortar shells started coming in and there was nothing I could do. The mortars were walking towards me, the explosions getting closer, and I couldn't move and I got hit a couple of times. But then my radio operator and my gunny sergeant just dove on top of me and laid on top as these mortars came through and I took a few more wounds. Fortunately, they weren't wounded—and I will take that with me, the camaraderie total, the feeling of brotherhood and the total esprit that Marines have for one another. They never leave one of their own, and it is something very special to be a Marine."

Captain Myron C. Harrington was commander of Delta Company, 1st Battalion, 5th Marine regiment, that went into Hue with about 120 men. He said, "It was very well seasoned. I had been in Vietnam six months and had taken over the rifle company a few weeks earlier.

We spent two or three days operating with the 2nd Battalion of the 5th in the southern part of Hue when we got the word to join our parent battalion inside the Citadel. The communist forces had not bothered to take appropriate defense positions along the Perfume River where it bent back towards the Citadel. We moved downriver, crossed the river on Navy landing craft and maneuvered to a loading dock at the back of the Citadel. When we disembarked I was again struck by the visible carnage: houses blown apart and civilians laying in the gardens and out in the streets.

"We came in, and our mission was specifically to clear the southeast portion of the Citadel. It was an area about a thousand meters wide in frontage, and about two thousand meters deep. It was a rather a compact area that we were assigned, but you have to keep in mind that this was very densely populated. There were a lot of small houses and buildings crowded very close together, a lot of heavy vegetation, trees, scrub, shrubbery hedgerows. . . . And what made this very difficult of course was that the North Vietnamese were able to camouflage and fortify their positions and to provide a great amount of resistance as we moved in. They had been able to move into the city over a period of several days perhaps even weeks and stage their equipment, their weapons, and develop supply points inside the city. They were able to reconnoiter the whole area and find out where they were going to put their fighting positions in the event they would have to defend themselves."

Still, he said, "I don't think they expected they'd have to defend the city. I think they thought that perhaps if they took it over, the fact that it was the ancient capital and that it had such historical significance to the people of South Vietnam, perhaps that there would be a reluctance to go in and try to rout them out of the city."

Harrington's company moved into the Citadel to rejoin the 1st Battalion. His first thought was, "You know, look at this place. It was almost total devastation. . . . I think my most vivid memory was when I was talking with one of the other company commanders who had already been participating the battle, and he just frightened the hell out of me in telling me how bad it was. He told me of a fortified position along the wall that for two days the battalion had been trying to take, and

I thought in my mind right then and there that, you know, here I am with a fresh company, and I knew without being told that my mission the next day was to take this fortified tower position along the east wall."

The key terrain feature within the Citadel that his company was required to take was a part of the massive stone and brick wall 30 feet high that surrounded it. At each point of the compass of the Citadel — north, east, south and west — were huge arch towers with entry roads underneath. "As we moved in towards the eastern arch tower named Dong Ba we saw there was a very heavily fortified NVA position on top, which of course was set above the rest of the immediate environment, with the city stretched below. It was very crucial that we take the high ground before we would be able to advance through the lower portion of the city. So, our critical piece of terrain was securing this arch tower in the eastern wall. "

Harrington assembled his two platoons and the command group. He decided on a frontal attack. "There was little else that could be done. We lined up and took full advantage of the debris, the houses that were blown down, the overturned vehicles, the walls, the hedgerows, the ditches, and moved into these positions prior to moving out. There was target preparation from our artillery and naval gunfire for a few minutes, a very intense amount of noise. Then we developed a control and coordination problem because one platoon commander moved to an advantage point to see the area in front of him, and his command group took an RPG round which seriously wounded the lieutenant and his radio operator and put the radio out of commission. I lost contact with the platoon but, needless to say, we continued the attack by moving Marines up to the wall. Then these Marines, super guys, began crawling along the wall to the spider holes the enemy were manning, and with accurate fire and by throwing hand grenades into the spider holes we moved our way forward towards the tower. I got to the position where we could see the tower and we could basically observe what the enemy was doing."

Harrington saw that the inner wall of the Citadel at that point was very narrow, not wide enough to put a squad of Marines up there. He sent his men up one by one. "So, I had eight to 10 Marines up on the wall maneuvering, creeping, crawling along and actually clearing these spider holes one by one as they moved towards the tower. We were at the intersection of one of the main streets of Hue, which you couldn't tell because of the devastation and debris that was all over. We were able to cross the street at this point in a platoon rush of 15 to 20 men to a position where we could now face the tower from two sides, from the north and west. We assaulted the tower and the fortified positions behind it and occupied it, which was a critical point because it would enable our response to the flanking fire against our Marines as we were trying to move to the south."

Harrington noticed that this was part of the city where the very poor lived because the wreckage of their flimsy homes was everywhere, with sheets of tin roofing scattered amidst the rubble. "You could not even see where the hut beam structures were. Then we began getting fire from the high-rise building. We utilized artillery to neutralize the fire but for several days this flanking fire caused us a lot of trouble. We took the Dong Ba tower on the afternoon of the 14th of February. The significance of that tower ranked very high for a Marine because we're always looking to take the critical terrain, the high ground, and the arch tower represented the high ground, essential for our bastion for further operations and moving the battalion down through the inner portions of the Citadel. Securing the tower was a small turning point in our operation because once we got ability to entrench ourselves on the wall the North Vietnamese could never get us off of it."

Because of the close proximity of the North Vietnamese troops and the Marines, and the fact that there were historically and culturally significant statues, relics and buildings in the Citadel area, Harrington said there was initially a reluctance to use heavy armament "to go in and destroy the city in order to save it. But as we began to take more and more casualties, the higher command realized that in order to be successful and to get the North Vietnamese out we were going to have to lift the restrictions that had been imposed earlier on us as far as our firepower was concerned. As a result, very early in the battle we were able to bring in our recoilless rifle fire, our tanks, our artillery, our naval gunfire and limited air support. Of course, we did our best to make sure that the bombs and artillery did not get purposefully called down on historically significant areas."

The casualty rate was high because of the very intense combat engagement. "In many cases," Harrington said, "we were only 15 to 20 yards away from the North Vietnamese, the enemy. We were in constant contact and in very close contact for the two weeks we were fighting them."

The Marines had become accustomed to fighting in the rice paddies and out in the jungles in Vietnam. They had not participated in combat in a built-up area since Seoul city in Korea in 1950. Harrington said, "While we do train in that type of combat, our training was not completely efficient because our experience at that time was completely zero of how we were supposed to fight this. There was no one in our battalion to my knowledge that had been in or participated in the street battles in Seoul. I know my experience was absolutely zilch as far as combat in a built-up area. So initially when we went in we did not have any real concept as to how to fight this. We knew where they were, and we knew that we just had to go in there and rout them. I think each commander out there did not mean to take unnecessary risk, and we tried to utilize our fire support to the maximum. We tried to maneuver as best we could in this very confined, limited and constrained area to ensure that we did not present the maximum target to the enemy. But regrettably when you are that close, it's that intense and you're going to suffer a fairly high casualty rate. We had 17 killed in our company and a lot of wounded. At one point I was down to 30 Marines fit to fight."

Harrington described the mood during the fighting, which included several night engagements: "For the most part, just the concerns, the tension, the apprehension, the fears that you have of knowing they have a capability of coming at you — we were very alert. I wouldn't say it was 100 percent, because you couldn't stay 100 percent all the time. But we tried to maintain maximum alert, maximum readiness throughout the battle, which of course, at the end of the battle, those that were left were, you know, emotionally drained, physically exhausted. And it took a while to recover.

"One night in Hue city we had taken a significant position, and the NVA counterattacked and of course they used tactics as we did. They laid down a heavy base of fire with mortars and rockets and drove off the squad of Marines guarding the position. I didn't realize the squad had withdrawn, and the next thing I knew is that the North Vietnamese came over this pile of rubble, charging at us, and I was right in the midst of this. It was a very quick meeting, engagement with the enemy right on top of you and you were right on top of him, and you were either quick or you were dead. That was really the way the fighting went. You had to be very alert all the time. You could not relax. They had snipers. We killed a sniper in a tree about 25 yards away from my little company command post, and we suspected he had been there for several days shooting at us. Fortunately, he was a pretty lousy shot."

Captain Harrington's Marines were generally well disciplined, he said. But one day, he had a call that there was trouble in one of his platoons that were down in strength. "When I went down, I found that two of my lance corporals were fighting. When I angrily asked what the fighting was about, one responded, 'Well skipper, I want to command this platoon and I have a senior data rank on him.' So here were two lance corporals fighting over who was going to command basically the remnants of this platoon. I think that's an indication of the fighting spirit, the determination that these young men who were totally immersed in their duty, and they wanted the responsibility. As a company commander, it made me feel good that I had this caliber of individual. I had officers and staff, but these young Marines, corporals and sergeants, came through and performed magnificently."

Yet even in combat, in the heat of battle, you sometimes get concerned about little things, Harrington noted. "We had found a stray puppy, obviously only a few weeks old, and of course my radio man and a couple of other Marines and the command group adopted the little puppy and we took care of him. It was a great diversion for us in the early part of the battle. And then one day, for no obvious reason, the puppy died. He had been eating the food we had been eating and drinking the water we had been drinking. And we got very concerned about knowing why this puppy all of a sudden died. We got to thinking that maybe the enemy were using some kind of poisonous gas that was in the water we were drinking; so, we picked up the little carcass and put it in an ammo can and sent it back to the battalion aid station to have it examined. They sent back a message that said, 'Don't worry about the puppy, and get on with the battle.'"

He was asked his opinion of the South Vietnamese soldiers. "From the company commander's viewpoint, it appeared to me that the cooperation and coordination with the South Vietnamese was there. On numerous occasions, we used their artillery to support our attacks. Initially, we used some of their command structures set up by the Vietnamese 1st Infantry Division, located in the northeast corner of the Citadel, which along with the American advisory compound in the southern part of Hue were the only locations not taken by the communist attackers in the first attacks. As we moved down the Citadel wall the South Vietnamese were on the other side trying to clear out the enemy who were causing us considerable difficulty." He said there were several-story buildings that let the enemy fire down on his Marines as they moved along the wall trying to get to the arch tower. "As we were restricted to basically doing a frontal attack and as we moved through an area, the Vietnamese picked up the responsibility for our rear area security. In my particular case, I had no difficulty with the South Vietnamese forces."

And his assessment of the North Vietnamese soldier? "I would have to say that during the battle for the city, the North Vietnamese soldier was an extremely tenacious fighter. He did not flee and run when the Marines came in. He held his ground. He was well indoctrinated. He knew what his mission was. I think the indoctrination they go through is probably very intense. And I think they probably had this emotional attachment to the fact that they had liberated the ancient capital of Vietnam and they saw this as a great crusade. They were going to perhaps assist in reunifying the country because they had occupied the Citadel. So, I think there was an intense amount of dedication on their part. I think I would have to say that they were courageous fighters because they inflicted severe harm to our command, to the Marines. So, I think they fought very well."

Harrington believed that part of the communists' grand strategy was to capture and hold Hue to influence peace talks if they ever material-ized. "I don't think they were every going to give it up even if we had surrounded them on all sides and cut them off and tried to starve them out. We would eventually have to go in and dig them out, which is what we did. When you were fighting against a North Vietnamese soldier you were fighting against crack soldiers. And I think our Marines acquitted themselves really well. I think we ruined their battle plan when we went house-to-house, room-by-room. As bloody a fight as this conflict was, I think we were victorious because of our aggressiveness, our willingness to dig them out and to go in house-by-house and room-by-room."

The weather was also a factor in Marine tactics. "This was during the seasonal monsoon period in the northern part of South Vietnam, so during this whole battle it was very wet, drizzly, and it was very cold. And when I say very cold, for Vietnam it was very cold—probably in the 40s or low 50s (Fahrenheit). The sun was not shining; so that it put a chill on you, and there was a very low cloud ceiling, which made the whole area looked so dull and gray. The smoke rising from the battle gave a kind of eerie look to it. The weather had a significant effect on us primarily because it was wet, cold and overcast with low ceilings, which meant that air support was very difficult to obtain. It hindered our total coordination of our air-ground concept of Marine operations in that we would not be able to use air so much, and this did hamper our ground operations a little bit."

Harrington and his staff were also challenged by the potential for looting. "You can imagine, when these store fronts would be blown out, that there were all these items laying around, the young Marines would naturally gravitate to these, and we did have some small problems there. But the commanders for the most part kept strict control, and you can control it. A Marine had his pack, you can't put a whole lot in a pack. And I think that some of the stories that came out, that the Marines were looting and carrying away all sorts of things, were unfounded. Yes, we did pick up food in the streets, for example, because our resupply was having difficulty getting food in. So, when we could get food, we took the food, and when we found blankets and things of this nature that would make our life a little bit more comfortable, we took these items. But we took nothing of substantial value, and I know, for example in my company, we had a shakedown prior to leaving the area to ensure that none of the Marines were walking out with anything of cultural or historical significance to the city. But it was a problem, and we had to pay strict attention to that. But I think that the biggest problem in fighting in the city was of course communications control and coordination."

Hue was a major story for the American press, causing concern to both President Johnson and General Westmoreland who worried about the impact on American public opinion. But Harrington said, "My views are very much in a positive vein. I was very impressed with the professionalism of the press that was with me. As the battle kind of flowed, the press moved up from the southern side and over to the northern portion of the Citadel and joined us. Initially in the first four or five days we were there we did not see many of the press because of the intensity of the battle, but when things got to a more normal state, so to speak, they came on many occasions. I was very impressed not with the foolhardiness of these individuals but with their intense amount of dedication as they tried to cover the story. Many of them exhibited a great deal of personal courage, I thought, by just being so close, and they were. I had two reporters who were wounded. I think most of them were very fair, very descriptive in depicting the battle and honest in their reporting. I really don't have any complaints. I was very impressed with them."

The Citadel was finally captured on January 24. Harrington said, "The taking of the imperial palace grounds was left to the South Vietnamese armed forces. I think there was a political decision that was made here that said, 'Look, it's our ancient city. We want to recapture the Citadel. We appreciate what you Americans have done for us, but it would just look better in the eyes of the world and our people if would could get in there and do it.' And that's my feeling of probably what transpired. We were not asked to support their attack from our fight positions, to participate in the taking of the palace grounds itself. A Vietnamese unit went in and was able to retake that with very little difficulty in the latter stages of the battle, and they raised their flag to its rightful place over the main Citadel gate."

Harrington later reflected on the role of his unit in the fight for Hue: "I think all of us who had come through the battle had a great sense of achievement. I think that we realized, because of the intense amount of press coverage that we had gotten during the battle, that it was a significant one that would go down perhaps as one of the most significant battles of the Vietnam War. I think the fact that we had done well and accomplished our mission gave us a great sense of pride and satisfaction in doing the job. And of course, we were very tired because of our ordeal. It had been something like 36 days, I think it was, that I had not had a bath, so it was good when we could go down to the Perfume River—which was not perfumed, to say the least—and take a bath. It was a great feeling of relief that we had survived this battle. And a great sense of pride and satisfaction in the achievement of these young Marines that accomplished this task."

Both Captain Myron C. Harrington and Captain George R. Christmas, who were interviewed at length for this book, received Navy Cross medals for their bravery and leadership during the battle of Hue. Captain Christmas remained in the Marines for 34 years, attaining the rank of lieutenant general. Fifty-three Marines died in the Hue fighting and 380 were wounded. The South Vietnamese had 213 killed and 879 wounded. Around 2,000 North Vietnamese and Vietcong soldiers were estimated to have been killed.

It was left for the South Vietnamese authorities to come to terms with the war's brutality. Military historian Lieutenant Colonel Pham Van Son wrote, "The battle of Hue lasted 26 days. It was the bloodiest and most destructive battle in the offensive. This was true not only of the fighting but also because of the mass murders by the communists. The whole city was marked by the passage of death. No house was left untouched by the war. The Vietcong, when they had the opportunity, used the people as if they were operating in territory they occupied in the countryside. They called people from their homes for 'political study' meetings, classified them into categories—civil servants, soldiers, police and just plain civilians. Except for the last category, all the people summoned were detained overnight at the government delegate's office on the right bank of the Perfume River. They were allowed to go home next morning. People speculated that the enemy was starting a three-stage mass arrest and murder scheme.

"A more serious situation existed in the Gia Hoi area which was under even firmer enemy control, and they succeeded in carrying out all three stages of the scheme," the historian wrote. "First, they sealed off the occupied area, herding the people together and classifying them into categories. The just plain citizen category was told to form civic organizations. This process was designed to have the enemy keep tight control over the populace. Each of the organizations had a representative to take orders from the enemy. These plain citizens were told to continue to work normally and to keep public order. Then enemy troops and agents came to each house confiscating all private radios in an apparent effort to cut the people off from the outside world. At the same time, they spread the word that the entire Thua Thien province and the whole country had come under their control. In the next step, they called on all government employees, such as public servants, soldiers and police, to surrender their individual weapons and report to their military place of duty in order to benefit from clemency measures. Those failing to comply would face serious measures. Large numbers of such people turned themselves and their weapons in to the communists and were allowed to return and stay home for two days. None were forced to do anything, and the enemy's move was apparently designed to deceive the public.

"The third stage was the actual mass arrest and terror drive against these former employees of the local government. After two days of having been freed people were asked to attend political meetings by the enemy cadre men who came to their homes afterwards and took some away. A number of people never came back or were never heard of again. The number of missing increased with each passing day. These people had been murdered somewhere in the city after attending the political meetings. They had never suspected they would meet tragic death nor were they aware at the time they were going to die."

Pham Van Son's history continued: "Survivors and enemy agents captured later in the war recounted that the victims had been told to dig air raid trenches during the daytime then they were led to them in the right to be massacred by machine-gun fire or simply buried alive. It was doubtful that they ever believed they were digging their own graves. Some victims were murdered and shoved into graves as soon as they finished them. They had been public servants, soldiers and those who had experienced personal feuds with pro-communist elements during the local political disturbance of previous years. Major mass graves were later found at the Gia Hoi high school, the Tang Quang Tu pagoda, The Bai Dau area, with 30 mass graves, and at the tomb of Emperor Tu Duc, where 20 mass graves were found. The bodies recovered from these and other mass grabs showed evidence of atrocious, painful deaths. A number of bodies were headless or limbless or both. Others had their hands tied behind their backs. Still others were tied together in groups of 10 or 15, indicating that the victims had been shoved into mass graves and buried alive.

"Among the victims were three West German doctors at the Hue medical school, and the wife of one of them. They had come to Vietnam to teach at the Hue University under a technical aid program. They had been abducted on the first day of the Tet Offensive, and their bodies were not found until spring. Vietnamese officials killed during the battle included the Hue deputy mayor, Tran Dinh Phuong, who was murdered right in front of his home, his body eventually buried there eight days later. The public prosecutor of the Thua Thien provincial court, Major Buu Thanh, was abducted and never heard from again. His son was also led away while pleading for the release of his father.

"Witnesses in Hue recounted that in the early stages of the occupation enemy troops were forbidden to violate people's property. Some of them even provided food to the people, using captured Vietnamese military trucks to carry rice from government warehouses to each home on the third day of Tet as a gift from the People's Liberation Army. This symbolic gift on the part of the enemy was aimed at winning the friendship of the local people. Apparently, it achieved its objectives with some naïve people. The behavior and policies of the enemy in the later stages of the occupation, resulting in the losses of innumerable civilian lives and great amounts of private property, served as a brutal warning."

"What was left in the path of war were scenes of sickening, almost irreparable destruction. The city was virtually reduced to rubble. Emaciated, haggard people wandered around, aimless and bewildered. The evidence of the huge loss in human lives was seen on housewives and children in their white mourning turbans as they roamed the streets shopping for meager, cheap food. Or they scrambled amidst the rubble looking for whatever might be useful. It was feared the people of Hue might starve since surface roads were still unsafe and airlifts were difficult and almost impossible due to adverse weather conditions. Sometimes cloud cover was down to 300 meters.

"Thievery and looting were widespread. War victims stole from their fellow sufferers. All deserted houses were emptied of everything usable from kitchen utensils to furniture and valuables. Robbed victims sought to steal from others. Many houses displayed scribbled signs saying 'occupied house,' the signs designed to discourage prospective thieves. Some 80 percent of the city's houses and buildings were destroyed or damaged in the battle."

The military historian went on: "The quarter-mile square Imperial Palace suffered extensive damage. The stately Ngo Mon Gate, which took several rounds of canon fire, threatened to collapse. Its roof was badly torn. The gold plate throne in the palace was intact but the other pieces of furniture in the Imperial Hall were broken, or knocked down among the debris on the floor. Most of the precious Chinese vases, which were several centuries old, were broken or reduced to pieces by the blast waves of artillery explosions and bombings. The Citadel's three square miles was practically left in shambles. The main Nguyen Thanh street and adjoining areas were only an indiscriminate mass of rubble. The tall walls of the Citadel were torn in several places.

"The civilian battle casualties, excluding those missing or buried alive by the enemy, were the highest in the city's history: 944 civilians were killed and 784 wounded. Some 4,456 civilian houses were totally destroyed, and 3,360 damaged by more than 50 percent."

Some estimates indicate as many as 3,000 people, including government officials, soldiers on leave, anti-communist intellectuals and others, were murdered by the communists in Hue. Bui Tin, a former communist colonel who was a high-ranking official with the North Vietnamese government during the war, wrote in his autobiography published in 2002 that, "The Hue massacres did happen, and the mass graves found there after the Tet Offensive were real. General Tran van Quang who commanded the B5 front (covering Quang Tri and Thua Thien provinces) was later reprimanded for letting that happen. As far as I know, there was no order from above demanding the mass extermination of prisoners of war or of civilians. Our battle discipline was clearly delineated and it was strictly forbidden to beat up, kill or verbally abuse prisoners of war."

20

THE SIEGE OF KHE SANH

I ADJUSTED MY STEEL COMBAT HELMET and pulled tightly on the chinstrap, looking across the airstrip to a loadmaster putting the finishing touches
on a freight shipment. He was signaling he was getting ready for us to
join seven tons of ammunition on a U.S. Air Force C-123A bound for
the embattled Marine combat base of Khe Sanh. I pulled a heavy flak
jacket over my khaki clothing and straightened up, ready to rush to the
transport plane revving up to begin its journey. The C-123A aircraft
used on the dangerous Khe Sanh run were formally named "Providers"
but the aircrews that braved the uniquely perilous daily resupply runs
stoically nicknamed the aircraft "mortar magnets" or "rocket bait." All
of the planes as they approached and departed Khe Sanh were without
exception shot up, some with dozens of holes. Several had been shot
down, or destroyed on the ground. I zipped up my flak jacket as the call
came to board, and we clambered into the aircraft's cavernous interior.
From a distance, my colleague photographer Koichi Sawada of UPI
and me, the only passengers, may have looked like Marines going into
battle, and we were indeed headed in that direction. But we were not
Marines but wire service staffers carrying not M-16 rifles but cameras.

It was early afternoon of February 29, 1968, as our aircraft gained
height and leveled off at around 8,000 feet, the gray-green mountainous countryside below stretching from the South China Sea to Laos.
These resupply flights were necessary to save Khe Sanh from falling to

a communist North Vietnamese siege, already in its 40th day, with no end in sight. The Associated Press reporter I was relieving, Lewis M. Simons, had told me earlier in Danang that the 6,000 Marines and supporting Vietnamese rangers, concealed in fortified bunkers or manning trench lines at Khe Sanh, were anxiously awaiting "the big one." That simple phrase denoted the long-predicted massive assault against the base by several thousands of North Vietnamese regular troops. They were believed to be intent on a battlefield success against the United States to match their decisive victory over French forces at Dien Bien Phu 14 years earlier, a battle that ended the war.

Khe Sanh was being pounded daily by heavy guns hidden in caves in the Co Roc Ridge across the border in Laos, with the 130 mm and 152 mm artillery pieces routinely emerging briefly to fire and then retreating into their hiding places behind doors of steel. At about 15 miles from Khe Sanh, they were beyond the range of American guns. The heaviest Marine ordnance in Khe Sanh were the 155 mm artillery pieces that had a range of only nine miles, and were thus unable to counterfire. The complete encirclement of the combat base by enemy forces in the ridgelines of the Khe Sanh valley also allowed gunners concealed in the heavy jungle and forests to hammer the vulnerable Marines with persistent mortar and rocket fire, along with machine-gun and small-arms bullets. The cargo our transport plane was carrying, boxed up and stacked in nets at the rear of the plane, included artillery and mortar shells, always in dire need at Khe Sanh to counter the communist ground forces moving ever closer.

The loadmaster warned us 20 minutes into the flight that our arrival would be hairy, and it would begin within a few minutes. He said with alarming detail, "There is no safe corridor for aircraft and we will be subject to heavy fire from small arms, 12.7 heavy machine guns and larger caliber anti-aircraft cannons. To survive, it means speed and precision. Just follow my instructions." I'd been at Khe Sanh before. So had Sawada. But experience was meaningless when your safety depends on maybe outrunning an exploding mortar shell.

At around 5,000 feet with the pockmarked red clay surface of Khe Sanh ahead of us, our pilot pushed the C-123A's nose down on a steep dive, the two pod-mounted auxiliary jet engines roaring with the strain, the aircraft's flaps extended. I resisted an urge to vomit and watched the tangled vegetation of the valley floor approach rapidly. Then our aircraft lifted up and landed at the east end of the airstrip on the nearly two-mile square plateau 300 feet above the valley floor that was home to the Khe Sanh base. Our plane taxied towards the unloading zone at the west end of the airstrip and slowed down but did not stop rolling, even as the cargo doors were opened and the loadmaster pushed out the ammunition boxes that were conveniently riding steel rollers attached to the aircraft's floor. He yelled to us, "Time to go." And as I made my way to the opening, I was sure the aircraft was speeding up. I leapt and sprawled out into the red dust, as did Sawada. The C-123A's auxiliary jet engines were still roaring. I saw it turning on to the airstrip and suddenly saw it airborne. I figured later that time on the ground in total for the aircraft was less than one minute. I heard shouting and the cry, "Get your asses over here," as thunderous explosions marched down the airstrip. Mortars. I dashed towards an unshaven Marine as he was pointing to a shell crater about 30 yards distant. Sawada beat me to it, even though he was carrying heavy camera gear. I sprawled in on top of him.

The paroxysm of mortar and rocket fire tailed off as the sky over Khe Sanh cleared of aircraft for the time being. I raised my head from the trench to see what the Marines were now calling "sandbag city," and watched soldiers quickly unpacking the ammo cargo we had arrived with, shouldering the smaller cases and heading to the underground storage bunkers. Six weeks earlier, the Khe Sanh combat base had been a neatly laid out military community with comfortably prefabricated regimental mess halls, an extensive field medical center, petrol, oil and lubrication areas, and a construction battalion headquarters, all above ground. A massive, unexpected communist artillery, mortar and rocket attack in the early hours of January 21 had destroyed most of the structures, exploded the huge ammunition dump, and signaled the beginning of the siege.

By now, everything of value was underground with the exception of the vital Marine air tactical control tower that stood sentinel beside the airstrip, a large white "Welcome to Khe Sanh" sign painted on the red metal paneling below the glassed-in observation windows. Its lower level was dressed in rows of sandbags, some shredded by shrapnel. The wreckage from the disintegrated surface buildings that I had seen on my earlier visit had disappeared, salvaged by Marines to better fortify their makeshift bunkers dug into the red soil next to the trench lines that circled the base. We saw that even the tanks were half buried in protective sandbags, as were the artillery batteries.

Sawada and I made a dash for the hospitable bunker of the Seabee squad from the 32nd Naval Construction Regiment that had been in place in Khe Sanh for most of the past year, its primary mission to keep the airstrip open. It had voluntarily undertaken another mission, the care and feeding of the journalists who arrived shaken and scared from the journey in. The Seabee bunker was deep and by Khe Sanh standards comfortable, with a few available cots and military C-rations to nibble on, and relaxing Marines to chat with. It's most attractive feature was a high ceiling under six feet of rock and steel sheeting, supported by heavy wooden beams, and believed impervious to any incoming shells other than those fired by the big Russian-made artillery behemoths buried in the caves of the Co Roc Ridge in Laos.

By late afternoon, the fog was returning to shroud Khe Sanh in a spectral light, limiting the visibility of the vigilant enemy snipers along the ridge lines and allowing outside activity to speed up. A Seabee near me yawned, and I followed him outside. He mounted a battered bulldozer, one of the few operating machines in the whole camp, and set off to deepen a command bunker near the trench lines. I walked beside an accompanying Marine whose job it was to alert the driver, deafened by his own machinery, whenever he heard the whistle of an incoming shell. The signal was for his companion to dive to earth, to be immediately followed by the driver. But on this trudge, there was no incoming.

That evening we dined on combat rations around a rough wooden table deep in the bunker with some of the Seabees. These institutional military "C-Rations" sustained all of Khe Sanh for the whole siege. I chose a box labeled turkey loaf from a stack in the corner and opened a small can and ate it cold, with cheese crackers for desert. Our Seabee hosts entertained us with military food folklore, including ingenious ways of adding variety to the half dozen or so menus available at the time. One tossed a can at me labeled ham and lima beans and said, "have some ham and motherfucker," a military-wide derisive description of one of the more unpopular food items. Another suggested a can of "beans and baby dicks" or as the label read, beans and frankfurter chunks in tomato sauce.

There was little time to digest the food. Lieutenant Junior Grade Martin J. Kux came down the bunker stairs with a flash message sent a few minutes earlier to the embattled combat base from the 3rd Marine Division headquarters at Phu Bai. Unit commanders were told to pass on the word. "We will be hit with heavy enemy artillery fire at 9 p.m.," Lieutenant Kux told his Seabee detachment. "This will be followed by a heavy ground attack. Take this very seriously; this is the first time we have received a flash of this nature."

Seabees were proud of their motto, "We Build and We Fight," earned in exemplary service in the Pacific in World War II and in Korea. In the previous three years they built much of the American base infrastructure located in the northern provinces of South Vietnam. Tonight though, it was time to fight. The several young Seabees in the bunker pulled on their steel helmets, clasped their M-16s and crouched down. Two hours to wait. A Seabee spoke up, "There's 6,000 of us, 40,000 of them. Let's kill our seven each and go back to bed." No one laughed. Then Lieutenant Kux telephoned the bunker to say the base had gone on red alert, meaning that the enemy troops were massing. The Seabees fell silent. Beyond the thinly sandbagged trench lines of Khe Sanh, red and white lights bobbed down a ridgeline visible through a curtain of mist, indicating the communist troops were moving in. "God, they don't even care about being seen," a Seabee sentry said as I peered into the night beside him.

We learned that Marine intelligence was postulating that the 66th Regiment of the 304th Peoples' Army infantry division, the lead North Vietnamese element in the victorious battle of Dien Bien Phu, was preparing to mount an attack on the most vulnerable outfit at Khe Sanh, the 37th South Vietnamese Ranger Battalion that was manning trench lines at the east end of the air strip. Overrunning that unit would allow the communists to spill their forces into the heart of Khe Sanh. In the evening before I arrived, communist sappers had slipped through the darkness and prepared the battlefield in advance, cutting holes in the barbed wire defenses of the Vietnamese rangers and removing mines and trip flares. Fortunately, their preparations were detected the next morning.

By mid-evening not only the whole base was on alert but so too was an American war machine code-named "Operation Niagara" by General Westmoreland — so called, he said, "to invoke the image of cascading shells and bombs. The key to Khe Sanh is firepower." The first part of Niagara was a comprehensive intelligence-collection effort by recon airplanes, radio intercepts and electronic sensors. Part two involved carefully coordinated around-the-clock shelling and bombing by all available aircraft and artillery — Air Force, Navy and Marine — and unquestioned priority on B-52 strikes. Westmoreland said he slept in a cot in the Combat Operations Center of his headquarters in Saigon so that he would be immediately at hand for any decision that had to be made on targets and troop deployment. Over the previous 40 days of Khe Sanh's siege, Operation Niagara was crucial. Its computerized targeting centers in support bases, and the available aircraft on alert in a dozen airfields in Vietnam and in the Pacific areas where the mighty B 52 super fortress bombers were on call, delivered massive firepower to destroy all direct threats to the men President Johnson was publicly calling "my boys," the embattled defenders of Khe Sanh. Niagara became known as the heaviest artillery/air support ever given to ground forces.

As the Marines hunkered down in the trench lines and bunkers in Khe Sanh anxiously awaited the predicted attack, so did officials in Washington, D.C., worry, aware that the drawn-out siege was alarming an increasing number of Americans. President Johnson was reportedly more preoccupied with the fate of the distant combat base than any previous battle of the Vietnam war, openly fretting with worry over Khe Sanh. He had a terrain model of the combat base set up in an annex of the situation room, with a large aerial map on the wall. Wire service photographs showed him poring over the model as he discussed tactics with his military aides. When he was in the Oval Office, the president used his switch console to view three large television screens, each tuned to a major television network. There were wire service tickers from AP,

UPI and Reuters in an annex where he kept up with breaking news. He told journalists in the early days of the siege that the Joint Chiefs of Staff had promised him never to let Khe Sanh fall, to never let it become "an American Dien Bien Phu."

In an interview after the war, General Westmoreland told me, "I do not know if President Johnson gave a direct order to hold Khe Sanh as specific as that. But I made it clear that I had no intention of doing anything else. I don't remember receiving any orders to hold it. I assumed from the president's interest that he expected it to be held, and I assured him that it would be. I think the communists had two purposes in mind. One was a military purpose and one was a psychological purpose, which was associated with political connotations all connected with public attitudes in the United States. The military objective was to outflank our defenses south of the demilitarized zone and move down into populated areas and connect with their force that infiltrated Hue. The psychological objective was to render a defeat — a spectacular defeat, such as Dien Bien Phu — and I believe they planned it as a repetition of Dien Bien Phu, and they were sufficiently self-confident to believe they could defeat us with the same strategy."

The other side seemed eager for battle. This message was intercepted as it was aired to North Vietnamese army soldiers late February: "The Marines can be defeated. It is important that we keep our strength. Remember you are here to fight. You are the chosen ones. Remember your comrades who have fallen on past days. They must be avenged. You are equipped to fight the invaders. The Marines will not stand up to your might. Soldiers of the free republic, you have been blessed with the honor of running the invaders from our brothers' land."

I waited with Sawada in the Seabee bunker for "the big one" as the minutes ticked by, and weighed the professional opportunity to score a major news coup as against the possibility of not living to tell the tale. Then the action began, almost on schedule. But the first salvos were fired not by the North Vietnamese but by the Marine combat bases' several batteries of howitzers and mortars and recoilless rifle canons. Shells roared over our bunker on the way to enemy lines, the harsh sounds barely muffled by our thick protective roof. We would learn later that camouflaged electronic sensors, unobtrusively distributed in the brush and jungle surrounding the base to detect movement, had indicated an assembly point where large numbers of enemy troops were gathering. It was that target that drew the fiery attention of Khe Sanh's defensive weaponry. But the communist assault troops were already on their way, and at 9:30 that night they revealed themselves in a furious assault.

In his red dirt, shoulder-deep trench on a knoll in the southeastern perimeter, Captain Walter Gunn, a lantern-jawed, rangy U.S. Marine advisor, clung to the earth as he and the Vietnamese soldiers beside him came under a rain of rocket and mortar fire. Communist sappers were attempting to crash through the outer barbed wire defenses while the defenders kept their heads down. As rockets flying red tails whirled into the base, Captain Gunn and the defenders began responding with machine-gun and rifle fire, and assumed that the main attack would soon follow as a North Vietnamese infantry battalion maneuvered behind the attacking sappers. They were slugging it out bullet for bullet. Then heavy enemy shelling was hitting across the base, with direct artillery fire hitting Marines' lines in the northeast corner, killing five Marines. A mortar shell slammed into the six-foot-deep rock roof of our Seabee bunker with a crash but hardly scarred it. Within 15 minutes, while the communist sappers were still trying to crawl through the outer-most wire defenses, Westmoreland's Niagara arrived, flooding the North Vietnamese assembly areas with napalm and high explosive bombs that were radar-directed from Marine and Navy warplanes. A nine-aircraft flight of B-52 Stratofortress on a mission further north was redirected to Khe Sanh, each air plane unloading its 35-ton bomb payload within a mile of the combat base. The thunderous, earthshaking explosions shook dirt from our bunker's ceiling and I felt momentarily deafened.

The red alert was canceled at 2 a.m. The communist attackers did not even breech the wire, so fierce was the firepower response to their actions. The whole base seemed to relax with a collective sigh. The "big one" did not happen this night, but the worrying amongst the beleaguered defenders of Khe Sanh would not end and until the siege was lifted.

For the Marine "grunts," the foot soldiers in the trench lines carved into Khe Sanh's red dirt, there was no real respite from the tension. Private

James Hebron was aged 18 on the perimeter line in the early weeks of the Khe Sanh siege. "One of the problems of being a grunt in Vietnam was that people back home knew a lot more of what was happening than we did. We just didn't have any information," he said in an interview after the war. "You get a little snag of information here and there but it just turns out to be rumor-mongering more than anything else. We heard rumors that there was anything from 20- to 80,000 enemy out there. And the truth being that any given point there were no more than four divisions or 40,000 people out there. But that's still 40,000 against 5,600 hundred Marines. That is not very welcome odds.

"I got goosebumps up and down my spine one morning and said, 'Oh Jesus,' when I looked behind me and, lo-and-behold, they were putting barbed wire behind my position. I've never seen anything like that even in a John Wayne movie; I thought that was really freaky. It meant one of two things. They either didn't trust us to dig our trenches deep enough or else they expected us to get overrun. And neither thing was geared to make you feel very confident in your ability to survive the next couple of days. I remember Lieutenant Colonel J.F. Wilkinson came around the trenches and asked anybody if they needed anything, food or anything like that. And if I seem, well, melodramatic in hindsight, a bunch of us got together and we swore oaths up and down that none of us would ever leave the trench alive, a heroic kind of nonsense I guess but we all believed it. And we all felt that this is it, you know. We all pulled out our grenades and put them on a shelf in the trench and waited. We did not quite know what we were waiting for. But we expected a massive invasion.

"The thing that helped us of course was air power, and the really tremendous B-52 raids. You couldn't see the airplanes so high in the sky. All you saw was that when the bombs exploded the air was ripped apart and the earth trembled under you and you were bouncing in the air. The closest were a few hundred yards from our line. So, the trench would shake and the sand bags would come lose, and there would be this tremendous vibration. I think that morale was surprisingly good. And it was great to be the center of attention. We saw newsmen walking around and we thought, 'Hell, we have got to be safe now.'"

Jimmy Bryant, a Marine from New York City, recalled in an interview after the war the pressures faced in the crude bunker life: "It was five Marines to my bunker and we shared it with large rats. They actually owned Khe Sanh. We were just roomers there. Some of them were very large. I have seen rats in New York where I was from, but I had never seen them as big as they were out there. When I first arrived on the line, my buddies told me how to sleep. You took a blanket and you tucked it in starting from your feet. Tuck your feet in completely then run up your side, tucking all the way. Then you laid your weapon across your chest and you flapped the back of the blanket and you pulled it in. That way you were like in a cocoon. And you slept like that. A guy didn't do it the first night he was there. He refused to sleep with his face covered, and a rat jumped him and bit a chunk out of his face. After that they never had to remind me about the required sleeping routine. The rats would walk over you and you could feel them walking, and they wouldn't attack you because they didn't have a feature to go after.

"Each day," Bryant continued, "we woke up to the first incoming shells. We usually ate after the second incoming. And we would go on patrol after the third. We would be hit five or six times a day with incoming. You wouldn't know when it was coming. Some of the guys wanted out so bad that they would jump into the trench line with their feet sticking out hoping to get a piece of shrapnel to cut their leg or foot. They wanted out that bad. After I'd been there awhile I understood why some people made marks like rat bites and get cuts on their hands and take 12 treatment shots in the stomach. They would rather have that than be out in the Khe Sanh bush."

The Seabee bunker where I was made welcome was a few hundred meters but a world apart from the trench lines. A young officer from the 26th Marine Regimental headquarters came by after breakfast and we walked quickly through morning fog to the lines of the Vietnamese 37th Ranger Battalion that had fought off the attack the previous night, about 600 meters away and outside the defended Marine perimeter. North Vietnamese shelling from Laos had resumed at dawn, a routine that varied only with the numbers of rounds expended. The "whomp" of the big gun firing gave soldiers a second or two to duck. A mortar shell is signaled by its whistle the instant before it explodes. Six days earlier on February 23, the intensity of enemy shelling reached its peak, with 1,307 rounds of enemy artillery, rocket and mortar fire smashing into Khe Sanh. The sandbag defenses failed the 12 Marines who were killed in the trench lines, and the 51 who were wounded. A chance hit on an ammunition supply point destroyed nearly a ton of ammunition. Westmoreland's Niagara was effective against communist troop movements but incapable of ending the artillery duels that had begun on the first day of the siege and continued until the combat base was finally abandoned.

Captain Gunn was relaxing in the cramped underground command bunker of the Vietnamese ranger battalion with one of the officers, Lieutenant Truong Truoc. They wore triumphant smiles because of a report that the bodies of 79 communist soldiers were scattered on the small ridge outside the wire. Only a handful of rangers had suffered minor injuries. Gunn offered to take me for a walk as rangers were coming out of their bunkers, welcoming the morning with a stretch. An automatic weapon cracked from a nearby ridge. Two rangers fell seriously wounded. "That's the trouble with this place," Gunn said, scratching his chin after seeing that the wounded were rushed to the medical center. "Stand up and you get blown away."

The South Vietnamese ranger unit Gunn advised was grafted on to the American Marine lines a month earlier, apparently a political decision in Saigon because there was no allowance made for them on the primary perimeter defense trench lines manned by Marines from the 26th regiment. The North Vietnamese attackers appeared to have determined that the rangers were the weakest link in the protective chain around the combat base and constantly threatened them. Captain Gunn said communist diggers had pushed their zig-zag trench lines to within 50 yards of the perimeter wire in the preceding days of rain and fog. American attack aircraft routinely dropped napalm and 250-pound bombs on the approaching enemy, and as the previous evening proved, attacks could be beaten off. But Gunn suggested the digging would resume as soon as the enemy regrouped.

The waiting game was as damaging to the Vietnamese ranger morale as it was to the American marines, "We don't like just sitting here; it's not good for the rangers. We have to get out and fight or we're no good," said the battalion commander, Captain Huan Pho. Earlier patrolling outside the wire enabled the Vietnamese rangers to engage with the communist enemy in fighting that was much more personal to them than to the Americans. Fewer patrols were now allowed as the siege tightened on the base. "If my men stay in Khe Sanh much longer they will be demoralized, desperate," the captain said, adding that he had no liaison with his headquarters since arriving 40 days earlier. With little available water, none of his men had had a bath and their hair was growing over their ears. They didn't like American C-rations and yearned for fish and rice, which was not available. Adding to their discomfort were the communist loudspeaker appeals to the rangers to surrender, with the propaganda voices emerging from the underbrush asserting that the North Vietnamese would overrun the base and kill everyone. American advisors said most of the young rangers had a "better dead than red" attitude and had proven it with a determined defense, but agreed that morale was fading.

The use of the Khe Sanh combat base as an appetizing bait to dangle in front of an enemy believed to be seeking "an American Dien Bien Phu," as President Johnson had put it, was already under critical scrutiny as the tightening siege entered its sixth week. American firepower was indeed strikingly effective in preventing the loss of the combat base, if taking it was indeed the communist goal. But the primary American goal was to kill enough North Vietnamese troops to convincingly weaken the Hanoi government's decade-long policy of supporting the insurgency in the South Vietnam. That was not happening. Many months of furtive preparation had allowed the North Vietnamese to prepare the high, jungled ridgelines with deep bunkers and gun positions that were proving impervious to American firepower; meanwhile, neighboring Laos was host to the heavy Russian-made artillery guns daily blasting the combat base. The body count, the integral measure of American success in the war, was becoming meaningless in the face of North Vietnamese willingness to continue committing the flower of its youth to the goal of driving America from Vietnam and unifying the country.

I met with Colonel David E. Lownds, the 47-year-old commander of the 26th Marine Regiment and base commander, at his 11 o'clock morning press briefing in his concrete underground bunker. A handful of journalists were there, and Lownds was the lure that kept bringing us back to cover this dangerous place. What he offered was full access to the most gripping continuing story of the Vietnam war — as much the drama of 6,000 men surviving in the most hostile environment that distant war planners could devise, as it was about moving forward American military and political goals. The proud Marine Corps, sure of its revered place in American military history, had proven a willing host to the growing numbers of journalists in Vietnam. The numbers had increased from the handful that greeted the first Marine combat units landing on the beaches at Danang on March 8, 1965, to the several hundred media people covering the Tet Offensive. Not that many of them came to Khe Sanh. The Marines offered access but not guaranteed survival.

General Westmoreland, concerned about the emerging image of the Khe Sanh siege as a slaughterhouse, was unhappy about the freedom the Marines were giving to the press, but could do nothing to stop it. He told me in an interview after the war, "Because the visibility given in the United States by the media and particularly by television there was great consternation in Washington. The president and in turn his advisors were very much influenced by television accounts and by press accounts, because they would get the information before they would get official reports, official reports that could be evaluated and could be verified. Reports about the Khe Sanh battle in the media were quickly transmitted as events of the moment. Mr. Johnson and his advisors were concerned to the point that they over-evaluated the importance of that battle and the prospect of their being defeated there, to the point that they assembled the Joint Chiefs of Staff and wanted their assurances that it could be held. The chairman of the Joint Chiefs, General (Earle) Wheeler, called me, and I told him to tell the president not to worry about Khe Sanh, that I had no concerns about it, and if there was any mishap which I did not expect — it was my full responsibility and I took it there and then."

I had first met Colonel Lownds on a visit in January. The extreme pressures from the enemy and from his nervous high command in the weeks since then had made no discernible difference in the officer's distinctive appearance: slim, ramrod straight, with a trim moustache giving a droll cast to his appearance in combat uniform and camouflaged helmet.

Lownds' confidence and candidness were the qualities most admired by visiting reporters, as was his willingness "to shoot the breeze" when time allowed. Lownds knew of what he spoke, a veteran of World War II, when he'd been wounded both in Saipan and Iwo Jima during the legendary Marine battles, and of fighting in the Korean War. In an interview after he had retired, I asked him to compare his experiences. "Khe Sanh was unique. You ask these Marines who have had it indoctrinated into them to 'Go, go, go. You've got to be aggressive, and you've got to see your objective. Your mission is to get there, dammit. You get there, dammit; you get there and do it.' Now all of a sudden in Khe Sanh, you say to this same group, 'Your mission now is to just sit down.' Every time I'd walk the line I'd hear impatient Marines, anxious to do battle, say, 'Hey, we're going to go today, Colonel, are we going to go today?' And I'd say, 'No, you're going to stay right here.' But they made the adaptation; those young men accepted their role and they did it."

When we met with Colonel Lownds in his bunker after the attack the previous night against the Vietnamese rangers, he let us crowd around a large operational map of the Khe Sanh area, pointing out the suspected locations of the two North Vietnamese infantry divisions targeting the combat base. The mobility of the communist units, with survival skills honed during their nearly three years of heavy fighting against the much better-equipped and firepower-supported American infantry, made them elusive targets. By emerging from the tangled brush and shell-shocked terrain of the slopes of the Khe Sanh plateau, the enemy got close but not close enough to push through the perimeter wire of the base, succumbing to the blinding fury of Operation Niagara. Lownds was gratified with the outcome, but he had a caveat. "Well, last night was not their best effort. I don't believe we will get off that easy."

In an interview with Lownds 10 years later, I brought up the controversy of locating the Vietnamese rangers outside the Marines' lines. He said, "When they came in, they came in as an afterthought. I guess it was figured I needed more help. I put them in front of a Marine unit because I thought that the main attack was going to come through that area. I would have had to reshuffle my whole front line, my whole perimeter in order to fit a new unit in there. So, what I did was: OK, we'll put these people up in front there, and they were close enough that so that the Marine battalion behind them could support them with fire. Well, you know, you pay your money and you take your chances. It was not for political reasons. My thinking was I needed more strength in that particular area. They were near the end of the airstrip. I couldn't dig trench lines across the airstrip so I needed strength in case the enemy came over the top end of the airstrip and they'd hit this unit that was blocking. They did a great job."

In that same interview, I brought up General Westmoreland's criticism of Lownds' unpreparedness when the communists launched their first attacks on the combat base. He said, "I was criticized for not digging in properly when the heavy shelling began in January, but in fact we were prepared for the patrol mission I had been given, not a siege. The press quoted senior army people as saying we were not digging six-foot-deep bunkers. I approached it like an amphibious landing on a beach, which we are trained for. You dig yourself a good foxhole and then get ready to move on. Digging deep it not what you do in the initial phase of a Marine operation. You're digging and getting ready to jump off to the next objective. But when the strategy comes that you are going to stay for a set-piece battle, then you start digging deeper. Anyone that was up there saw it, it did get deeper and deeper and deeper. And every time my Marines would stop digging, we'd say dig another foot. And they'd say, 'We've already struck China. Are we going to invade or what?' — because it is so damn deep. But basically, you go with your priorities. Are you going to dig a 20-foot-deep bunker, or are you going to put protective wire and land mines out front? There has to be priorities. Priorities are set by the commander. He'll decide this particular day we're going to get wire out in front of us, and we're going to get our mines put in front of us. That means you don't lay wire and dig at the same time unless you got three hands and most of us—some people do, but most of us don't."

Sitting around drinking coffee after our briefing in his Khe Sanh bunker, I asked Colonel Lownds if he was concerned about parallels between the siege of Khe Sanh and the fate of Dien Bien Phu, considering that the same communist general, Vo Nguyen Giap, masterminded both actions. Every reporter who visited was asking him this question, and he had the patience to respond to my query. "The comparison is not a good one," he said. "We hold the high ground, which the French at Dien Bien Phu didn't. We have enough artillery and air support, and this was where the French went down. They did pretty well until the point where they lost their artillery. When they lost their artillery, they went down."

The colonel produced a letter that was written by a Frenchman who said he had fought at Dien Bien Phu. "To paraphrase, he says there is no similarity," Lownds said. "You have leaders which I feel are competent, you have artillery and you have enough sense to keep the high ground around you. I have no compunction of saying that you will be there as long as you want to." In his autobiography, "A Soldier Reports," General Westmoreland wrote that he was confident in his decision not to abandon Khe Sanh, "I asked my command historian Colonel Reamer Argo to study Dien Bien Phu and compare it to Khe Sanh. He gave a gloomy presentation saying that like other sieges in history, they failed because the defenders lost all initiative. I knew Khe Sanh was different because of our tremendous air and artillery support and the ability to move other troops into the area by air or land. Argo's presentation nevertheless stunned my staff. Deliberately getting the attention of all, I said, 'But we are not, repeat not, going to be defeated at Khe Sanh. I will not tolerate you talking or even thinking of this possibility.' Then I strode deliberately from the room."

I had noticed in my Khe Sanh visit that nearly every bunker with makeshift overhead cover along the trench lines had what looked like antennas sticking out from them, as did more stable sandbagged structures near the airstrip and around the ammo dumps and medical center. I asked Lownds about it and he laughed with pleasure. "Well, perhaps because of my personality and the way I handle problems, a lot of people figured I hadn't done my homework to handle a job like this. But I had read Bernard Fall's book on Dien Bien Phu and I'd been in hundreds of guerrilla exercises, so I figured I was prepared. I was aware that the North Vietnamese had pinpointed the French command bunkers, and they lost their command communications. Imagine what that must have meant? I noticed a week or so ago that the enemy gunners were starting to zero in on our communication antennas. So, I said: OK, they're starting to zero in on the antennas here. What do we do? So, I told a Marine go put up antennas everywhere, and he said, 'What, everywhere?' 'Everywhere, no matter what it is, as long it's above ground and shows any activity. Just put up sticks and let them guess which ones are the right ones."

As I was returning to the Seabee bunker at mid-afternoon with a Marine escort, we heard a C-123 transport plane taking off amid the crash of incoming mortar rounds. As we ducked for cover, there was a less familiar noise, the reverberating crunch of collapsing metal. We saw Seabees and other Marines racing across the airstrip where the transport plane had crashed, its nose buried in the trench lines along the southern base perimeter. Smoke was coming from the fuselage that soon began to burn with yellow flames. The crew and the handful of passengers miraculously escaped injury. But the enemy gunners who had targeted the plane were not finished. They fired in three more rounds that injured several soldiers. My escort watched the blazing aircraft as I took pictures, and he commented, "That's half a million dollars down the drain, but we saved everybody aboard, the first time we've done that in a dozen wrecks. This is fine."

Night came back to Khe Sanh along with the fog, closing its curtain over shell-pocked pathways, mounds of sandbags, rusting carcasses of downed helicopters and planes and crippled jeeps, and watchful Marine sentinels in the trench lines. In the deeper bunkers where no natural light penetrates, night and day have no meaning. The meaning down there is the thump of the incoming shells and the continuing wonder if the stout roofs can take a direct hit.

Colonel Lownds had told me that North Vietnamese sappers were tunneling closer to his perimeter, and while the encroaching trench lines were visible he was worried about underground tunnels. He pulled out a bunch of letters from people back home with ideas for locating them. The latest instrument his men were using were brass divining rods normally used for finding water. "No matter how stupid anything is—and I don't say that brass rods are stupid—we use it," said Lownds. "If some country boy from the Kentucky hills says he has a gadget that he says he used to hunt foxes with and wants to try it to find tunnels, I say, 'Go ahead, try everything.'" Lownds had read his military history and was aware that the communist Vietminh dug under a strongpoint at Dien Bien Phu and blew it up in their final stages of the battle in 1954. He suggested I visit C Company of the first battalion in the morning before the fog lifts to watch the divining rods in action.

As planned, a Marine escort dropped me off at the sandbagged company headquarters located across the airstrip from the unloading area where underground tunnels were suspected. I met Lance Corporal D.E. Ingris, a tall Missourian who, after vigorously shaking my hand, planted a steel helmet on his head, threw a flak vest over his shoulder, and stepped along the red clay slope of the company perimeter. His shoulders bent forward, he clasped two steel rods in front of him parallel to the ground and slowly moved forward. None of his buddies in nearby bunkers tittered as Ingris solemnly stepped to the right and the left. They watched intently. Ingris followed his brass rods up and down the red slope, looking for the telltale twist of the rods that might indicate a hollowing in the deep earth below that could be a tunnel. He told me that back home on his farm he could sometimes find water this way. A dozen sets of divining rods were being distributed among the Marines from a shipment sent to Khe Sanh from the United States, where Marine engineers were experimenting with them. In this most sophisticated war, the diving rod, regarded by many as a worthless gadget, had entered the inventory of the embattled Marines at Khe Sanh.

The possibility that the North Vietnamese communists who surround them in their thousands might be tunneling under this two-mile square plateau had been a constant worry for the Marines. The possibility became a fact the previous week when their worst fears were realized: An enemy rocket slashed through the wire at the northwest perimeter of the base and opened up newly dug tunnel six feet below the surface. The commander of the sector, Lieutenant Marshal "Skip" Wells, told me, "I never took that tunnel threat seriously before. We are well equipped to handle the communists in a frontal assault head on. But these tunnels, they could blow up the wire from underneath, knock out the airstrip, infiltrate men. They worry us." The tunnel uncovered by the rocket was eighteen inches wide and too small for a Marine to crawl through to investigate. It ran under the perimeter wire and toward the small road that splits the Marine trenches, "a logical place if they wanted to burrow under us to get to the airstrip just feet away," Wells said. The Marines pumped tear gas into the tunnel opening and threaded barbed wire through it.

Wells said he practiced with the brass rods over a culvert and saw that it actually worked. Searching for tunnels, he said, "We have used the rods . . . but gave up after going down around five feet, figuring we were in the wrong place. Now we know that the Vietcong are digging at least six feet underground, we will re-dig those holes." The officer said the frequent shelling of Khe Sanh ruled out the use of sensitive seismographic equipment, but his men had been crouching on the ground testing stethoscopes, and driving in engineering stakes in addition to using the divining rods.

Colonel Lownds was well aware that the security of Khe Sanh depended on the courage of Marine infantry companies holding the summits of three strategic hills outside the base, hills 881, 861 and 991. "They are the key hills. They are our eyes, and we can never lose them because they would become the enemy's eyes looking right down on us." For that reason, there was more heavy ground fighting around those hills than around the Khe Sanh combat base. I never managed to visit the hills in my reporting trips to Khe Sanh. My Associated Press colleague John T. Wheeler covered more of the Khe Sanh story than any other journalist, and wrote this piece about the Marines on Hill 881:

"Each day on much shelled Hill 881, grimy bearded Marines taunt a large North Vietnamese force surrounding them with what probably ranks as one of the most dangerous American flag-raising ceremonies in the world. Communist mortar men, always ready to fire at any sign of movement on the hill, see the tattered American flag go up on an improvised flag pole each morning and listen to a Marine bugle play 'To the Colors.' The flag and bugle were the idea of Captain William Dabney, commander of the 3rd Battalion, 26th Marines. Hill 881, captured from the communists last spring, is under the heaviest pressure. Dabney and his men have been on the hill for 60 days, and he knows what that flag means. 'He's got an extra percentage working for him when he puts that flag up; nobody is going to take it down if the Marines there have their way,' said battalion operations officer Major Mathew Caulfield."

"Each day," Wheeler's story continued, "whether fog shrouds their movements or not, Marines stand at attention in their trenches and salute formally as the flag is raised and the bugle sounds, 'To the Colors.' The last note has barely faded when the Marines dive to the ground in anticipation of North Vietnamese mortar fire that always comes. It takes several seconds from the time a mortar shell is fired until it hits. The flag raising and morning bugle call have caught the imagination of all the Marines at Khe Sanh, most of whom are unabashedly proud of their patriotism. Technically, the American flag is not supposed to be raised alone over Vietnamese territory, but to the Marines here the whole complex, together with other much fought-over demilitarized zone areas, have taken on an emotional significance. The Marines argue that because it was their blood alone that took and hold the hills around Khe Sanh, it is the American flag that belongs there. Because of high winds the flag atop Hill 881 has become tattered. So far Dabney has not been able to replace it. None is available, and with food, water and ammunition stored at Khe Dinh base, the flag priority is low and is well down on the hill supply list. 'What we need is a flag as tough as those guys on Hill 881,' Major Caulfield said. 'Maybe someone at home will send them one.'"

I left Khe Sanh after my five-day visit the way I arrived but in reverse. I crouched down in a bomb crater at the airstrip at mid-morning with several wary Marines under orders to return home. It was the only way out. We watched a C-123 transport plane twist through the air as it came in for a landing and taxi quickly towards the unloading area. The cargo doors swung open as it passed by us, and the loadmaster began rolling out wooden crates. We started running towards the plane then, because it was speeding up as mortar rounds began exploding down the airstrip. I am not a particularly athletic person, but I managed to outrun a least two of the Marines sweating under their heavy backpacks. We grasped the loadmaster's outstretched hands and he pulled us aboard and closed the cargo doors as the old transport's auxiliary jet pods burst into action, thrusting us backwards as we gained speed and elevation and out of shooting range of the belligerents below.

I was to learn later that "the big one" that everyone was expecting at Khe Sanh — the attempt by massed North Vietnamese regular troops to overwhelm the combat base by brute force — was actually the failed attack on South Vietnamese rangers that took place during my last visit on February 29. It became "the big one" because no others of a larger size had preceded or followed it, and enemy forces began soon afterwards departing into bases in the high ridges and in Laos. It begged the question of what the real intent was of the enemy buildup at Khe Sanh.

The seventy-seven-day siege ended on April 8 when advance units of the U.S. Army's 1st Cavalry Division, with little resistance, arrived to link up with cheering Marines on the bomb-blasted Khe Sanh plateau. Six weeks later, Colonel Lownds was photographed at President Johnson's side at the White House when his 26th Marine regiment received the presidential unit citation. Six weeks later the combat base was abandoned on the orders of the new American military commander in Vietnam, General Creighton Abrams, who saw Khe Sanh as more of a liability than an asset. Casualties from all the Marine units fighting in the Khe Sanh area were 354 killed and nearly 2,000 wounded. Several hundred more Americans had been killed in helicopter and transport plane crashes en route to or in departure from Khe Sanh. Communist deaths were estimated at from 5,000 to 10,000.

In my interview with him after the war, I asked Colonel Lownds if there was a battle in Khe Sanh in the classic sense. He said, "The fact that the enemy didn't penetrate or overrun some of my units is a credit to the people who were working for me. Yeah, there was a battle, but where was the battle won? The battle was won on the perimeters and not within the perimeters. It was won on the outside. Now on the hills there was battle, you know that as well as I do. Our people there did their jobs and very frankly it was a key to winning. Now if the enemy can't close (on Khe Sanh) does that mean the enemy troops there didn't do their job? Does that mean that the thousands of troops out there didn't engage in hand-to-hand combat with us, and you might ask, why didn't they? All we know is that there were troops out there, and we know they never got to our wire. So, was the battle won before it started? I don't know. You answer it."

And how did he feel about the base being abandoned? "I'm a Marine. I still am. I'm retired but I'm a Marine, and Marines have a funny habit. That is, they do what the hell they are told to do. If the decision was made by people above me that Khe Sanh was no longer required, you know, I don't have any feelings one way or the other. I was told to go there, told to stay there. I went there. I stayed there. You do what you're told to. But you know who I am, I am not a tactician. I like to think I knew a little bit about tactics, but I'm certainly not a strategist and know about moving armies and stuff like that. I was told to do a job. and I did it. I did it only because I had the young men that could do it. And after all they are the ones that really went into battle at Khe Sanh."

Although Colonel Lownds was noteworthy for his tolerance and pro-visioning of the journalists who trekked to his door over the course of the siege, he noted, "I did have some concerns about the press. It became known to reporters that my main water supply was from a stream outside the base that came from way back in the hills. The enemy could have cut it, poisoned it or something, but it never happened. I guess he didn't realized how important that water supply was. And you know, the press never did write anything about it, and for that I am eternally grateful."

Lownds told me one of his favorite stories about the visiting press. "The senior officer running the Marine air war, General (George Shepard) Bowman, on a given day when things had been particularly bad, he had an aircraft drop in ice cream. Not everybody got it, but many people did. Do you know when Easter came they dropped colored eggs in? I'm willing to bet right now that if you went back and checked the records that we didn't lose two dozen eggs. Now that's a credit to whoever was packing them. God bless you, whoever it was. But anyway, command headquarters sent up an Italian lady journalist and it was right after a national magazine ran a cover that said, 'The Agony of Khe Sanh'.

When this lady got me alone, she said, and I can't quite get the accent, 'Ah, colonel, I sees the apple, I sees the orange, I sees the ice cream, but I no sees the agony.'"

In the course of just over two months, from mid-February to early April, tactical aircraft flew an average of 300 sorties daily around Khe Sanh, close to one every five minutes, and expended 35,000 tons of bombs and rockets. B-52s flew 2,602 sorties and dropped over 75,000 tons of bombs, Marine howitzers within the combat base and the army's 175 mm guns at Camp Carroll fired more than 100,000 rounds or nearly 1,500 rounds per day. It was an awesome display of firepower, given the bomb delivery capacity of the B-52, one of the heaviest and most concentrated in the history of warfare.

Even though he professed confidence in a favorable outcome of the siege of Khe Sanh, General Westmoreland admitted considering an even greater escalation in weaponry if necessary to achieve his goals. In his autobiography "A Soldier Reports," he wrote, "There was another possibility at Khe Sanh, tactical nuclear weapons. Early in the fight, President Johnson phoned General Wheeler to ask if there was a chance that he might have to make that decision, for he had no wish to face it. Although I recognized the controversial nature of the subject and that employing nuclear weapons would be a political decision, I nevertheless considered it would be prudent for me to acquaint myself with the possibilities in detail. Because the region around Khe Sanh was virtually uninhabited, civilian casualties would be minimal. If Washington officials were so intent on 'sending a message' to Hanoi surely small tactical nuclear weapons in defense of the base, even the threat of them — would be a way to tell Hanoi something, just as two atomic bombs had spoken convincingly to Japanese officials in World War II. Although I established a small secret group to study the subject, Washington so feared that some word of it might reach the press I was told to desist. I felt at the time and even more so now that to fail to consider this alternative was a mistake."

General Westmoreland told me in an interview after the war: "A Dien Bien Phu did not materialize at Khe Sanh, but the operation was given such visibility in the United States that it did play into the hands of the enemy psychologically. I think it should be recognized that the strategy of the enemy was to defeat us politically at home. I think they were smart enough to realize that they could not defeat us on the battlefield. But they realized we were vulnerable to political defeat because they defeated the French that way. They were sufficiently confident to believe they could defeat us by the same strategy. And indeed, they did."

21

SUNDAY, MARCH 31, 1968

I T WAS A DAY LIKE NO OTHER for Lady Bird Johnson. the wife of President Lyndon Baines Johnson. It began early because her older daughter, Lynda, was coming in on the "red eye special" from California about 7 a.m. after kissing her husband, Marine Captain Charles Robb, goodbye at Camp Pendleton as he departed for Vietnam. "I wanted to be right there at the door with open arms to meet her," Mrs. Johnson wrote in her diary, "but I begged Lyndon not to get up. 'No. I want to,' he insisted. So, the operator called us in what seemed the gray early morning and both of us were downstairs at the entrance to the Diplomatic Reception Room at 7 when she stepped out of the car."

Mrs. Johnson remembered her daughter "looked like a ghost, pale, tall, and drooping. We both hugged her and then we all went upstairs. I took her into her room, helped get her clothes off, and put her to bed. She'd had a sedative on the plane, slept a little but not much. I think partly emotion and partly the sedative made her look so detached like a wraith from another world. When I went back to Lyndon's room, his face was sagging and there was such pain in his eyes as I had not seen since his mother died. But he didn't have time for grief. Today was a crescendo of a day. At 9 in the evening (of March 31, 1968), Lyndon was to make his talk to the nation about the war, but the speech was not yet firm. There were still revisions to be made and people to see it."

A month earlier, as the battle of Hue came to a close and the fate of the combat base at Khe Sanh remained in the balance, President Johnson was at his Texas ranch pondering the consequential decisions thrust upon him by the communist Tet Offensive. To make matters worse he received a dismaying on-the-scene report from Saigon from the chairman of the Joint Chiefs of Staff, General Earle Wheeler.

In a February 27 message to the president, Wheeler said, "This offensive has by no means run its course. All commanders on the scene agree that the initial enemy attack nearly succeeded in a dozen places and the margin of victory — in some places survival — was very very small indeed. Whether he intends to expend himself fully at the current level of intensity or to hold out enough to fight next year is not known. However, the scope and severity of his attacks and the extent of his reinforcement are presenting us with serious and immediate problems. The enemy has undoubtedly been hurt, but he seems determined to pursue his offensive — apparently, he has the capability to do so. There has been a substantial withdrawal of ARVN (South Vietnamese regular troops) from the countryside in order to protect the cities. Therefore, unless ARVN forces re-enter the countryside quickly it may go by default. In many areas the pacification program has been brought to a halt. The Vietcong are prowling the countryside, and it's a question of which side moves fastest to regain control."

Wheeler also conveyed an unexpected request from the U.S. military commander in Vietnam, General William C. Westmoreland, for a substantial increase in the number of American forces there. His wish list called for an additional 205,179 soldiers to be sent to Vietnam by the end of the year, with 105,000 by May 1 and the rest in two increments. The result of that request, if implemented, would boost America's military commitment to Vietnam far beyond what the president had determined was politically acceptable.

The beginning of a convulsive, month-long debate in Washington that proceeded in secret and changed America's political and military landscape was already underway even before Johnson returned to the White House. Some of his senior foreign policy advisors were reacting with alarm to Westmoreland's surprising troop request. A meeting at the State Department on February 27 revealed a clear divide between the hawks and the doves.

"This is unbelievable and futile," commented Harry McPherson, special counsel to the president, in the official notes of the meeting.

Secretary of Defense Robert McNamara, in his last official day in office: "I do not understand what the strategy is in putting in 205,000 men. It is neither enough to do the job, nor an indication that our role must change."

Assistant Secretary of State William Bundy: "We must prepare for the worst. South Vietnam is very weak. Our position may be truly untenable. Contingency planning should proceed toward the possibility that we will withdraw with the best possible face and defend the rest of Asia. We can say truthfully that Asia is stronger because of what we have done in past few years."

Incoming Secretary of Defense Clark Clifford: "Look at the situation from the point of view of the American public and the Vietnamese. Despite optimistic reports, our people, (and world opinion) believe we have suffered a major setback. Problem is, how do we gain support for a major program, defense and economic, if we have told people things are going well. How do we avoid creating a feeling that we are pounding troops down a rathole? What is our purpose? What is achievable? Before any decision is made we must re-evaluate our entire posture in Vietnam. Unfortunately, the president has been at the ranch with hawks."

McNamara: "Agreed. Decision must not be hasty. Will take a week at least to work out defense and economic matters, if we go big."

A contrary view was expressed by two key officials, according to the note-taker: "Secretary of State Dean Rusk and presidential advisor Walt Rostow think the enemy took a beating in the Tet Offensive. Rostow says captured documents show enemy was disappointed, may be unable to mount heavy coordinated attack on cities. Rusk reminds that enemy took 40,000 casualties. No U.S. units out of operation. Rostow says if we can reinforce Westmoreland now he should be able to handle the situation until good weather comes to I Corps and North Vietnam."

The note-taker concluded the report of the meeting with this assessment: "General impression is prevailing uncertainty, radically different proposals were offered and debated. None rejected out of hand. We are at a point of crisis. McNamara expressed grave doubts over military, economic, political, diplomatic and moral consequences of a larger force buildup in Vietnam. Question is will those profound doubts be presented to president?"

The month-long Tet Offensive had already placed enormous physical and emotional strain on President Johnson. He returned to Washington from Texas after having watched CBS anchorman Walter Cronkite's controversial broadcast calling for negotiations, seen by many as symptomatic of the public's growing criticism of the war. Johnson was being hard-tugged in opposite directions. The allies were pressuring for a negotiated settlement. He was hearing from Moscow and Paris that the North Vietnamese were interested in peace talks. And conversely Westmoreland and the Joint Chiefs of Staff were lobbying for an all-out military effort. He faced the double election year dilemma of choosing between escalation or what might seem retreat. Johnson by now, said his biographer Doris Kearns Goodwin, was going through "the most difficult period in his entire life. The way he described it was that he was being stampeded on all sides."

One way or another, the president had reached a turning point in the war. He called for the man he had chosen to take over the Pentagon, Clark Clifford. He ordered him to form a task force to be operative immediately and to render an urgent A-to-Z assessment of U.S. options in Vietnam. Clifford, a veteran of Democratic politics, was Johnson's trusted and politically like-minded friend and legal advisor. He had worked for the Kennedy administration on the foreign intelligence advisory board and had been a Johnson advisor at the 1966 Manila conference on Vietnam. Late in 1967, Johnson had asked him to visit all of America's Vietnam allies to persuade them to make a greater contribution to the war as election year approached and more military help was needed. Clifford spent several weeks trying. He said in an interview after the war, "I kept finding that the important officials of these nations who were much closer to the trouble, did not share the degree of concern that was apparent in our country. Some were right on the border and yet they did not see the same danger as we did. And it troubled me deeply. I had accepted the philosophy and reasoning that was widespread at that particular time — that this was communist aggression in Southeast Asia and that it was in our own enlightened self-interest to help the South Vietnamese stem the tide of Soviet and Chinese expansionism."

Clifford said on returning from Asia he passed on to Johnson his concerns, to be told "they were only tightfisted with arms and money, and that they were still behind the war." Despite Clifford's worries, the president asked him to be the new secretary of defense. "At that time, I supported President Johnson fully. I supported the war. I thought it the right course of action," Clifford said. "I had been a confidant of Johnson for 25 years, and I think he thought it would be a strengthening fact if I was to replace Secretary McNamara. The result of that shift proved to be quite paradoxical."

Clifford's task force team to assess America's Vietnam options was drawn from all major departments, and its members were to provide a frank analysis of future prospects. It included a former chairman of the Joint Chiefs of Staff, General Maxwell Taylor, who had also been an ambassador to Saigon, Richard Helms, the director of the CIA, Assistant Secretary of State William Bundy, and Walt Rostow, the special assistant to the president for national security. Clifford made clear that his Tet inquiry resulted from Westmoreland's huge troop request because America had sent "more than we ever intended." He was aware of the feelings of his predecessor, Robert McNamara, about bombing the North, saying, "He had concluded that the bombing was valueless; it risks the lives of our men (the air crews), it killed civilians and was not precluding North Vietnamese from moving to the battle area."

Clifford began his policy assessment with a cross-examination of Defense Department chiefs, a task that left him questioning his commitment to American policy goals. In an interview after the war, he said, "I swear to you it was a revelation to me. I spent four days down in the 'tank,' that's the situation room of the Pentagon where you're in touch with every U.S. location in the world," he said. "I tried to get answers to questions like, 'How long in your opinion — and you are the military experts — do you think the war will last?' — and could get no satisfactory answer. 'Now if we send 200,000 more men will that be the end, or must we send more?' 'Well, we really don't know.' 'Well, are we actually prevailing? 'It all depends on how you look at it.' I could not get sound and solid answers."

Clifford talked with one American general who had "moved a thousand men" in a sweep of a war zone. "I said, 'How did it go?' And he said, 'Badly.' I said, 'What was the trouble?' And he said, 'Damn it, they won't come out and fight'." Clifford said, "It reminded me of the complaint by the British general in the Revolutionary war that the American troops would not come out and fight. We hung behind brick fences, rocks and trees and knocked off those redcoats. And this was the same kind of problem." Clifford said he began doubting that "even if the U.S. doubled or trebled" its forces it would end the war, "because the other side was not fighting that kind of war."

Despite Clifford's growing doubts, his task force submitted an interim memorandum to President Johnson that did not suggest a new strategy and compromised on Westmoreland's request, neither approving or rejecting it. The president was told, "There can be no assurance that this very substantial additional deployment would leave us a year from today in any more favorable military position. All that can be said is that additional troops would enable us to kill more of the enemy and provide more security if the enemy does not offset them."

On March 10, the New York Times published an account of Westmoreland's large troop request, shocking many and turning an increasing number of newspaper editorialists against the war. In the official history of the Joint Chiefs of Staff, the troop request was described as "a maneuver instigated by General Wheeler with General Westmoreland as a willing accomplice." The purpose, according to the history, was to raise the previously-determined troop ceiling, "secure a major mobilization to rebuild the national strategic reserve, and obtain authorization for expanded operations in Southeast Asia. Instead they brought about a reversal of what they intended."

In an interview I had with General Westmoreland after the war, he suggested he had been duped into requesting the large troop reinforcement by the chairman of the joint general staff. "General Wheeler acted on the assumption that there would be mobilization of the reserves, and asked me what I would like to be made available to be deployed to my command if needed, in accordance with the new strategy. He was of course very much interested in building up the general reserves for use in Europe and elsewhere. We came up with a plan which was in effect a contingency plan, which amounted to some 200,000 troops. But in order to implement a new strategy I didn't need that many troops, and a certain number of them would be deployed when ready and others would be prepared to use if at all required. It was based on wishful thinking on our part, an assumption that the administration would decide to take the fight to the enemy and force them by military means to the conference table — and we had the manpower, we had the plans, we had the capability to do that.

"Now unhappily this top-secret plan was leaked to the press, and the headlines were that I was seeking 206,000 troops, and the article was in the context that I was desperate; one report said that Westmoreland had panicked and had asked for these reinforcements to save the day. Now that was far from the case, but this had a profound impact. And it put pressure on Mr. Johnson that pretty well closed the door to any other course of action except withdrawal."

Further symbolizing the president's problems, according to Doris Kearns Goodwin, "was that Robert Kennedy, the very person he had feared his entire presidency, would come back and haunt him about John Kennedy. And he had come in March to finally announce that he was going to try, as Johnson put it, to reclaim the throne for the lost brother." The other Democratic "peace candidate" Senator Eugene McCarthy, long considered by most observers as a long shot, almost tied the president in the New Hampshire primary.

On Sunday, March 10, Lady Bird Johnson wrote in her diary: "This was a day of deep gloom — that is to say, gloom was purveyed in the newspapers and on TV. It weighted the air around me and I felt it in my very bones, though it was not very apparent to Lyndon. His voice was hearty, he had lively stories to tell when he stopped to talk with us. His work on the phone and reading reports ground on and on. I never took off my hat to him more, or felt more tender toward him. Secretary Rusk came by right after church. Tomorrow he goes up on the Hill to testify before TV. I admire him with all my heart, He is a great bulwark of strength, but even he looked weary. Afterward, Lyndon told me something very touching, that Dean had said to him. 'Your courage keeps me going. These days are an exercise in sheer spirit.'"

"It was well after 2 p.m. when Lyndon phoned to say he was hungry. We had a delicious lunch of crabmeat crepes and salad, hardly calculated to be reducing, but he's been so good so long. Afterward Lyndon said, 'Let's walk around the south grounds.' He took a golf club and hit some balls towards Eisenhower's green, and we walked around in beautiful sunshine. There are a few crocuses out and the buds are beginning to swell. In the West Garden, one of the magnolia soulangianas has a single bud opening. Then we went over to the bowling lane, but Lyndon left after the first game to get a nap. Lyndon sent word for me to come in. He hadn't really slept. He'd read and talked on the phone. Earlier I had asked him, 'Suppose someone else were elected president, what could Mr. X do that you could not do?' He said, 'He could unite the country and start getting some things done. That would last about a year, maybe two years.' I think that is what weighs heaviest on Lyndon's mind. Can he unite the country, or is there just too much built up antagonism, division, a general malaise, which may have the presidency — or this president — irrevocably as its focal point?"

Mrs. Johnson continued, "Lyndon called Hubert (Humphrey). There's still laughter in Hubert, but Muriel (Humphrey's wife) said that even this most happy and philosophical man has been weary and shaken over the last few days. I thought there was hurt in his voice when he described some of the actions of certain senators on the Hill. Hubert said, 'It's bad, and it's going to keep on being bad, through the primaries. I think we may as well brace ourselves for more of the same until the middle of June.' Those sties are coming back on Lyndon's eyes, first one and then the other, red and swollen and painful. I thought wryly that his life sounded more and more like the tribulations of Job. Nevertheless, he is remaining calm, even-tempered, serenely philosophical about policies. But about the war itself, he is deeply worried."

On March 19, shortly after Robert Kennedy had announced his candidacy for the presidency, the House of Representatives passed a resolution calling for an immediate review by Congress of American war policy. Doris Kearns Goodwin said that at this period Johnson feared "becoming paralyzed not just that he might lose, but worse than that — that in the middle of all those forces he would literally become paralyzed."

Clark Clifford decided the same day to confront President Johnson directly with his just-finished confidential inquiry. The report from his trusted friend and an important official was another setback for the president, as he discovered what was becoming apparent to the defense secretary's deputy, Paul Nitze. In an interview after the war, Nitze described Clifford to be initially "a great hawk," and watched "as the great hawk became the great dove. Clifford did not just change his mind; he reversed it 180 degrees. He wanted to get out of Vietnam right away." Nitze, an advocate of negotiations, found himself "as much in disagreement with Clifford after his change of mind as I was before."

Clifford pulled no punches. "I reported my personal view to President Johnson, and said that it was very clear to me that the one course of action that the United States should take was to get out of Vietnam; it was a real loser," he said. "I think the major impact on the president was the fact that I had supported the war, supported it strongly. He knew me very well after 25 years, and the fact that I had gone into the position, went through this exhaustive inquiry and then changed, I think that had more impact on President Johnson than perhaps any one development." Unsure just how effective his wrecking-ball approach to Vietnam policy might have been, Clifford said he "continued to persuade anybody who would listen to me to get out of the war."

On March 23 Westmoreland was informed by the president that he would be replaced and brought home to be chief of staff of the army. In a discussion at the White House the previous day with Senator Richard Russell, the chairman of the Senate Armed services committee, Johnson said he had planned to move the general out of Saigon in February, but resisted because of what he saw as unfair congressional criticism of Westmoreland's performance. He asked the senator, "Do you think there would be any reaction, that I was demoting Westmoreland and that he'd been a failure? George Christian (White House press secretary) thinks there would be." Russell responded, "There would be some among people that don't like him, undoubtedly. But nobody in the services would think so."

Westmoreland told me after the war, "I was center stage, and the war became considerably unpopular. And needless to say, a lot of that rubbed off on me. But that is an occupational hazard. I was not elated with some of the venom that was cast my way, but as a soldier prays for peace, he must be prepared to cope with the hardships of war and bear its scars. I have borne these scars. But when you go into the military profession you do so with the understanding such will be the case. I did my utmost to carry out my duties loyally and conscientiously and professionally. And with the satisfaction of knowing that I conducted myself that way, I have no regrets. And I have nothing to apologize for."

President Johnson, faced with continuing personal uncertainty over the course of action he should take in Vietnam, but with his recent public speeches suggesting his commitment to a military solution of the war, sought a consensus. A key development in the course of the presidential decision was his convening of another meeting of "The Wise Men," the retired presidential advisors who had twice previously in the course of the war backed his policies wholeheartedly. The venerable group met on March 24, and included General Omar Bradley, State Department elder Dean Acheson, former Deputy Defense Secretary Cyrus Vance, and McGeorge Bundy, previously National Security advisor to both Presidents Kennedy and Johnson. But the briefings they received from department heads and experts at informal lunch and dinner gatherings were generally not optimistic. The following day they met with the president at the White House, and Dean Acheson summed up the group's majority view, declaring that "we can no longer do the job we set out to do in the time we have left and we must begin to take steps to disengage."

In a March 26 meeting at the White House with the newly-named commander of American forces in Vietnam, General Creighton Abrams, and General Wheeler, the president was in an obviously emotional state. He expressed his frustrations with the weakening economy and growing public discontent, "complicated by the fact that this is an election year. I don't give a damn about the election. I will be happy to just to keep doing what is right and lose the election."

He said, "There has been panic in the last three weeks caused by Senator Ted Kennedy's critical report on corruption in the South Vietnamese military and government. The leaks to the "New York Times" hurt us. The country is demoralized. You must know about it. And now the release that Westmoreland wants 200,000 men, and a call-up of 400,000. That would cost $15 billion. That would hurt the dollar and gold. A worker writes a paper for the Clifford group and it's all over Georgetown. The people are trying to save us from ourselves. You must bear this in mind. I will have overwhelming disapproval in the polls and elections. I will go down the drain. I don't want the whole alliance and military pulled in with it."

Johnson had decided to make a speech to the nation in the evening of March 31 to explain his policies. His legal counsel Harry McPherson was tasked with drafting a speech to Johnson's liking that defended his hardline approach to the war ("Our will is being challenged... We shall not quit... I ask you now to support the new efforts I have described this evening... with determination to see this conflict through...").

But in late March the speech for the president's television address on Vietnam underwent significant revision. A memo written by the State Department's office of the historian said, "From 11:03 a.m. to 2:15 p.m. on March 28, Secretary of State Dean Rusk, Assistant Secretary of State William Bundy, Secretary of Defense Clark Clifford and special counsel Harry McPherson, met to discuss drafts of the speech on which McPherson had been working. When the meeting began, Clifford noted his sense that the leaders of the American business and legal communities no longer supported the war effort. 'Whatever the specific reasons, these men now feel we are in a hopeless bog,' he asserted. 'The idea of going deeper into the bog strikes them as mad. They want to see us get out of it.'" Clifford then proposed that the speech introduce a new element, namely a halt to the bombing north of the 20th parallel. Notes of the meeting have not been found, but in his memoirs McPherson describes how Clifford's assertion was received:

"Amazingly, the conversation thereafter was concerned with the mechanics of informing our commanders and allies, and with redrafting the speech — not with whether the country should instead be rallied to sustain the effort. No one argued for a continuation of the bombing around Hanoi, or for committing large numbers of fresh troops. Here were five men, all associated with the war; all of whom had either urged its prosecution, helped to form its strategies, argued its rationale, or wrote the leader's speeches. And not one of them spoke out against 'winding down the war' — which would mean inevitably accepting a result that was less than satisfactory by the standards they had set for it."

The hardline speech that McPherson was working on was set aside, and work began on a new alternative draft that emphasized negotiations and de-escalation. In the end the group decided to give both the hardline and the de-escalatory drafts to the president. In his memoirs, Clifford related how it was determined which speech the president favored:

"The next morning, shortly after 10 o'clock, President Johnson called McPherson to discuss changes to the draft. As Harry began looking through the old draft for places where the president wanted to make changes, he suddenly realized that the president was working on the alternative draft! Suppressing his excitement, he took down the president's changes one by one, but as soon as their conversation was over, Harry called me. 'We've won,' he shouted. 'The president is working from our draft.'"

At 9:55 a.m. on March 31, President Johnson departed the White House for Mass at St. Dominic's Catholic church, a somber gray Victorian-gothic structure with twin spires in a poor section of southwest Washington. He was accompanied by his youngest daughter Luci and her husband Patrick Nugent. The church was simple and restful and a favorite sanctum of the president. After the hour-long service they stopped off at the apartment of Vice President Hubert Humphrey and his wife Muriel who were leaving for Mexico later in the day. Mrs. Johnson had stayed back at the White House to rest, and wrote in her diary, "Sometime during the morning Buzz (Horace Busby, an aide to Johnson) came in, took up his place in the Treaty Room, and began to work on the speech. I had spent a good part of Saturday and part of Friday making suggestions on it myself. I read it over again for what was the umpteenth time. And then, I believe in his bedroom, Lyndon said to me and Arthur and Mathilde Krim (close friends), 'What do think about this? This is what I'm going to put at the end of the speech' And he read a beautifully written statement that ended, 'Accordingly, I shall not seek and I will not accept the nomination of my party for another term as president.'

"The four of us had talked about this over and over, and hour after hour, but somehow, we all acted and felt stunned," the first lady continued. "Maybe it was the calm finality in Lyndon's voice, and maybe we believed him for the first time. Arthur said something like, 'You can't mean this,' and Mathilde exclaimed in an excited way, 'Oh, no, no.' And then we all began to discuss the reason why and why not, over and over again.

"At lunch Mathilde's eyes were full of tears, and Luci had obviously been crying forthrightly. Lyndon seemed to be congealing into a calm, quiet state of mind, out of our reach. And I, what did I feel — so uncertain of the future that I would not dare to persuade him one way or the other. There was much in me that cried out to go on, to call on every friend we have, to give and work, to spend and fight, right up to the last. And if we lost, well and good. We were free. But if we didn't run we could be free without all this draining of our friends. I think that was what was uppermost — what was going over and over in Lyndon's mind — was what I've heard him say increasingly in these last months, 'I do not believe I can unite this country'."

At 3:37 p.m., according to his daily diary, Johnson asked his secretary. Juanita Roberts, for the withdrawal remarks made by President Harry Truman at the annual Jefferson-Jackson dinner 16 years earlier, in March 29, 1952. Presiding over the increasingly unpopular Korean War and expected to run for a second term in office, Truman made the surprise announcement at the end of a speech justifying the Korean War. "We have been willing to sacrifice to stop aggression, willing to send our money and goods to help men in other countries stand up against tyranny, willing to fight in Korea to stop World War III before it begins. If the bloody harvest of world war were ever to begin anew, most of us would never see a peaceful world again." Predicting his successor would be a Democrat, Truman, who had taken office on the death of President

Franklin D. Roosevelt in 1945, said, "I shall not be a candidate for re-election. I have served my country long and I think efficiently and honestly. I shall not accept a nomination. I do not feel that it is my duty to spend another four years in the White House."

Around 6 p.m., President Johnson had a White House meeting with Anatoly Dobrynin, Moscow's ambassador to Washington, to discuss aspects of his speech that emphasized his search for peace. The Russian diplomat wrote in his autobiography that he also met later with other officials, and as he was leaving the White House he ran into Johnson again in a hallway. "The president stopped me and after a moment of hesitation, he said he wanted to tell me in strict confidence that at the end of his television address he intended to announce that he would not run for another term as president. He expressed the hope that this hard decision he had made to withdraw would help pacify the fierce controversy over Vietnam during the election campaign and help settle the entire Vietnam conflict.

"'I want to show them I have no obsessive lust for power that many believe. I want to spend the rest of my time serving the country, not the party,' Johnson said. The President told me that I was the first foreigner to learn about his decision, and so far, only four or five Americans knew about it, including his wife. Johnson spoke with difficulty and could hardly hide his emotions. He did not look well. It was clear he had thought long and hard before taking the decision. He could not but realize that as he was doing this nearly a year before the end of his presidential term his further ability to influence the events in the country and abroad would be considerably diminished during the remainder of his term in office. It looked like a desperate move, a last-minute attempt to prove to those who accused him of relentlessly pursuing the war merely to save his own face and ensure his reelection, that he was ready to sacrifice his second term in the nation's highest office to calm the public, and from that position try to conclude an honorable settlement in Vietnam."

Clark Clifford noted in an interview for the Lyndon Johnson Library that President Johnson began to give out little hints of his future intentions, such as in late 1967 when they were returning from a trip to Southeast Asia. "He made a comment to me about it and he said something like,

'Good Lord Almighty, why anyone would want to go on with this terrible job, everybody just beating me over the head. Thank heavens I'll be through soon.' And you'd kind of laugh and say, 'Yeah, that's right, except you won't.' And then he'd kind of look at you and smile a little. Then the next day he'd have a good night's rest and something would happen that would go right and he'd be right on top of the job again. It came to me as a complete and total surprise on Sunday evening, March 31."

Clifford found out about the president's true intentions later that same day when he'd been working on the final drafts of the evening speech. He said Johnson called, saying, "'Why don't you bring your wife Marnie down about half an hour or 45 minutes before the program and come on over to the house and we'll visit together, and then I'll go over and put on the speech.' So, I think we got there maybe 45 minutes before the speech was to go on. I remember Mr. and Mrs. Walt Rostow were there, and my wife and I were there, and I think that's about all. Maybe Horace Busby was there. We sat around and talked about 20 minutes before the sergeant came out and said that the president wanted to see me in his bedroom. And I went in and he handed me the last two or three paragraphs of his speech and said, 'I'd like you to read it.' And I read them, and you could knock my eyes off with a stick. I said, 'You've made up your mind?' He said, 'I've made up my mind.' I said 'You're actually going to do it?' He said, 'I'm actually going to do it.' I said, 'All right, it's your decision, then it becomes my decision. You're sure you've thought it through?' He said, 'I've thought out every phase.' So, I said, 'Well, by God, I've got to tell Marnie. I can't let her hear it over the TV.' He said, 'That's all right.'

"So, I went out. This was upstairs on the second floor at the west end of the hall. I remember Mrs. Clifford and Mrs. Rostow were sitting together on the sofa. I went up and told both of them together what he was going to do. They looked like they'd seen ghost. Neither one of them could believe it. They were absolutely and completely destroyed. Then I went down with the president to his office while he made the speech," Clifford said.

Lady Bird Johnson joined them. She wrote, "In the familiar Oval Office of the president, the floor a jungle of cables under the brilliant glare of TV lights. What a stage setting. Lyndon, very quiet at his desk. The lines on his face were deep, but there was a marvelous sort of repose overall. And the seconds ticked away. I went to him and said quietly, 'Remember pacing and drama.'"

While President Johnson had assured his family and closest friends of his firm intention to quit, a degree of uncertainty remained even as he cleared his throat to begin his speech. Johnson had intended to make a similar announcement at the conclusion of his State of the Union address in January, but he never did take out of his pocket the paper on which he had written the climactic paragraph. And he stated in his autobiography that while he had made the decision not to seek a second term and to stop much of the bombing campaign and several other pertinent decisions, "I could have unmade any of them or all of them right down to the time I sat behind my desk to speak on television on the night of March 31. Had the enemy in Vietnam launched a large and devastating new series of attacks, our reaction would have been strong. If I had then become convinced that withdrawing from politics would have undermined our men in Vietnam or harmed out country, I would have changed my mind. Hanoi's actions or statements could have caused us to call off or alter the bombing proposal at the last moment. War or a serious incident could have erupted elsewhere in the world. Any one of a dozen things could have happened, and in each case, I could have reconsidered my decisions and changed course if necessary. But these things, thank God, did not happen. I went forward with decisions that had taken place in my mind years, months and days earlier. I repeat: No president, at least this president, makes a decision until he publicly announces that decision and acts upon it. When did I make the decisions that that I announced on the evening of March 31, 1968? The answer is: 9:01 p.m. on March 31, 1968. And they are the same decisions I would make in retrospect."

Lady Bird Johnson recalled, "It was a great speech, and I wanted him to get the greatest out of it — and I did not know what the end would be. The speech was magnificently delivered. He's best, I think, at the worst of times, calm and strong. Those who love him must have loved him more. Those who hate him must at least have thought, 'Here is a man.'"

Addressing the nation, President Johnson proclaimed to the world his willingness to "move immediately towards peace through negotiations." As a move in that direction, he announced that he was "taking the first steps to de-escalate the conflict" by unilaterally reducing the level of hostilities. "Tonight," he said, "I have ordered our aircraft and our naval vessels to make no attacks on North Vietnam, except in the area north of the demilitarized zone where the continued enemy buildup directly threatens allied forward positions and where the movements of their troops and duopolies is clearly related to that threat."

Continuing his peace theme, Johnson announced that the United States was "ready to send its representatives to any forum, at any time, to discuss means of bringing this ugly war to an end." For this purpose, he designated Ambassador Averell Harriman as his "personal representative in such talks". He called on North Vietnamese President Ho Chi Minh to "respond positively and favorably" to his overture.

At the same time, he made it clear that the U.S. objective in Vietnam had not been changed. The goal, Johnson said, was not the "annihilation of the enemy" but rather the creation of conditions that would permit the people of South Vietnam "to chart their course free of any outside domination or interference from us or anyone else."

Then came the politically monumental announcement that even those closest to the president were uncertain he would make: "What we won when all our people united just must not now be lost in suspicion, distrust, selfishness and politics among any of our people. Believing this as I do, I have concluded that I should not permit the presidency to become involved in the partisan divisions that are developing in this political year—the presidency of your country. I do not believe that I should devote an hour or a day of my time to any personal partisan causes or to a duty other than the awesome duties of this office. Accordingly, I shall not seek, and I will not accept, the nomination of my party for another term as your president."

Lady Bird Johnson wrote, "Lynda and I had been sitting down, behind us Luci and Pat, and they were standing. Luci threw her arms around Lyndon. She was obviously holding back her tears but just barely. Lynda kissed him and Pat shook his hand. We walked out of the president's office to return to the second floor, and I looked back at him and there he was standing, holding his hands behind his back, his head tilted up, with the oddest, most faraway expression on his face."

The president took Clark Clifford upstairs with him, who recalled, "A group of people, maybe 25 or 30, mostly people around that worked for him there in the White House and some others that had been invited in, were all there. It seems to me we had a drink and a little supper, and boy, it was like a wake. Nobody wanted him to do it. Everybody was shocked and surprised."

Clark Clifford soon moved towards resolving any lingering misunderstandings about what exactly were President Johnson's intentions concerning future military commitments to Vietnam. In an April 11 press conference at the Defense Department, he announced a new troop level ceiling for American forces in Vietnam of 549,000, and that "considering the increased effectiveness of the South Vietnamese forces, this will permit us to level off our effort and in due time to begin the gradual process of reduction." In a meeting with several senators soon afterwards, Clifford stressed the need "to keep part of public attention focused on the idea that we have come to a ceiling in our forces and are looking to slow but ultimate disengagement."

Assessing the impact of the Tet Offensive on the Johnson administration's war policies, assistant secretary of state William Bundy told me in an interview after the war: "Militarily the attack had been repulsed, but what has clearly happened was a demonstration of how serious things were, that we had not been making the progress that people in the administration were saying. It had seriously weakened domestic American continued support for the war, and that forced the situation where President Johnson eventually decided that he couldn't go on being president, of course, and on March 31 included in the end of a major speech on Vietnam his own abdication from the presidency. But it also meant that we would not add the very large number, 205,000 troops, that our own military wanted, that we would instead hold the level roughly where it was. We would continue to resist very vigorously within South Vietnam along with the South Vietnamese, but that we would attempt a partial bombing stoppage and see if that led to negotiations.

Which it did. Eventually of course to the total stopping of bombing on November 1968.

"That was the first real move toward peace, a move to level off the war. Essentially it represented a conclusion that there was not a military solution in Vietnam that was possible that lay within the political capacity of the United States and the American public to carry it through. That's what it amounted to."

My view of President Johnson's remarkable March 31 decision was from the battlefield, where I reported for The Associated Press for the duration of the war and where, over the previous six years, I had watched America's commitment to South Vietnam evolve. It grew from the Kennedy administration's cautious use of military advisors and covert operations against a communist insurgency to become the full-scale application of combat troops and massive supportive firepower to counter North Vietnamese infiltration during the Johnson years.

The momentum of this enormous effort was hard to slow down. But when President Johnson finally signaled a withdrawal, it did slow down, even as the survival of South Vietnam as an independent state was imperiled by America's departure. Historically, the decision of this president to sound the retreat from an unpopular war — a war much of his own making, a war of tragic miscalculations and losses but also of individual soldiers' courage and spirit that I saw firsthand — was unique. The president's decision in the aftermath of Tet spared his nation from even greater misadventure, even as it blemished his own reputation as a leader.

AFTERWORD

I **VISITED HANOI, THE CAPITAL OF VIETNAM,** late in 2017, invited to speak to an audience of successful American businessmen from the Houston-based Young Presidents Organization who were making their first visit to the scene of their nation's most controversial war. The several hundred wealthy visitors were in their teens or younger when the Vietnam War had convulsed American politics and divided society; their arrival all these years later signaled their interest in confirming that this former enemy and single-party Communist state was ripe for capital investment. The visit came with Donald Trump in the White House and rumblings of a possible war in another far-away communist nation, North Korea.

We were staying in the Sofitel Legend Hotel Metropole, one of the finest in the city, built in 1901 as a showcase of French colonialism and upgraded in recent years to accommodate important visitors. Convincingly describing the long-distant war and its terrors to gatherings in the ornate, comfortably-furnished conference rooms was made easier by my colleague, Huynh Cong (Nick) Ut, the Pulitzer Prize winning AP photographer, who had traveled with his dramatic pictures of the war.

Three days after arriving I noticed the presence of hard-faced American security men prowling the hallways and the extensive grounds of the hotel, and rumors began circulating that President Donald Trump, on a visit to Danang to attend a meeting of Southeast Asian countries, would be spending the night at the Metropole during a layover in Hanoi. Within hours I saw that all public hotel entrance-ways were closed off. The presidential motorcade arrived early evening and Trump was ushered inside through a newly canopied private entrance. Anxious to keep an appointment, I prevailed on a young American Embassy official for help and he led me through the extensive hotel kitchens to the sidewalks outside where Vietnamese security men were blocking off surrounding streets to traffic. President Trump's comments at a state dinner late that evening received plaudits from the visiting American businessmen, as he heaped praise on Vietnam's economy, saying the southeast Asian nation "is one of the great miracles of the World," and that the parts of the country he toured "are really something to behold."

Trump was the fourth American president to visit post-war Vietnam over the previous 17 years, an indication of the incredible shift of the national interests of the United States since the Vietnam war years. The Hotel Metropole itself was a reminder of those conflictive times. I first visited the hotel late in 1972 during a reporting visit to Hanoi when years of American bombing had reduced the outskirts of the city to rubble and the landmark hotel to a neglected guest house. It was here where anti-war activist Jane Fonda was housed by government authorities during her controversial propaganda visit earlier in 1972. Another cultural icon, musician Joan Baez, was in residence a few months later during President Richard Nixon's brutal "Christmas Bombing" campaign aimed at forcing Hanoi to sign the peace agreement that ended America's direct role in the war. Baez turned her experiences in the Metropole's concrete underground bomb shelters into material for her anti-war ballad, "Where are you now, my son?" the audio enhanced by sounds of the actual B-52 bombing she recorded from her upstairs hotel room. The bomb shelters still exist but visits are discouraged; The floors are slippery, the mildewed walls lit by a few yellowed light bulbs that show, tacked to the concrete in one corridor, a picture of Joan Baez.

Other reminders of the massive American air war that devastated much of North Vietnam's industrial and population centers are similarly rare beyond the elaborate war museums reflecting the official view of the conflict. In Hanoi. Nick Ut and I did visit two of the few remaining surviving Vietnamese figures from the war years. One was 90-year-old Madame Nguyen Thi Binh, the Vietnamese communist leader who negotiated at the critical Paris Peace Talks on behalf of the Vietcong. She served later in the communist party's central committee. Madame

Binh had just celebrated her 90th birthday party when we visited, and presented us with a copy of her autobiography where she writes of her contacts during the war with American peace activists, some of whom, she said, she still keeps in touch with.

Another significant but lesser known Vietnamese figure we met in Hanoi was General Dong Sy Nguyen, the field commander of the critically important Ho Chi Minh trail communist supply line from 1965 to war's end. The 87-year old officer described the battle to keep the trail open as key to the communist victory. "The Americans commanded the air with their bombers, but we commanded the ground, and we had a million troops in reserve to keep defending it," he said.

In the south of Vietnam, the cities of Ho Chi Minh/Saigon and Danang are being transformed by massive construction projects into clones of Singapore and Hong Kong, and by millions of people born since the war ended in 1975 and now engaged in vigorous commercial pursuits. The offices of the former western news bureaus in Saigon and many of the French colonial buildings in the heart of the city have long been swept away by the construction boom, replaced by soaring business towers and hotels. The new Reverie Hotel on Nguyen Hue street where the visiting Young President Organization members stayed in Saigon, claimed to be the first six-star hotel in Asia. The luxurious amenities included a "pillow menu" that was new to me. It offered a selection of seven including an anti-snore pillow, a buckwheat one and a "Swedish memory pillow." I settled for the one already on my bed.

Visitors arriving in today's Vietnam looking for traces of the war usually settle for a visit to the museums, or go the Cu Chi tunnels west of Saigon, widened for western visitors, from which Vietcong guerrillas, concealed in their underground hiding places, played a deadly cat and mouse game with American soldiers seeking them in the jungles above. Some travel to the old Khe Sanh marine combat base on the Laos border, resurrected by local authorities into a disappointing replica of the real thing.

There are places where memorials of the war relate more to experiences of local combatants rather than to tourists. Nick Ut and I traveled to the hamlet of Ap Bac, an hour south of Saigon in the verdant Mekong

Delta farmlands where early in the war, on January 2 and 3 in 1963, the first significant battle was fought. A South Vietnamese infantry force backed by armor and American-piloted helicopters attempted to overrun a small Vietcong propaganda team operating a mobile broadcasting unit in Ap Bac, but a reinforcing guerrilla company fought off the attack. There were heavy casualties on the Government side. Several American helicopters were shot down, with Americans killed. The battle was minor one compared to later fierce engagements, but it attracted the attention of the young western press corps in Saigon. As an AP reporter at the time, I drove to the battle scene with David Halberstam of the New York Times. Neil Sheehan then of UPI and Nicholas Turner of Reuters flew in by helicopter. The senior American military advisor there, Lt. Colonel John Paul Vann, was angry with the government troop performance and he volubly complained to us about it. The resulting headlines riveted attention upon the failure of American advisory efforts in Vietnam, attention that was to continue throughout the war.

I was not expecting to see anything but a sleepy hamlet as Nick and I drove along the byways of the delta to Ap Bac. Tall coconut palms shaded the narrow roads, and wooden bridges crossed the many canals along the way. Then we turned on to a path along the broad paddy field that I remembered was the staging area for the government attack in 1963. I looked across the expanse of ripening rice beyond a farmer weeding his crop. Beyond him there was a billboard, a large wooden one, Then another. Two more, each had a bold, colored depiction of the climatic scenes in the long-ago battle. A U.S. helicopter enveloped in fire was crashing into a canal. Two U, S. armored personal carriers, red flames licking at their turrets, were burning, their attack on the hamlet, 100 yards away, stalled. A fourth billboard in the distance depicted an exploding bomb.

A few young students gathered around us as we walked towards the hamlet. They pointed to a memorial pagoda and showed us a small museum. The billboards, they said, had been erected a few years earlier when the museum was opened. Inside the building were pictures with detailed captions in Vietnamese explaining the battle and its significance as an example to the growing "people's" revolution that the Americans could be beaten. Of pride of place was the mobile broadcasting unit that had escaped capture by government troops and was used for Vietcong propaganda for the remainder of the war.

The people of Ap Bac continue to celebrate their long-ago victory even though in the war that followed many of their compatriots died before victory was finally achieved. Many Americans, however, still struggle to come to terms with defeat and the cost of the war to their country in blood and money and national reputation. The long finger of blame points to the major political figures involved over the course of the two decades that the United States was directly involved in South Vietnam, with President Lyndon Johnson usually the prime target because of his decision to commit American ground forces to the war in 1965 in a fruitless attempt to achieve military victory.

The custodians of the Johnson Presidential Library in Austin, Tex., aware of his unfavorable reputation, convened a Vietnam War Summit in April, 2016, to examine the Johnson Administration's historical record in the context of the 21st century. LBJ's daughters Lynda and Lucy and their husbands hosted the event. Former Secretary of State Henry Kissinger, still active in his 90th year, headed the speakers list that included former Secretary of State John Kerry and anti-war activist Tom Hayden. I was invited to attend to discuss coverage of the war with my Vietnam colleague Dan Rather of CBS News. I had had no direct contact with the president in my journalism career but I was made aware during my Vietnam assignment that my coverage angered him because it sometimes challenged his optimistic public assessments of eventual success. In inaugurating his library in May 1971, Johnson said, "It's all here. The story of our time – with the bark off. There is no record of a mistake. or an unpleasantness or a criticism that is not included in the files here." In that spirit, I made sure my hour's conversation in the library auditorium with Rather fully addressed the unsuccessful efforts by his administration to constrain and disrupt press coverage of the war.

After the Tet Offensive and the events described earlier in this book, direct American military involvement in Vietnam dragged on for five excruciating years, with defeat for a demoralized South Vietnam government two years later. Today America is involved in what some describe as a "forever" war, with the United States active militarily in the Middle East and Africa with seemingly no way out. As one who covered the Fall of Saigon in 1975, and watched the frantic disorder of America's departure and the measured arrival of the victorious communist forces, my thoughts at the time were "never again", never again would America make the mistakes in foreign and military policy it made in Vietnam because it had learned the hard way to avoid such disasters.

The main lessons:

Understanding the nature of the conflict. In Vietnam the United States was fighting a war against communism while the North Vietnamese and the Vietcong were fighting primarily for nationalism and an independent country.

Support at home. In Vietnam the war effort lost the support of Congress, the media and the citizenry that guaranteed failure.

Understanding that if you get into a war you have to get out. In Vietnam there was no clear understanding of the type of war being contemplated, no idea of what victory looked like, no alternative military strategy and no international backing.

Limited wars don't work. In Vietnam the communist enemy vowed to fight on indefinitely while seeking sanctuary when necessary in neighboring countries that were out of bounds to American counterattack.

Remembering the successes. The counterinsurgency doctrine in Vietnam that sought to gain and retain the respect of village elders and provide linked security zones essential for population safety came too late to save the war effort, but would be useful in the similar environment in Afghanistan's war zones.

The media didn't lose the Vietnam war: Isolating today's all-volunteer military from routine news coverage threatens to lose the soldier's connection to the broader society. The country is proceeding on parallel tracks, with the military and military family on one track and then there is everyone else. The military is becoming a warrior class disconnected from the population.

—Peter Arnett, 2018

GALLERY

THE ARNETT INTERVIEWS

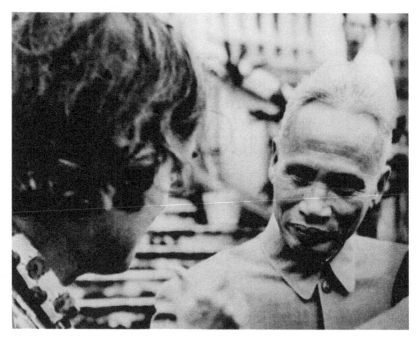

North Vietnamese Prime Minister Pham Van Dong is interviewed by Peter Arnett in Hanoi, 1972. (Peter Arnett Collection)

General William Westmoreland and Arnett during an interview in Charleston, SC, 1978. (Peter Arnett Collection)

Ambassador Henry Cabot Lodge and Arnett during an interview in Boston, MA, 1978. (Peter Arnett Collection)

Ambassador Frederick Nolting and Arnett during an interview in Washington, DC, 1978. (Peter Arnett Collection)

Ambassador Kenneth Glabraith and Arnett during an interview in Cambridge, MA, 1978. (Peter Arnett Collection)

Assistant Secretary of State William Bundy and Arnett during an interview in Washington, DC, 1978. (Peter Arnett Collection)

Historian Arthur Schelsinger Jr. and Arnett during an interview in Cambridge, MA, 1978. (Peter Arnett Collection)

Historian Doris Kearns Goodwin and Arnett during an interview in Cambridge, MA, 1978. (Peter Arnett Collection)

Novelist Tim O'Brien and Arnett during an interview in Boston, MA, 1978. (Peter Arnett Collection)

Journalist Wilfred Burchett and Arnett during an interview in Washington, DC, 1979. (Peter Arnett Collection)

Ambassador/General Maxwell Taylor and Arnett during an interview in Washington, DC, 1979. (Peter Arnett Collection)

Major General William DePuy and Arnett during an interview in Washington, DC, 1979. (Peter Arnett Collection)

North Vietnamese General Vo Nguyen Giap greets Arnett before an interview in Hanoi, 1985. (Peter Arnett Collection)

ACKNOWLEDGMENTS

My task in writing this book was to describe the Vietnam War as seen by the policymakers, the diplomats and the soldiers of that era, a sort of literary reenactment that will help the reader better understand how and why America became involved in a disastrous war in such a distant place. As a reporter for the Associated Press, I covered the war from the battlefield, always aware that the fate of the military campaign depended as much on the executive decisions and debates at home as it did on the vagaries of combat in the jungles and mountains of Vietnam.

The climax of this book comes with my account of the 1968 Tet Offensive as seen both from the battlefield and from the White House. Few actions in America's military history have raised as much continuing controversy as the Tet Offensive, the surprise attack by communist forces against South Vietnamese cities and towns during the Lunar New Year celebrations in 1968, and the resultant brutal battles in Hue and the U.S. Marine base at Khe Sanh.

Even though American military commanders described the successful repulsion of the Tet Attacks as a disaster for the enemy, President Johnson was persuaded by influential aides not only to set a limit on troop reinforcements and to order a bombing halt over much of North Vietnam. but also to abdicate from the presidency by announcing that he would not run for reelection. Tet became the turning point of the war.

I relied not only on my own reporting for this book, but also on the vast repository of formerly classified government documents and White House discussions and debates that has been declassified during the past decade, particularly from the administration of President Lyndon

B. Johnson. I also retrieved from my own files detailed interviews with primary decision makers assembled after the war, many of the interviews made by me.

My initial ideas for this book were encouraged by Peter Costanzo, the digital publishing specialist at The Associated Press. Peter had been untiringly supportive of a previous book I had written about Vietnam for the AP, titled "Saigon Has Fallen," and I was fortunate in that he quickly assigned Chris Sullivan, a top AP editor who worked on that previous book to assist me on this new one. Chris' long experience handling the wire service's National Reporting Team was invaluable as we moved through the book chapter by chapter.

The AP's editorial, photographic and research staff worked diligently to prepare the book for publication. My thanks to team members Mike Bowser for the cover design and Sean M. Thompson from AP photo archives. Valerie Komor, Director of Corporate Archives, who has long been the custodian of the reportage and memorabilia from the news organization's Vietnam era, was helpful as usual, as was her colleague, processing archivist Francesca Pitaro. Thanks also to Lauren Easton from publicity.

I appreciated the perceptive comments from my journalist son Andrew who has visited Vietnam several times with me over the years, and who reviewed the chapters I emailed to him regularly. My wife Nina and daughter Elsa, also very familiar with the subject matter, encouraged me to persevere in this new literary effort.

Peter Arnett started as an intern at his local newspaper at age 18, which inspired him to become an international journalist. Less than a decade later, he was traveling the globe for The Associated Press, the first of several major American news organizations he would work for during his career. In 1966 he was awarded the Pulitzer Prize for his coverage of the Vietnam War. Arnett joined CNN in the early 1980s, earning a television Emmy for his live television coverage of the first Gulf War in 1991. Born in New Zealand in 1934, Arnett later became an American citizen and currently resides in Fountain Valley, CA.